THE DISTRICT GAZETTEER OF
CHHATTISGARH

THE DISTRICT GAZETTEER OF
CHHATTISGARH

Editor

S.C. Bhatt

GYAN PUBLISHING HOUSE
NEW DELHI-110 002

THE DISTRICT GAZETTEER OF CHHATTISGARH

Rs. 490

ISBN : 81-212-0773-8

Published in 2003 in India by
Gyan Publishing House
5, Ansari Road, New Delhi-110002
Phones : 3261060, 3282060, Fax : (011) 3285914
E-Mail : gyanbook@del2.vsnl.net.in
Website: http:\\www.gyanbooks.com

Lasertypesetting by : Varsha Graphics, Delhi
Printed at : Mehra Offset Press, Delhi

CONTENTS

PREFACE

You have the District Gazetteer of Chhattisgarh State before you. As you browse through its pages, you will feel like travelling across the length and breadth of the district. It is a well-known fact that the district is a very important administrative unit for a state government or the Union Territory Administration in India. As parts of the administrative control, all the planning and development activities whether concerning to its towns or villages, is planned, implemented and monitored at the district level by the appropriate district authority.

State of Chhattisgarh is famous for its natural storage of minerals and ores. It contains about 525 million tonnes of dolomite reserves, accounting for 24 per cent of the country's share. With substantial deposits of limestone, iron ore, copper ore, rock phosphate, manganese ore, bauxite, coal, asbestos and mica, the mineral revenue that will accrue from Chhattisgarh, will exceed Rs 600 crore annually. The information regarding the occurrences of minerals and ores, is mentioned in this volume district wise, with latitude and longitude references.

All the information, facts and figures collected by the heads of various departments of the districts have been incorporated with much care in this valuable study.

Hopefully, this volume would prove to be immensely useful and become an invaluable academic companion to all researchers and scholars, administrators, planners, tourists, librarians and all those who wish to gain micro-knowledge of this tract of Indian sub-continent. Undoubtedly this work would also be beneficial to all those who are interested in the history, development and future of the new State.

I would like to express my deep sense of gratitude to the Resident Commissioner, Chhattisgarh, Census Commissioner, India and his team of dedicated officers, to the professors and the librarians, for their academic guidance and encouragement provided by them in giving final shape to this volume.

S.C. Bhatt

INTRODUCTION

On November 1, 2000, India gave birth to a new state, i.e., Chhattisgarh. The new state is carved out of India's largest state of Madhya Pradesh. The state of Chhattisgarh has its capital at Raipur and the High Court at Bilaspur. The capital may be shifted later to Nandghat, about midway between Raipur and Bilaspur on the banks of Shivnad River. Agriculture is the main activity of the people of this state and it is enveloped by Maharashtra, Andhra Pradesh, Orissa, Bihar and Uttar Pradesh and, of course, Madhya Pradesh.

The genesis of the demand can be traced to early 20th century during a meeting of Raipur District Congress Committee, the idea of a separate entity of Chhattisgarh was mooted. The leaders who took part in that meeting were of the view that the region of Chhattisgarh was culturally and historically distinct from the rest of Madhya Pradesh. The latest state comprises 16 districts of the erstwhile Madhya Pradesh — Bastar, Bilaspur, Dantewara, Dhamtari, Durg, Janjgir-Champa, Jashpur, Kanker, Kawardha, Korba, Koriya, Mahasamund, Raigarh, Raipur, Rajnandgaon and Surguja.

The name Chhattisgarh, or "thirty six forts', was formerly applied to the territories of the Haihaivansi dynasty of Ratanpur, which comprised the greater part of the then districts of Durg, Raipur and Bilaspur. Far removed from the routes of armies and protected from invasion or disturbances by the precipitous ranges which fringe the plain on three sides, the Haihaivansi kingdom continued to enjoy a peaceful and uneventful existence until the middle of the eighteenth century; while the people, isolated and almost barred from intercourse with the outside world, have developed or retained peculiarities of dress, manners, and language which distinguish them from the residents of adjoining tracts, to whom they are known as Chhattisgarhis. The Chhattisgarhis dialect resembles the form of Hindi spoken in Oudh. The people are generally held to be characterised by lack of intelligence, by backwardness in their method of agriculture, and by a more primitive habit of life than their neighbours. The headquarters of the Commissioner was at Raipur town. The population of the Division in 1881 was 2,495,655 and increased to 2,924,663 in 1891 or by 17 per cent.

The census of 1901 showed a decrease to 2,642,983,02 by 10 per cent, the Chhattisgarh plain having been visited by two severe famines during the previous decade. On the outskirts of the plain and surrounding the British districts were situated the territories of fourteen Feudatory states, whose administration is controlled by a political Agent under the supervision of the Commissioner.

KORIYA

It was a tributary state in the then Central Provinces. Till 1905 it was included in the Chhotanagpur state of Bengal. It was bounded on the north by Rewa State; on the east by Surguja; on the south by Bilaspur district and on the west by the state of Chang Bhakar and Rewa. It consists of an elevated table land of coarse sandstone, from which spring several abruptly scarped plateaux, varying in height and irregularly distributed over the surface. The general level of lower table land is about 1800 feet above the sea. On the east this rises abruptly into the Sonahat plateau, with an elevation of 2477 feet. The north of the state is occupied by a still higher table land, with a maximum elevation of 3367 feet. In the west a group of hills culminates in the Deogarh Peak (3370 feet), the highest point in Koriya. The lofty Sonhat plateau forms the water shed of streams which flow in three different directions: on the west to the river Gopath, which has its source in one of the ridges of the Deogarh peak and divides Korea from Chang Bhakar, on the north-east to the Son; while the streams of the southern slopes feed the Heshto or Hasdo, the largest river of Korea, which runs nearly north and south throughout the state into Bilaspur district and eventually falls into Mahanadi. Its course is rocky throughout, and there is a fine waterfall near Kirkwahi.

The state was ceded to the British government in 1818. In early times there had been some indefinite feudal relations with the state of Surguja, but these were ignored by the British government. The chief call themselves Chauhans, Rajputs, and profess to trace back their descent to a chief of the Chauhan class who conquered Koriya several centuries ago. The direct line became extinct in 1897.

The solution of the chief with the British government are regulated by a *sanad* granted in 1899, and re-issued in 1905 with a few verbal changes due to the transfer of the state to the Central Provinces. Under this *sanad* the chief was formally recognised and permitted to administer his territory subject to prescribed conditions, and tribute was fixed for a further period of twenty years, at the end of which it is liable to revision. The chief was under the general control of the Commissioner of Chhattisgarh.

MAHASAMUND

It was a tehsil of Raipur district, the then Central Provinces. It was constituted in 1906 on the formation of the new Durg district. It contains the greater part of the old Raipur tehsil, including the large *zamindari* estates lying on the south and east of the Mahanadi, and the Phulpjhar *zamindari* transferred from Sambalpur in 1905, together with the Rajim, Raitam, Sirpur, and Khalari tracts forming the ordinary proprietary area of that *tehsil* east of the Mahanadi. Mahasamund contains 2042 villages, with an area of 5,284 square miles and a population of 398,075 persons in 1901, compared with 360,305 in 1891. The density was 75 persons per square mile. The headquarters are at Mahasamund. It includes the *zamindari* estates of Fingeshwar, Bindra-Nawagarh, Khariar, Narra, Suarmor, Kauria, and Phuljhar, with a total area of 4584 square miles.

JANJGIR

It was the eastern tehsil of Bilaspur district, the then Central Provinces. In 1901 its area was 1467 sq miles, and the population was 285,236. On the formation of the new Durg district, the constitution of *teshil* was considerably altered. A tract lying south of the Mahanadi containing the Bilaigarh, Katgi, and Bhatgaon Zamindaris with the Sonakhan estate, and the Sarsewa group of villages was transferred to the Baloda Bazar Tashil of Raipur District while the three northern *zamindaris* of Korba, Chhuri, and Uprora were transferred from the Bilaspur teshil to Janjgir. On the transfer of Sambalpur district to Bengal, the Chandarpur-Padampur and Malkhurda estates of that district were added to this *teshil.* The revised figures of area and population for the Janjgir *teshil* are 3039 sq miles and 418,209 persons. The population of this area in 1891 was 451,024. The density is 138 persons per sq mile. The headquarters are at Janjgir, a village of 2,257 inhabitants, adjoining Naila station is on the Railway 26 miles east of Bilaspur town. It includes the zamindari estates of Champa, Korba, Chhuri, and Uprora, with a total area of 1748 sq miles.

JASHPUR

It was a tributary state in the then Central Provinces till 1905, it was included in the Chotanagpur state of Bengal. It was bounded on the north and west by the Surguja state, on the east by the Ranchi district of Jharkhand, and on the South by Gangpur, Udaipur, and Raigarh, Jashpur consists in almost equal portions of highland and lowland. On the Ranchi side the magnificent table land of Uparghat attains an average elevation of 2200 feet above the sea, and is fringed by hills which in places rise 1,000 feet higher on the east the Uparghat blends with the plateau of Chhotanagpur proper, while on the west it springs from the lowland regions known as the Hetghat in a scarped fortress like wall, buttressed here and there by projecting masses of rock. The Uparghat again is divided by a slight depression from the still loftier plateau of Khuria, which occupied the north western corner of the state, forming the watershed between the IB and the KANHAR, a tributary of river Son. This plateau consists of trap rock topped with volcanic laterite, overlying the granite and gneiss which form the surface rocks at lower elevations. The lowlands of the Hetghat and of Jashpur proper lie in successive steps descending towards the south, broken by ranger of low hills, isolated bluffs, and bare masses of geneiss and other metamorphic rocks. The granite of this low region frequently rises into bare round knolls, the most conspicuous of which is called the Burha from its fancied resemblance to an old man's bald head. The principal peaks are RANIJULA (3527 feet), KOTWAR (3393 feet) and BHARAMURIO (3390 feet). The chief river is the IB, which flows through the state from north to south. Several waterfalls are found along its course, the finest, being formed by the rush of its waters over a square mass of trap-rocks where it passes from the high table-land of the Uparghat into the flat country of Jashpur proper. Owing to numerous rapids, the river is not navigable below these falls. The smaller rivers of Jashpur are mere hill streams, all of which are fordable except at brief intervals during the rains. In the north, these are feeders of the Kanhar and flow towards the valley of Ganges, while on the south they run into the IB and contribute to the river system of Orissa. Gold is obtained in small quantities from the banks and bed of the IB river, near the Gangpur border, by the Jhora Gonds, who wash the soil, they make over the gold to the Raja and are paid by him in rice. Iron is procured in a modular form in the hilly tracts, and is smelted by aboriginal tribes for export. The forest consists largely of *Sal, Shisham,* and ebony, but owing to their distance from the railway there is as yet little demand for the timber.

The state of Jashpur was ceded to the British government by the provisional agreement concluded with Mudhoji Bhonsla in 1818. Although noticed in the second article of this agreement as a separate state, Jashpur was at first treated in some measure as a fief of Surguja, and the tribute, the amount of which was last fixed in 1899 at Rs 1250, still paid through the state. The chief, however, is not bound to render any feudal service to Surguja. The population increased from 113,636 in 1891 to 132,114 in 1901. They dwell in 566 villages, and the density is 68 persons per square mile. The large increase is due chiefly to the inducements held out to immigrants to settle the state, where the area of cultivable waste is very large. The people have also benefited by the introduction of sugar cane and wheat cultivation, and roads have been constructed from the capital to the borders of Ranchi, Surguja, Udaipur, and Gangpur. The most numerous castes and tribes are Oraons (47,000), Rautias (12,000), Korwas (10,000) Ahirs or Goalas and Nagesias (9000, each) and Chiks and Kaurs (7,000 each), according to the census 1901. A rebellion of the Korwas gave considerable trouble some years ago. Pondrapat and table-lands of the Khuria plateau afford excellent pasturage, and Ahirs or cowherds from Mirzapur and elsewhere bring large herds of cattle to graze, the fees paid by them being a considerable source of income to the state. Many Ahirs have settled permanently in Khuria. The trade is confined to foodgrains, oilseeds and jungle products, and is carried on by means of pack-bullock.

The revenue of the state from all sources in 1904-5 was Rs 1,26,000, of which Rs 50,000 was derived from land, Rs 11,000 from excise and Rs 7,000 from forest. The expenditure in the same year was Rs 1,05,000, including Rs 22,000 spent on administration, Rs 35,000 on domestic charges, and Rs 6,000 on public works. The state maintains 199 miles of roads.

KANKER

It was a feudatory state in the then Central Provinces. It was bounded on the north by Durg and Raipur districts, on the east by Raipur, on the south by the state of Bastar and on the west by

Chanda. The headquarters were at Kanker, a village with 3,906 inhabitants, situated on a small stream called the Dudh, 39 miles by road from Dhamtari station on the Raipur-Dhamtari branch of Bengal–Nagpur Railway. Most of the state consists of hill and forest country, and except in the eastern portion along the valley of Mahanadi there are no extensive tracts of plain lands. The Mahanadi enters Kanker at a short distance from its source, and flows through the eastern part of the state, receiving the waters of numerous small streams from the hills. Gneiss of a granitoid character is the prevailing rock formation.

The ruling chief belongs to a very old Rajput family, and according to traditions his ancestors were raised to the throne by a vote of people. During the supremacy of the Haihaivansi dynasty of Chhattisgarh, the chief of Kanker was shown in an old record as in subsidiary alliance with the ruling power, and as having held the Dhamtari tract on condition of furnishing a military contingent of 500 strong whenever required. In 1809 the chief was deprived of Kanker, but was restored to it in 1818 by the British Resident administering the Nagpur territories, on payment of a tribute of Rs 500. This was remitted in 1823 on the resumption by the government of certain manorial dues, and since then no tribute has been paid. Chief Lal Kamal Deo was installed in 1904. The population in 1901 was 103,536, having increased by 26 per cent, during the previous decade. Gonds form more than half the total, and there are also a number of Halbas. Chhattisgarhi and Gondi are the languages spoken.

The total revenue in 1904 was Rs 1,56,000. The principle heads of receipt being land revenue (Rs 67,000), forest (Rs 60,000) and excise (Rs 20,000). The principal items of expenditure were Rs 45,000 for the maintenance of the ruling family, Rs 13,000 on general administration, Rs 8,300 on police, Rs 4,200 on education, and Rs 3,400 on land revenue settlement. During 12 years since 1892 to 1903, a total of Rs 1,14,000 has been expended on public works, under the supervision of the engineer of the Chhattisgarh state division.

The mineral rich state is economically very poor. It will have utilise depend on the neighbouring states of Orissa and Andhra Pradesh. Agriculturally it is a very productive area, called the country's rice bowl. It supplies foodgrains in a very good numbers of rice mills. Chhattisgarh produces more than 1500 hundred varieties of rice. About 85 per cent population here is dependent on agriculture. With substantial deposits of limestone, iron ore, copper ore, rock phosphate, manganese or bauxite, coal, asbestos and mica. Chhattisgarh is one of the mineral rich states of India. Dolomite reserves of Chhattisgarh is estimated about 24 per cent of the country's share. It has healthy bauxite reserves of an estimated 13 million tonnes, an impressive reserves of iron ore at about 2,000 million tonnes and coal at 29,000 million tonnes. Tin ores reserves exceed 27,000 million tonnes. The mineral revenue that will accrue to Chhattisgarh will exceed Rs 600 crore annually. Deobogh in Raipur district contains deposits of diamonds. Prospecting of diamonds has begun here and when extraction starts in about two years' time, it is expected to generate an additional Rs 2,000 crore a year for the state. Chattisgarh also accounts for more than 70 per cent of India's total production of tendu leaves that are used for making bidi. Aluminium, Iron and steel, industries are famous enough in the world.

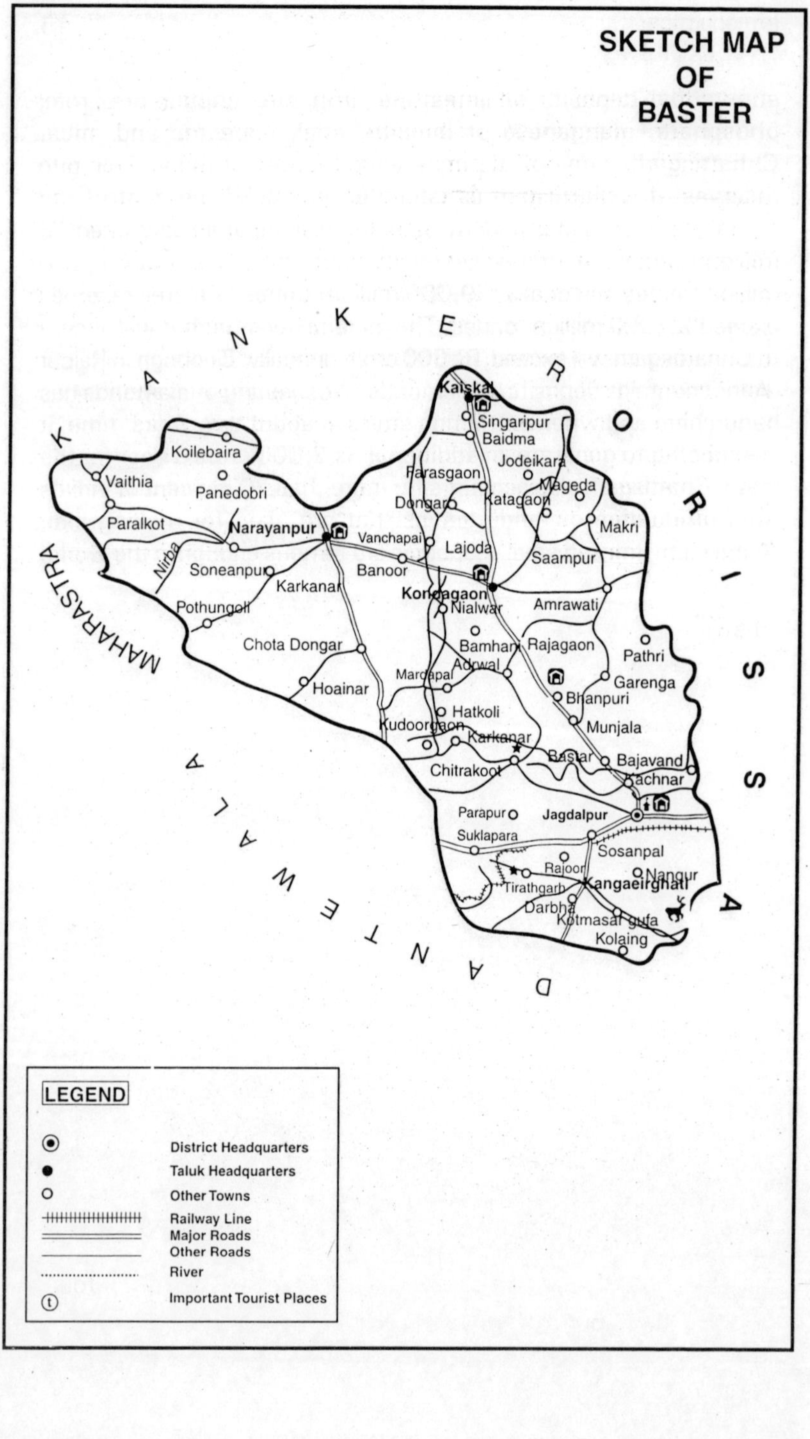
SKETCH MAP OF BASTER
KANKER
ORISSA
MAHARASTRA
DANTEWALA
Nirba
Kaiskal
Singaripur
Baidma
Koilebaira
Vaithia
Panedobri
Paralkot
Narayanpur
Parasgaon
Jodeikara
Mageda
Dongar
Katagaon
Makri
Vanchapai
Lajoda
Saampur
Soneanpur
Banoor
Karkanar
Kondagaon
Nialwar
Amrawati
Pothungoli
Chota Dongar
Bamhani
Rajagaon
Pathri
Adrwal
Mardapal
Hoainar
Garenga
Bhanpuri
Hatkoli
Munjala
Kudoorgaon
Karkanar
Bastar
Bajavand
Chitrakoot
Kachnar
Parapur
Jagdalpur
Suklapara
Sosanpal
Rajoor
Nangur
Kangaeirghati
Tirathgarh
Darbha
Kotmasar gufa
Kolaing
LEGEND
District Headquarters
Taluk Headquarters
Other Towns
Railway Line
Major Roads
Other Roads
River
Important Tourist Places

BASTAR

LOCATION AND AREA

Latitude: 18.4° North to 19.9° North
Longitude: 80.5° East to 82.1° East
Attitude: 553 m

Bastar district is situated in the extreme south of Chhattisgarh State and lies between latitudes 18.4° and 19.9° North and between longitudes 80.5° and 82.1° East. The district is bounded on the north by Kanker and Dhamtari districts; on the west by Chandrapur district of Maharashtra, on the south by Dantewada district; on the east by the state of Orissa. Bastar district was constituted in 1948. Of the two constituent feudatory States forming the Bastar district, Bastar district was bigger than the other. The name of the district seems to have been derived from then Bastar State. There are two explanations regarding the etymology of the name Bastar. According to one, the word Bastar is corrupt form of the Hindi word Vastra meaning cloth and refers to the legend of the gift of a piece of cloth by the tutelary diety to the first chief of the State.

The district headquarters is located at Jagdalpur.

HISTORY

The secluded wilds as it used to be till recently the early history of Bastar district is obscure. On the basis of some inscriptions and copper plates (Epigraphia Indica, Vols. IX and X) it appears that a Nagvanshi dynasty had established their rule in the central part of the district in the 11th century with Barsur and perhaps also Kuruspal near Chitrakot, as their capital This kingdom of the Nagvanshis was known as Chakrakot. No record is available regarding the southern and northern parts of the district on the basis of which any historical reconstruction could be attempted regarding these areas. An inscription found at Sihawa (Raipur district) and dated 1192 A.D., however shows that the founder of the erstwhile Kanker State was Bir Kanhar

Deo who had come to Sihawa from Jagannath Puri, and third ruler in his line had shifted to Kanker where he established capital and extended his domain over the present Kanker and Bhanupratappur tehsils and also possibly the northern parts of Kondagaon and Narayanpur tahsils. The rule of the Kanker chiefs also extended upto Dhamtari tract of Raipur district. The Kanker dynasty was in subsidiary alliance with the powerful Haihayvanshi dynasty of Chhattisgarh.

The Chakrakot kingdom of central Bastar was often raided by many a king from the south and it subsequently formed part of the Warangal kingdom of the Kakatiya dynasty who were feudatories of the Chalukyas. On the decline of the Chalukyas. the Kakatiyas became independent. These Kakatiyas were great patrons of learning and Mallinath, the great commentator flourished under their patronage.

The most notable chief of the warangal Kaktiyas was Pratap Rudra Deo who lost his life in 1424 A.D. in a battle with Ahmad Shah Bahmani. It was his brother Annam Deo who left Warangal and established his Kingdom at Bastar. Annam Deo can thus be said to be the founder of the erstwhile State of Bastar about 1424-25 A.D.

Bastar (now a village 12 miles north of the district headquarters) continued to be the capital of the State till Dalpat Deo's regime who shifted to Jagdalpur. Dalpat Deo's step brother joined hands with the Marathas and in about 1750 a Maratha army under Nilu Pandit invaded and captured the capital but they were fiercely attacked and cut to pieces, Nilu Pandit escaping with his life hidden in a sack carried off by a Banjara. The shifting of the capital from Bastar to Jagdalpur took place after 1750.

During the reign of Daryao Deo, the successor of Dalpat Deo, there was a revolt by the Halbas but it was ruthlessly suppressed. About a century later in 1876, there was a revolt by the Murias. During the heydey of their rule, the Marathas exercised only a nominal control of this district. Being cut off, the district was spared the frequent attacks by invading armies and but for minor internal discords, the ruling dynasties of Bastar and Kanker continued to dominate the area.

The first European who appears to have made attempts to visit Bastar was Captain Blunt in 1795. He had to return without much exploration because of the hostility of the tribals. Captain Fenwick was the first European to visit Bastar in 1850. He was followed by Take in 1855 and by Glasfurd in 1860-62. In 1910, there was large scale disorder in erstwhile Bastar State when the tribals started all-round rioting. It was, however, merged in Madhya Pradesh after Independence and were constituted into the present district.

POPULATION (2001)

Total population of the district according to 2001 census is 1302253 persons, comprising 648068 males and 654185 females. Rural population of the district is 1172265 persons (581666 males and 590599 females) and urban population is 129988 persons (66402 males and 63586 females).

The tehsil-wise population breakup, i.e., rural-urban and male-female population distribution is represented according to 2001 census in the following table:

Tahsil	*Total Rural Urban*	*Persons*	*Males*	*Females*
Keshkal	T	155056	76988	78068
	R	155056	76988	78068
	U	—	—	—
Narayanpur	T	108304	53822	54482
	R	108304	53822	54482
	U	—	—	—
Kondagaon	T	332081	104991	167090
	R	305309	151637	153672
	R	26772	13354	13418
Jagdalpur	T	706812	352267	354545
	R	603596	299219	304377
	R	103216	53048	50168

The decennial growth rate of population of the district as a whole in relation to the State between the period 1991 and 2001 is presented below

State/ District	*Decennial growth rate of population (per cent) 1991–2001*		
	Total	*Rural*	*Urban*
Chhattisgarh	18.06	14.23	36.24
Bastar	18.28	18.17	19.28

LANGUAGES AND RELIGION

Main languages spoken in the district are Hindi. Bengali, Marathi Oriya and Telugu.

GEOGRAPHY AND PHYSICAL FEATURES

Nearly the whole of the northern part of Kondagaon and Narayanpur tehsils is in undulating forest plateau, about 2000 feet high and over this plateau, there are disconnected chains of hills. To the west and southwest of Narayanpur and bounded on the south by the Indrawati, is the extensive mass of hills known as Abujhmar, still the *terra incognita* of the State. The Abujhmar region varies from 2000 to 3160 feet in height. The highest point on the Tulsidongri range in the eastern part of the district is 3928 feet.

The district is rich in forests. The district could be divided into four distinct belts from the point of view of its distribution. (i) Mixed forest of the north, (ii) Central moist region comprising the sal belt, (iii) the teak belt and (iv) the dry region comprising mixed forest.

In the northern portions of the district, the forest trees are Teak (*Tectona grandis*), Sal *(Shoraaro-busta),* Sirsa *(Dalbergia latifolia),* Bijasal (*Ptetocarpus marsupium*), Kusum *(Schleichera trijuga),* Palas (*Butea frondosa*), Mahua (*Bassia latifolia*), Tendu (*Diospyros melanoxylon*), Harra (*Terminalia chebula*), Aonla (*Phyllanthus emblica*), Saja (*Terminalla tomentosa*) Kauha *(T. arjuna),* Salai *(Boswellia serrata)* Char (*Buchanania latifolia*) and others. This region is not so important for timker as for the income from other sources, e.g., collection of forest produce.

The moist region comprises the central region and here the predominant tree is sal, locally known as sargini, accompanied by the usual species. The next belt, the Teak belt or the intermediate belt is less extensive than the moist region and comprises a tract along the south western border of the district.

The dry region consisting of mixed forest is extensive and is interspersed between the moist and intermediate belt but more generally confined to the western half and southern parts of the district. Here are found trees of a mixed variety viz. dhawra (*Anogeissus latifolia*) Bhirra (*Chloroxylon swietenia*), rhoni (*Soymida febrifuga*) and others like char, tendu, aonla, harra and so on.

In the rocky regions, the trees are generally stunted and deformed. Common trees in the rocky region are salai, hangu (*Balanites rexburghli*), khair (*Acacia catechu*), harra, palas, semar (*Bombax malabaricum*) and others.

In the region around village settlements are found the common trees which need no mention here. Palms fill an important place in the domestic economy of the people. The Palmyra palm (*Borassua flabellifer*), locally known as tar, grows gregariously in the south-west. From this people extract tari. The next most important is sulphi (*Caryota urens*). Unlike the palmyra palm, sulphi is not a gregarious species and grows in the shady valleys of hills of depressions of undulating plains. It thrives best in the central regions of the district. The sulphi yields a sap, known by the same name and provides a delicious juice. Other palm trees are the wild date palms (*Phoenix Sylvestris*) and *P. acaulis,* which are locally named as chhind and the buta chhind (*P. farinifera*). From the stem of this buta chhind is obtained a grub which is a delicacy for the tribes.

RIVERS, CANALS AND WATERWAYS

River Indrawati the main geographical feature of the district, flows across the southern limit of it with a tortuous course. It enters this district from Orissa near the confluence of its tributary, the Bhaskal, 13 miles upstream of Jagdalpur. At Chitrakot, 24 miles by road and 35 miles by river downstream from Jagdalpur the Indrawati plunges off the edge of the 2000 feet plateau of north-east Bastar in a beautiful horse-shoe fall. 94 feet high. On reaching the western border of the district, it turns to the south and forms the district boundary until it joins the Godavery below Sironcha. Other important rivers of the surrounding are the Sabri, the Tel, the Narangi, the Gudra, the Net Bherat, the Kotri, the Dantewara, the Dudh and the Mahanadi. The Sabri forms the boundary of the district with Orissa State in the east for about 77 miles. The Tel rises in the district and flows southwest to the Godavery. The Narangi and the District Baordig are the two important tributaries of the Indrawati draining most of the north-eastern areas of the district. The Gudra, the Nei Bherat and the Kotri are the tributaries of the Indrawati debouching into it from the north, the former two take into them most of the drainage from the Abujhmar hills. The Kotri or the Paralkot river rises in the Panabaras area of Durg district and flows south via Partabpur and by the side of the Paralkot range. The Kotri and the Nei Bherat join the Indrawati in a trijunction of unforgettable beauty beneath the fortfied rocks of the Bhairamgarh in a wild expanse of hills and forest unbroken by a single clearing. The Dudh rises about 15 miles west of Keskal and flowing north-east via Kanker town joins the Mahanadi. Except the rivers in the extreme north-eastern parts of the district, the drainge system of Bastar district comes under the Godavery drainage.

TOWNS, VILLAGES AND AMENITIES

The district at present comprises 4 tehsils and 2 towns.

The urban population of the district as percentage of total population in the census years 2001 is indicated below. It also shows the sex ratio (females per 1000 males) and density (population per sq km in the urban population of the district in relation to the State:

State/ District	*Urban population as percentage of total population*	*Sex ratio 2001 (Females per 1000 males)*			*Density (Population per sq km)*
	2001	*Total*	*Rural*	*Urban*	
Chhattisgarh State	20.08	990	1005	935	154
Bastar	9.98	1009	1015	958	87

AMENITIES

Good number of villages having one or more amenities in the district are education, Medical, Drinking Water, Post and Telegraph, Market/Hat, Communications Approach by Pucca Road and Power supply.

COMMUNICATIONS

Baster is connected by road transport from Raipur district. The district is well connected by roadways. The National Highway Number 43 touches Keskal in the North, Kondagaon in the Centre and Jagdalpur, the district headquarter in the south. The National Highway Number 16 also touches Jagdalpur. The Rail communication facility is available in the southern part of the district.

AGRICULTURE AND IRRIGATION

The percentage of irrigated area to total cultivable area is low, being 2.3 per cent. Canal is the main source of irrigation in the district. Paddy is the main crop of the district. Wheat, gram, groundnut and jowar are grown throughout the district.

ANIMAL HUSBANDRY

Livestock is a chief wealth next to agriculture. Cows and buffaloes are common livestock found in the district. In order to improve the overall standard of living, the Animal Husbandry Department has been focussing the district. Still, the milk production is not much satisfactory.

INDUSTRIES

The district is very backward in respect of manunfacturing industries. Household industry plays an important role in the economy of the district. The most important household industry is bidi making, and it is followed by flour mills and oil mills.

HANDICRAFTS

Bell metal works at Jagdalpur; Cane and Bamboo works at Bastar; Jewellery works at Jagdalpur; Stone work at Jagdalpur; Terracota at Jagdalpur; Wood-work at Bastar.

TRADE, COMMERCE AND EXPORT

The following table provides information on important commodities manufactured in exported from and imported in the towns of this district. It also gives information on number of banks available in these towns.

Name of town	*Most Important Commodities*		
	Imported	*Exported*	*Manufactured*
Kondagaon	Edible oil	Timber	Handicraft articles
Jagdalpur	Pulses	Kosa cloth	Kosa cloth

TOURISM

Places of archaeological interest in the district is at Dhanora. Dhanora is important for the ruins of 20 tanks and about 25 mounds which may be of archaeological value.

Kanger, It is a famous National Park of Chattisgarh State. It occupies an area of 200 sq kms. It lies at the border area of Orissa but touches the Jurisdiction of Bastar district. Tiger, panther, deer are the main attraction of the sanctuary).

Tirathgarh and Chitrakoot are the places where tourists use to come in big numbers from other parts of the country and also from abroad every year.

Jagdalpur, the district headquarter is a place of pilgrimage where people from different parts of the country use to come every year.

FAIRS AND FESTIVALS

Important fairs and festivals organised in different parts of the district are Shivratri, Christian Mela, Kabirpanthi mela, Republic day, Holi, Chaitra Poornima, Dashra.

EDUCATION

According to 2001 census, (excluding the population in the age group of 0-6 years) is 479147 persons. Of these, 305540 are males and 173634 are females. In the rural areas of the district 386988 persons (253942 males and 133046 females) are literates and in urban areas 92186 persons (51598 males and 40588 females) are literates. The rate of literacy of this population to the total population, excluding 0–6 years age group according to 2001 census is shown as follows:

	Persons	Males	Females
Total	44.58	57.09	32.17
Rural	40.28	53.24	27.50
Urban	80.75	88.61	72.56

In terms of the number of institutions per 10000 population, Kondagaon (M) has the highest average of primary and middle level institutions. Jagdalpur being the district headquarters town has low averages on all accounts.

COLLEGES (2000)

Government Danteshwari Girls College, Jagdalpur, (Established 1972). Enrolment 507, Teachers 9. (Affiliated College)

Government Degree College, Kondagaon (Established 1982), Enrolment 647, Teachers 10. (Affiliated College)

Government Engineering College, Jagdalpur (Estalished 1982). Enrolment 136, Teachers 17. (Affiliated College)

Government Post Graduate College, Jagdalpur (Established 1960), Enrolment 1015. (Affiliated College)

(Above named colleges belong to Pt. Ravishankar Shukla University, Established 1964.)

MEDICAL

Jagdalpur being the district headquarters town which has a District Hospital is having the highest number of beds in medical institutions per 1000 population.

MEDIA

AIR Station. All India Radio, Jagdalpur.

Newspapers. Dandanarayana Samachar, a Hindi daily, published from Bastar. The circulation of it is 36111. Hindsat a Hindi daily, published from Jagdalpur. The circulation of it is 26473.

ADMINISTRATION

(i) Administrative Division: Bastar

Tehsils: Keshkal, Narayanpur, Kondagaon, Jagdalpur.

Towns and Urban Agglomerations with their Population, Sex-Ratio, Decadal Growth and Literacy Rate (2001)

Town	*Population*	*Percentage Decadal Growth*	*Sex Ratio*	*Literacy Rate*
Kondagaon (MC)	26772	9.73	1005	73.86
Jagdalpur (UA)	103216	22.04	946	82.49
(i) Jagdalpur (MC)	73687	11.39	949	83.57
(ii) Frezerpur (CT)	9630	92.75	943	85.43
(iii) Hatakchora (CT)	6054	25.19	955	73.74

(ii) Parliamentary Constituencies and assembly segments (2001):

No. & Name of Parliamentary Constituencies:

19-Kanker (ST), 20-Bastar (ST).

No. & Name of Assembly Segments of Kanker Parliamentary Constituency which lies in Bastar district Kanker (ST):

148. Keskal (ST)—Keskal RIC and P.Cs. 19 to 26 in Pharsgaon RIC in Kondagon tehsil and the forest villages in the area.

157. Narayanpur (ST)—Koilibeda and Antagarh RICs and P.Cs. 23 to 25 in Narayanpur RIC in Narayanpur tehsil and the forest villages in the area.

Kanker was in Bastar Lok Sabha seat in 1957 and 1962. The communitywise breakup (OBE) in Kanker is Scheduled Castes (6 per cent) Scheduled Tribes (53 per cent) and Ahirs, Telis and Kalars around 5 per cent each. Gandas and Mehras among the Scheduled Castes and Gonds [44 per cent] Bhumias [4 per cent] and Halbas [3 per cent] among the Scheduled Tribes are most dominant.

Number and name of assembly segments of Bastar Parliamentary constituency, which lies in Bastar District.

Bastar (ST):

149. Kondagaon (ST)—Pharasgaon RIC (excluding P.Cs. 19 to 26) and Kondagaon RIC (excluding P.Cs. 35 and 37 to

43) in Kondagon tehsil and the forest villages in the area; and Narayanpur RIC (excluding P.Cs 23 to 25) in Narayanpur tehsil.

150. Bhanpuri (ST)—Bhanpuri RIC: and P.C. 38 in Bakawand RIC in Jagdalpur tehsil and P.Cs. 35 and 37 to 43 in kondagaon RIC in Kondagaon tehsil and the forest villages in the area.

151. Jagdalpur—Bakawand RIC (excluding P.C. 38), Jagdalpur (B) RIC and Jagdalpur (A) RIC (excluding P.Cs. 54 to 59) in Jagdalpur thesil and the forest villages in the area.

152. Keslur (ST)—P.Cs 54 to 59 in Jagdalpur (A) RIC and Keslur RIC in Jagdalpur tehsil and the forest villages in the area, and P.Cs. 7 to 9 in Chindgarh RIC in Konta tehsil

153. Chitrakote (ST)—Chitrakote RIC in Jagdalpur tehsil; and P.Cs. 1 to 9 in Dantewara RIC in Dantewara tehsil and the forest villages in the area.

The communitywise breakup (OBE) in Bastar is Scheduled Castes (4 per cent), Scheduled Tribes (74 per cent) and a sprinkling of other communities. Gonds (60 per cent), Bhumias (6 per cent) and Halbas (5 per cent) are the dominant Scheduled Tribes.

OBSERVATIONAL ORGANISATION

Surface Observatories

This district lies under meteorological sub-division, Madhya Pradesh, East. The facility is available at Jagdalpur. The instrument lies in

Latitude	:	19.1° North
Longitude	:	82.1° East
Altitude	:	553 m
Date of starting	:	3-10-1909.

Hydrometeorological Stations for Climatological Purposes

This facility is available at Pralkote. This instrument lies in

Latitude	:	19.8° North
Longitude	:	80.8° East
Altitude	:	
Date of starting	:	2-5-1970

Upper Air Observatories

This facility is available at Jagdalpur. There are three kinds of this observatories, they are:

(i) Pilot Ballon Observatories: information about upper winds

(ii) Radio sonde observatories: for pressure, temperature, humidity

(iii) Radio wind observatories: wind speed and direction

MINERALS AND ORES OCCURRENCES

Building Materials

Gray limestone and purple lime stone are quarried at many in Jagdalpur (19.1, 82.1) tahsil for road metal.

Slab of silicious platy shales are quarried of Devarapal (18.96, 81.81) for flooring purposes. The sub-arkosic rocks in the area are used as road metal and building material.

Clay

Clay occurs in the *nala.* One mile east of Jajol (18.96, 82.1) and Kotamsar. The reserves of the Kotamsar deposits have been estimated at about 400,000 tons.

Limestone

Occurrences of limestone have been reported from several localities in the Jagdalpur (19.1, 82.1) tahsil.

DISASTROUS WEATHER EVENTS

Drought

1981 September, 3rd and 4th week, aridity was less than 25 per cent, shortage of water, kharif crop badly affected.

1985, April and May, acute shortage of water, crops completely damaged.

June to August 1987, acute shortage of drinking water and fodder reported.

Flood

1983, 16 August, More than 100 houses damaged due to flood in the Godavari River. Several towns badly affected, road communications disrupted.

August 1986, 2nd to 4th week, there was severe flood in Narmada and Indravati river, 18 person died of which 14 persons from Bijapur tehsil of Bastar district alone, in the Bastar district 700 houses either collapsed or severely damaged; road communications disrupted.

Heavy Rains

12–13 July 1994, persons reported died, large number of cattlehead perished, water entered into hutments of low lying areas, kachha houses collapsed.

17–19 June 1996, roads damaged at several places, telecommunications and vehicular traffic disrupted.

DISTRIBUTION OF *SCHEDULED CASTE* POPULATION BY SEX (1991)

	POPULATION		
	Total	Males	Females
	1,32,881	66,407	66,474
Audhelia	14	8	6
Bagri, Bagdi	54	27	27
Bahna, Bahana	18	11	7
Balahi, Balai	34	16	18
Banchada	23	14	9
Barahar, Basod	68	34	34
Bargunda	1	1	0
Basor, Burud, Bansor, Bansodi, Bansphor, Basar	182	94	88
Bedia	17	9	8
Beldar, Sunkar	79	43	36
Bhangi, Mehtar, Balmik, Lalbegi, Dharkar	1,288	634	654
Bhanumati	50	23	27
Chadar	1,521	766	755
*Chamar, Chamari, Bairwa, Bhambi, Jatav, Mochi, Regar, ...	10,013	5,249	4,764
Chidar	665	342	323
Chikwa, Chikvi	100	55	45
Chitar	1,702	891	811
Dahait, Dahayat, Dahat	32	16	16
Dewar	303	166	137
Dhanuk	24	16	8
Dhed, Dher	6	3	3
Dohor	279	145	134
Dom, Dumar, Dome, Domar, Doris	1,637	799	838
Ganda, Gandi	27,095	13,332	13,763
Ghasi, Ghasia	2,660	1,359	1,301
Holiya	24	10	14
Kanjar	30	19	11
Katia, Patharia	1,217	617	600
Khatik	95	46	49
Koli, Kori	155	81	74
Khangar, Kanera, Mirdha	13	8	5
Kuchbandhia	52	22	30
Mahar, Mehra, Mehar	75,259	37,441	37,818
*Mang, Mang Garodi, Mang Garudi, Dankhni Mang, ...	64	28	36
Meghwal	17	10	7
Moghia	183	92	91
Muskhan	8	4	4
Nat, Kalbelia, Sapera, Navdigar, Kubutar	13	10	3
Pasi	81	48	33
Rujjhar	873	437	436
Sansi, Sansia	12	8	4
Silawat	26	19	7
Zamral	3	1	2
Unclassified	6,891	3,453	3,438

(Contd.)

DISTRIBUTION OF *SCHEDULED TRIBE* POPULATION BY SEX (1991)

	POPULATION		
	Total	Males	Females
	15,29,888	7,59,024	7,70,864
Agariya	123	59	64
Andh	32	14	18
Baiga	21	12	9
Bhaina	54	19	35
*Bharia Bhumia, Bhuinhar Bhumia, Bhumiya, Bharia, ...	809	391	418
Bhattra	1,51,418	75,197	76,221
Bhil, Bhilala, Barela, Patelia	295	135	160
Bhil Mina	6	4	2
Bhunjia	29	13	16
Biar, Biyar	84	44	40
Binjhwar	128	63	65
Birhul, Birhor	120	49	71
Damor, Damaria	69	31	38
Dhanwar	188	91	97
Gadaba, Gadba	1,901	893	1,008
*Gond; Arakh, Arrakh, Agaria, Asur, ...	12,63,293	6,25,789	6,37,504
Halba, Halbi	85,824	43,315	42,509
Kamar	944	472	472
Karku	178	99	79
Kawar, Kanwar, Kaur, Cherwa, Rathia, Tanwar, Chattri	1,260	660	600
Khairwar, Kondar	148	76	72
Kharia	35	19	16
Kondh, Khond, Kandh	47	23	24
Kol	102	51	51
Kolam	51	23	28
Korku, Bopchi, Mouasi, Nihal, Nahul, Bondhi, Bondeya	70	48	22
Korwa, Kodaku	10	7	3
Majhi	107	63	44
Majhwar	8	4	4
Mawasi	7	4	3
Munda	273	144	129
Nagesia, Nagasia	12	9	3
Oraon, Dhanka, Dhangad	2,587	1,395	1,192
Pao	25	11	14
Pardhan, Pathari Saroti	2,723	1,362	1,361
*Pardhi; Bahelia, Bahellia, Chita Pardhi, ...	1,287	668	619
Parja	898	462	436
Sahariya, Saharia, Seharia, Sehria, Sosia, Sor	42	23	19
Saonta, Saunta	1	1	0
Saur	24	14	10
Sawar, Sawara	883	440	443
Sonr	1,493	764	729
Unclassified	12,279	6,063	6,216

(Contd.)

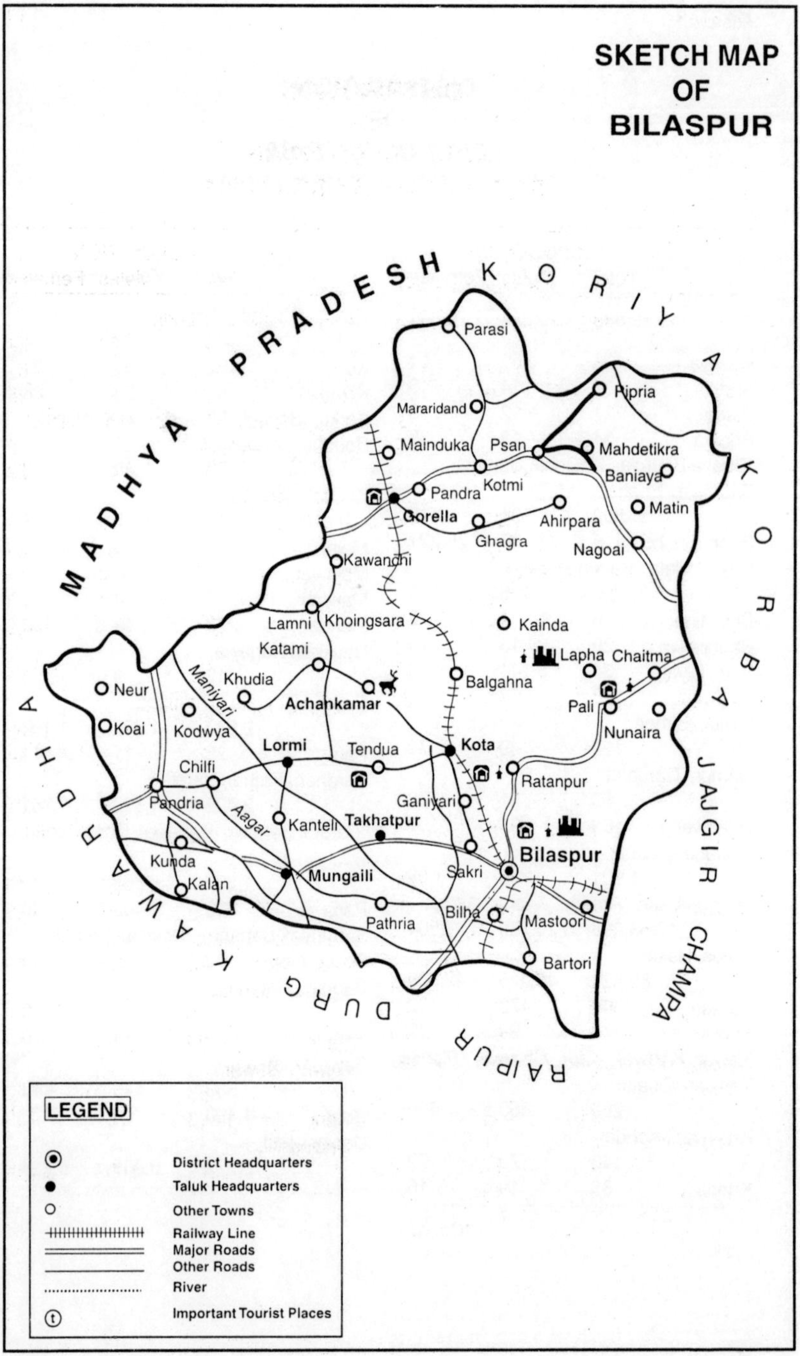
SKETCH MAP
OF
BILASPUR
MADHYA PRADESH
KORIYA
KORBA
JAJGIR
CHAMPA
RAIPUR
DURG
KAWARDHA
Parasi
Pipria
Mararidand
Mainduka
Psan
Mahdetikra
Baniaya
Pandra
Kotmi
Gorella
Matin
Ahirpara
Ghagra
Nagoai
Kawandhi
Lamni
Khoingsara
Kainda
Lapha
Chaitma
Katami
Khudia
Balgahna
Neur
Maniyari
Achankamar
Pali
Koai
Kodwya
Nunaira
Lormi
Tendua
Kota
Chilfi
Ratanpur
Pandria
Ganiyari
Aagar
Kanteli
Takhatpur
Bilaspur
Kunda
Sakri
Kalan
Mungaili
Bilha
Mastoori
Pathria
Bartori
LEGEND
District Headquarters
Taluk Headquarters
Other Towns
Railway Line
Major Roads
Other Roads
River
Important Tourist Places

BILASPUR

LOCATION AND AREA

Latitude : 22.0° North to 21° North
Longitude : 81.2° East to 82.5° East

Bilaspur district, in Bilaspur Revenue Division, is situated in the North-Western part of Chhattisgarh State. The district is bounded by Shahdol and Dindori district of M.P. from North and North Western side; Korba and Jangir Champa district on the east; Raipur and Durg districts on the south; and Kawardha district on the south-west.

The district gets Its name from the district headquarters town, Bilaspur which according to the local legend was founded more than 4310 years ago by a fisher woman named Bilasa Keotin. Bilasa was married woman but was desired by the king of the country and to escape from yielding to him, she burnt herself alive, her husband voluntarily sharing her fate. The habitation founded by her came to be known after her name.

HISTORY

Upto 1905, Bilaspur District covered a much greater area (8341 sq miles). During 1905-06 two important changes took place. Samabalpur district was added to Bengal in 1905 and consequently Malkharoda and Chandanpur-Padampur estates thereof, (area 333 sq miles) were transferred to Bilaspur District. In 1906. Durg district was reconstituted and an area of 363 sq. miles of Bilaspur was transferred to Durg. At the same time 706 sq. miles area was transferred to Raipur District. During the decade 1931–41, the district area was further reduced with the transfer of 80 sq miles to the "New Province" of Orissa which was constituted in 1936 during the decade 1951-1961. Sakti was transferred from Raigarh District to Bilaspur with consequential and other major internal changes, This new Sakti tehsil was expanded by the addition of 283 villages (42.32 sq miles) of Janjgir tehsil and 52 villages (49.20

sq miles) of Kharsia tehsil (which was abolished) of Raigarh District; 17 villages were transferred from Bilaspur tehsil to Mungeli tehsil, 2 villages from Janjgir tehsil were transferred to Rajgarh tehsil of Rajgarh District.

POPULATION (GENERAL, SC/ST)

Total population of the district according to 2001 census is 1993042 persons, comprising of 1009007 males and 984035 females. Rural population of the district is 1511488 persons 760610 males and 750878 females) and urban population is 481554 persons (248397 males and 233157 females).

The tehsilwise population breakup, i.e., rural-urban and male-female population distribution is represented according to 2001 census in the following table:

Tehsil	*Total Rural Urban*	*Total population* Persons	Males	Females
Pendra	T	287359	144340	143019
	R	259794	130336	129458
	U	27565	14004	13561
Lormi	T	208705	104854	103851
	R	196547	98590	97957
	U	12158	6264	5894
Kota	T	184601	91960	92641
	R	149743	74088	75655
	U	34858	17872	16986
Mungeli	T	297274	150020	147254
	R	265666	133689	131977
	U	31609	16331	15277
Takhatpur	T	217001	110054	106947
	R	200012	101404	98608
	U	16989	8650	8339
Bilaspur	T	496690	255810	240880
	R	160634	81913	78721
	U	336056	173897	162159
Masturi	T	198804	99946	98858
	R	193804	99946	98858
	U	–	–	–
Bilha	T	102608	52023	50585
	R	80288	40644	39644
	U	22320	11379	10941

The decennial growth rate of population of the district as a whole in relation to the state between the period 1991 and 2001 is presented below:

State/District	Decennial growth of population (per cent) 1981–91		
	Total	Rural	Urban
Chhattisgarh State	18.06	14.23	36.24
Bilaspur	17.59	12.75	35.92

LANGUAGES AND RELIGION

Main languages spoken in the district are Hindi, Marathi Sindhi and Urdu.

GEOGRAPHY AND PHYSICAL FEATURES

The district is bounded on the north, west and east by ranges of hills while the southern border is open and for the greater part marked by Mahanadi and Seonath rivers. The eastern outer wall of the Satpuras, known as the Maikal range, runs from the north-east to south-west along the north-western border. Irregular ranges of hills alternating with small elevated plateaus stretch along the northern part of the district. On the eastern border, the Sakti hills almost down to the Mahanadi, thus completing the semi-circular chain by which the wide plain country is surrounded. In the central plain region there are two isolated ridges, the Sonthi and the Dalha, and the latter rises abruptly from near Akaltara and is visible from long distances. The general slope of the district is from north-west to south-east. The level of plain country varies from about 1000 feet in the west of Maugeli Tehsil to 750 feet above MSL at the south-eastern extremity of the district. The highest point in the district is Lilwani (3696 feet).

RIVERS, CANALS AND WATERWAYS

Mahanadi and Seonath are two important rivers of the district.

TOWNS, VILLAGES AND AMENITIES

The district at present comprises of 8 tehsils and 14 towns.

The urban population of the district as percentage of total population in the census year 2001 is indicated below. It also shows the sex ratio (females per 1000 males) and density (population per sq km) in the urban population of the district in relation to the State:

State/ District	*Urban population as percentage of total population*	*Sex ratio 2001 (Females per 1000 males*			*Density (Population per sq km)*
	2001	*Total*	*Rural*	*Urban*	
Chhattisgarh State	20.08	990	1005	932	154
Bilaspur	24.16	975	987	939	241

AMENITIES

Villages having one or more aminities are Education; Medical; Drinking water; Post and Telegraph; Market and Hat; Communications; Pucca road and Power supply.

COMMUNICATIONS

Bilaspur tehsil as well as the district headquarters town is an important rail head, on the Calcutta-Nagpur trunk route of South-Eastern Railway. This district is also well-connected by road transport.

AGRICULTURE AND IRRIGATION

The district has a very big cropped area. Percentage of total irrigated area to gross cropped area is about 22 per cent. Canal and the tube-wells are major source of irrigation in the district. Paddy, wheat, and gram are grown in the substantial quantity in the district.

ANIMAL HUSBANDRY

Cows and buffaloes are common livestock found in the district.

Zoo

Kanan Pandari, Bilaspur Division, Bilaspur.

INDUSTRIES

There is no major industry in the district except a few rice mills, oil mills, etc.

HANDICRAFTS

Textiles (woven) works at Bilaspur.

TRADE, COMMERCE AND EXPORT

The following Table provides information on the important commodities manufactured in exported from and imported in the towns of the district.

Wholesale trading of grains and tendu leaves is done in the district.

Name of the Town	*Most important Commodities*		
	Imported	*Exported*	*Manufactured*
Pendra	Paddy	Rice	Chapda
Gorela	Wheat	Cement poles	Cement poles
Ratanpur	Cloth	Rice	Soaps
Kota	Wood	Cement sleepers	Cement sleepers
Lormi	Paddy	Rice	Bamboo basket
Takhatpur	Thread	Rice	Handloom cloth
Mungeli	Oil	Rice	Rice
Bilaspur	Kirana	Bidi	Aluminium Utensils
Sirgite	Iron	Iron articles	Iron articles
Bodri	Lime stone	Cement	Cement
Bilha	Paddy	Rice	Edible oil

TOURISM

Achanakmar: It is a wild life Sanctuary, spread over an area of 551.83 sq. km. The sanctuary is known for, tiger, panther, varieties of deers, bear, and wild hogs.

Pali, Ratanpur and Bilaspur are the religious point.

Lapha and Bilaspur are the sites of archaeological interest and there are forts.

FAIRS AND FESTIVALS

Important fairs and festivals organised in different parts of the district are mentioned below:

Madkooghat Mela, Magha Poornima, Shivratri, Narbadakund Bath, Christian Mela, Kabirpanthi Mela, Republic Day, Kutighat Fair, Holi, Chaitra Poornima, Dasahra.

EDUCATION

According to 2001 census, total literates (excluding the population in the age group of 0-6 years) is 1054658 persons. Of these, 660239 are males and 394419 are females. In the rural areas of the district 714188 persons (464800 males and 249388 females) are literates and in urban areas 340470 persons (195439 males and 145031 females) are literates. The rate of literacy of this population to the total population, excluding 0-6 years age group according to 2001 census are shown as follows:

	Persons	*Males*	*Females*
Total	63.68	78.98	48.08
Rural	57.57	74.76	40.03
Urban	81.92	91.23	72.02

With the increase in the population size of villages the literacy rate is found to be successively increasing which is obviously because bigger villages are well equipped with educational amenities. As per 1991 census 84.32 per cent of total inhabited villages have one or more educational institutions. Literacy is associated with urbanisation. Greater the urbanisation of an area, higher the literacy rate found there. This is, by and large, true in the case of urban areas of Bilaspur district, though there are exceptions like Gaurella, a small town which has a fairly high literacy rate.

COLLEGES 2000

CMD, Postgraduate College, Bilaspur (Established 1956), Enrolment 2805, Teachers 77. (Affiliated College)

DP Vipra Mahavidyalaya, Bilaspur (Established 1969), Enrolment 2110, Teachers 28. (Affiliated College)

Government Arts College, Lormi, Enrolment 199, Teachers 7. (Affiliated College)

Government Arts College, Seepat, Bilaspur (Established 1986), Enrolment 69, Teachers 6. (Affiliated College)

Government Arts and Commerce College, Bilaspur (Established 1984). Enrolment 611. (Affiliated College)

Government Arts and Commerce College, Bilha (Established 1984). Enrolment 452. Teachers 7. (Affiliated College)

Government Arts and Commerce College, Kota (Established 1985). (Affiliated College)

Government College of Education, Bilaspur (Established 1955). (Affiliated College)

Government Degree College, Pendra (Established 1982). Enrolment 520, Teachers 12. (Affiliated College)

Government Engineering College, Bilaspur (Established 1964) enrolment 794, Teachers 41. (Affiliated College)

Government Girls College, Pendra (Established 1989), Enrolment 66, Teachers 6. (Affiliated College)

Government Girls Postgraduate College, Bilaspur, (Established 1961), Enrolment 1989, Teachers 65. (Affiliated College)

Government JMP College, Takhatpur (Established 1965). Enrolment 367, Teachers 9. (Affiliated College)

Government Navin Girls College, Bilaspur, Enrolment 32. (Affiliated College)

Government Science College, Mungeli, Enrolment 137, Teachers 4. (Affiliated College)

Government Science Model College, Bilaspur (Established 1944). Enrolment 639, Teachers 39. (Affiliated College)

Government Women Physical Education College, Pendra (Established 1980). Enrolment 14, Teachers 6. (Affiliated College)

K.R. Law College, Bilaspur (Established 1968) Enrolment 832, Teachers 9. (Affiliated College)

SNG College, Mungeli (Established 1961). Enrolment 628, Teachers 9. (Affiliated College)

(Above named colleges belong to Guru Ghasidas University, Established 1983.)

MEDICAL

Medical facility of one type or other is available in villages of this district, which constitutes very good per cent of total inhabited villages.

MEDIA

Newspapers

Dainik Agradoot, a Hindi daily, published from Bilaspur, circulation 31335.

Dainik Bhaskar, a Hindi daily, published from Bilaspur circulation 28168.

Deshbandhu, a Hindi daily, published from Bilaspur, circulation 27928.

Lok Priya Nishpaksh Varta, Hindi weekly, published from Bilaspur, circulation 33070.

Highway Channel, Hindi daily, published from Bilaspur.

Pankhudiyan, Hindi quarterly, published from Bilaspur.

Chhattisgarh Reporter, Hindi weekly, published from Bilaspur.

ADMINISTRATION

(i) Administrative Division: Bilaspur

Tehsils: Pendra Road; Lormi; Kota; Mungeli; Takhatpur; Bilaspur; Masturi; Bilha.

Towns and Urban Agglomerations with their Population, Sex ratio, Decadal growth and Literacy rate (2001)

Town	*Population*	*Percentage Decadal growth*	*Sex Ratio*	*Literacy Ratio*
Pendra (TP)	12392	6.30	992	81.40
Gaurella (TP)	15173	6.88	950	82.67
Ratanpur (TP)	19838	23.46	950	70.69
Kota (TP)	15020	11.31	951	78.33
Lormi (TP)	12158	17.16	941	73.67
Takhatpur (TP)	16989	15.31	964	78.81
Mungeli (UA)	31608	20.00	935	76.34
Mungeli (TP)	27387	18.55	934	78.95
Bilaspur (UA)	330291	43.85	933	84.66
(i) Bilaspur M. Cor.	265178	27.51	–	–

(ii) Devri (CT)	11636	136.07	932	86.94
(iii) Sirgiti (CT)	12469	37.22	928	75.33
(iv) Lingiyadih (CT)	15769	–	961	77.42
Mehmand (CT)	5765	–	922	64.48
Bodri (TP)	13328	26.20	973	72.27
Bilha (TP)	8992	23.86	–	–

(ii) Parliamentary constituencies and assembly segments (2001):

No. & Name of Parliamentary Constituencies
14-Janjgir, 15-Bilaspur.

14-JANJGIR

No. & Name of Assembly Segments of Janjgir Parliamentary Constituency which lies within the jurisdiction of Bilaspur district.

118. Masturi (SC)—Masturi RIC., P.Cs. 111, 130 and 131 in Bilaspur RIC, and P.Cs.133, 135 and 136 in Sipat (Nargoda) RIC in Bilaspur tehsil.

119. Sipat—Sipat (Nargoda) RIC (excluding P.Cs. 133, 135 and 136), P.Cs. 107, 108, 132 in Bilaspur RIC, P.Cs.78 to 80. 97 and 98 in Ghutku I RIC and P.C. 96 in Ghutku RIC in Bilaspur tehsil and the forest villages in the area.

The communitywise breakup (OBE) in Janjgir is Scheduled Castes (17 per cent), Scheduled Tribes (28 per cent) Rawats (19 per cent) and Ahirs and Telis around 8 per cent each. Others found in large numbers are Kurmis, Malis, Kewats, and Brahmins Satnamis/Chamars (15 per cent) among the Scheduled Castes and Gonds (14 per cent) and Kawars (7 per cent) among the Scheduled Tribes are most prominent.

15—BILASPUR

Number and Name of Assembly Segments of Bilaspur Paliamentary Constituency which lies within the Jurisdiction of Bilaspur district.

110. Marwahi (ST)—Marwahi RIC, Gaurella RIC (excluding P.Cs. 26 to 28) and PCs to 33 and 37 In Kota RIC in Bilaspur tehsil.

111. Kota (Gen.)—P.Cs. 26 to 28 in Gaurella RIC, Kota RIC (excluding P.Cs. 31 to 33 and 37) and P.Cs. 64 to 67 in

Ghutku-I RIC in Bilaspur tehsil and the forest villages in the area.

112. Lormi (Gen.)—Lormi RIC (excluding P.Cs. 12 to 14, 17, 35 and 36) and Pandaria RIC in Mungeli tehsil and the forest villages in the area.

113. Mungeli (SC)—Mungeli and Kunda RICs and P.Cs.17, 35 and 36 in Lormi RIC in Mungeli tehsil.

114. Jarhagaon (SC)—P.Cs. 12 to 14 in Lormi RIC., Jarhagaon RIC and, Patharia RIC (excluding P.Cs. 84 to 91) in Mungeli tehsil.

115. Takhatpur (Gen.)—Takhatpur RIC., Ghutku-II RIC (excluding P.C. 96) and Ghutku-I RIC (excluding P.Cs. 64 to 67, 78 to 80, 97 and 98) in Bilaspur tehsil.

116. Bilaspur (Gen.)—Bilaspur Town including Railway Colony and P.Cs. 109, 110-A and 110-B in Bilaspur RIC in Bilaspur tehsil.

117. Bilha (Gen.)—Bilha RIC. and 112 and 117 in Bilaspur RIC in Bilaspur tehsil and P.Cs. 84 to 91 in Patharia RIC in Mungeli tehsil.

The communitywise breakup (OBE) in Bilaspur is Scheduled Castes (19 per cent), Scheduled Tribes (19 per cent) and Ahirs, Rawats and Telis around 10 per cent each. Kurmis, Malis and Brahmins are also present in sizable numbers Satnamis/Chamars (16 per cent) among the Scheduled Castes and Gonds (9 per cent) and Kawars (15 per cent) among the Scheduled Tribes are dominant.

OBSERVATIONAL ORGANISATION

Surface Observatories

This district lies under meterological sub-division, Madhya Pradesh, East. The facility is available at Pendra Road. The instrument lies in

Latitude	:	22.76° North
Longitude	:	81.9° East
Altitude	:	625 m
Date of starting	:	23-6-1903

Upper Air Observatories

This facility is available at Pendra Road. There are three types of upper Air observatories, they are:

(i) Pilot Ballon observatories: information about upper winds.
(ii) Radio sonde observatories: for pressure, temperature and humidity.
(iii) Radiowind observatories: wind speed and directions.

Seismological Observatories

This facility is available at Bilaspur. This observatory is used for routine determination of epicentre of earthquakes, preparations of bulletins, special study and research.

Aeronautical Meteorological Stations

This facility is available at Pendra. It maintains current weather watch at aerodromes or important locations along and near air routes, provide service for the use of air craft and air traffic control units.

MINERALS AND ORES OCCURRENCES

Bauxite

Occurrence of Bauxite is reported from Rajmergarh (22.7, 81.8), Deoshani Pahar (22.76°, 81.8°), Hazari Dadar (22.65, 87.7), Bij Pahar (22.53, 81.6), Dumar Dadar (22.5, 81.45), Ladra Dadar (22.46, 81.45), Sendurkhar Dadar (22.5, 81.45), Rukmidadar (22.48, 81.3), Pandripani (22.45, 81.21) and Majhgaon (22.6, 81.2), Laterite around Tawardabre (22.71, 81.76), Jalaswar (22.73, 81.76) and Choktipani (22.73, 81.8) are bauxite. These are either pisolithic in texture or are like light white to pinkish coloured clay.

On the Amarkantak (22.66, 81.73) plateau within the Bilaspur district, there is a fairly good deposit of bauxite in addition to a few minor segregations, along the boundary lines S.W. of Amakantak.

Building Materials

The massive granites around Awaldih (22.75, 81.93), Bhadora (22.75, 81.95) and Thengadand (22.65, 81.9) can be used as road metal, railway blast, aggregates and also as building stones.

The bedded dolomitic limestones are quarried for road metal near Setganga (22.1, 81.56). Mungeli (22.1, 81.68), Boirkachra (22.18, 81.28), Bhalpahari (22.2, 81.28) and Pandaria (22.21, 81.41). The flaggy dolomitic limestone exposed near Jaitpur (22.1, 81.48). Damapur (22.1, 81.46) and Chhatan (21.15,

81.6) are worked on a small scale for use as building material. The Cuddapah quartzite around Deosara (22.3, 81.31) can be used as road metal.

Clay

Occurrence of white clay deposits are reported from about 2 miles W.S.W. of Jogisar (22.63, 82.0). They occur in the shape of small pockets. The clay is plastic, light olive green light to pinkish white in colour and is admixed with grits. The thickness of the clay bodies varies from a foot to over 5 ft. below a blanket of 3 to 5 ft. of overburden.

Limestone

Extensive deposits of lime stone have been reported from around Gobripat (22.28, 81.98), Maharpur (22.25, 81.7) near Paraswara (22.31, 81.71) around Baradwar (22.23, 81.96) between Amne (22.21, 81.9) and Mahukapa (22.23, 81.9), Poghra (22.21, 81.98), around Belpan (22.2, 81.86) Limha (22.21, 81.83), Bijaipur (22.21, 81.8). It is estimated that the reserve of the material available from all the deposits will be fairly large. Chemical analysis of the lime stone shows the material is of poor quality but can be used as flux material by suitable admixture with higher grade lime stone.

Lime stones are found to occur around Choklipani (22.73, 81.78) and to the N.W. of Konchi 22.63, 81.79. They are burnt locally to be used as a source of lime. Silicious and impure limestone occur near Sagona (22.29, 81.3), Narsighpur (22.3, 81.5) Sildana (22.26, 82.1) and Kota (22.3, 82.1). Several small deposits of tufaceous lime stone occurring intercalated with shapes have been noted in a *nala* about one km. east of Rahmankapa (22.26, 81.3).

Manganese

Fragments of psilomelaone, pyrolusite and wad are scattered over the eastern slopes of a hill situated about a mile to the N.E. of Ratanpur (22.28, 82.23). Nodular fragments of psilomelane and pyrolusite with ramnants of quartz, chert and quartzite occur near Gorakana, (22.31, 81.43) and has been traced between Gorakona and Munmuna.

B.N. Sinha reports the occurrence of low grade manganese ores low phosphorus from near Kuarimunda (22.3, 82.1) and Kori (22.3, 81.9).

Kori (22.3, 81.9).

Mica

There are numerous pegmatite veins exposed Komochoki (22.6, 82.1) and some of them contain fairly large flakes of white mica, which are about 2 ins. across and occur in book 1 inch or more in thickness. The flakes are highly stained and crumpled.

Pyrites

An occurrence of pyrites as dissiminations in lime stone have been reported from the bed of the chapi *nala* near Sildana (22.26, 82.1).

DISASTROUS WEATHER EVENTS

Hailstorm

April 1st 1982, crops worth Rs. two crore in 113 villages damaged.

16-19 October, 1986, 50 to 60 per cent paddy crop damaged.

Drought

September 3rd and 4th week 1981, Kharif crop badly affected, aridity was less than 25 per cent, acute shortage of water.

April and May 1985, acute shortage of water, crops completely damaged.

February to May 1992, acute shortage of drinking water, crops badly damaged.

Heavy rains

23—26 August 1991, 10,000 persons in 125 villages affected, 118 houses collapsed, Rail services disrupted, Roadways were paralysed, telephone services in rural areas badly affected.

5 August 1994, vehicular traffic and telecommunication services disrupted at various places, standing crops damaged, big trees came on the ground.

1st July 1996, two persons died and several others injured in a house collapse, cows and oxen died due to fracture, water entered into hutments.

Lightning

17 June 1995, 2 persons died and six others injured, flowering crops damaged.

DISTRIBUTION OF *SCHEDULED CASTE* POPULATION BY SEX DISTRICTWISE (1991)

	POPULATION		
	Total	Males	Females
BILASPUR	6,87,221	3,48,238	3,38,983
Audhelia	3,780	1,850	1,930
Bagri, Bagdi	75	38	37
Bahna, Bahana	28	13	15
Balahi, Balai	204	116	88
Banchada	58	29	29
Barahar, Basod	477	222	255
Bargunda	25	10	15
Basor, Burud, Bansor, Bansodi, Bansphor, Basar	1,308	632	676
Bedia	10	9	1
Beldar, Sunkar	1,347	703	644
Bhangi, Mehtar, Balmik, Lalbegi, Dharkar	4,663	2,406	2,257
Bhanumati	228	92	136
Chadar	176	83	93
Chamar, Chamari, Bairwa, Bhambi, Jatav, Mochi, Regar, ...	5,80,987	2,94,852	2,86,135
Chidar	613	314	299
Chikwa, Chikvi	313	202	111
Chitar	202	133	69
Dahait, Dahayat, Dahat	279	130	149
Dewar	1,689	853	836
Dhanuk	155	77	78
Dhed, Dher	25	15	10
Dohor	34	22	12
Dom, Dumar, Dome, Domar, Doris	1,240	623	617
Ganda, Gandi	34,913	17,447	17,466
Ghasi, Ghasia	16,425	8,056	8,369
Holiya	26	11	15
Kanjar	40	21	19
Katia, Patharia	996	502	494
Khatik	371	182	189
Koli, Kori	2,104	1,047	1,057
Khangar, Kanera, Mirdha	27	10	17
Kuchbandhia	45	28	17
Mahar, Mehra, Mehar	14,780	7,578	7,202
*Mang, Mang Garodi, Mang Garudi, Dankhni Mang, ...	922	447	475
Meghwal	14	6	8
Moghia	15	11	4
Muskhan	38	14	24
Nat, Kalbelia, Sapera, Navdigar, Kubutar	905	444	461
Pasi	656	360	296
Rujjhar	365	182	183
Sansi, Sansia	122	60	62
Silawat	60	28	32
Zamral	13	9	4
Unclassified	16,468	8,371	8,097

(Contd.)

DISTRIBUTION
OF
SCHEDULED TRIBE
POPULATION BY SEX
DISTRICTWISE (1991)

	POPULATION		
	Total	Males	Females
BILASPUR			
	8,73,741	4,36,217	4,37,524
Agariya	9,207	4,563	4,644
Andh	157	65	92
Baiga	23,223	11,623	11,600
Bhaina	32,754	16,514	16,240
*Bharia Bhumia, Bhuinhar Bhumia, Bhumiya, Bharia, ...	11,600	5,702	5,898
Bhattra	130	65	65
Bhil, Bhilala, Barela, Patelia	445	240	205
Bhil Mina	221	103	118
Bhunjia	167	75	92
Biar, Biyar	1,307	667	640
Binjhwar	29,709	15,102	14,607
Birhul, Birhor	338	158	180
Damor, Damaria	116	65	51
Dhanwar	24,701	12,424	12,277
Gadaba, Gadba	3,354	1,606	1,748
*Gond; Arakh, Arrakh, Agaria, Asur, ...	4,45,957	2,22,334	2,23,623
Halba, Halbi	339	192	147
Kamar	56	30	26
Karku	274	135	139
Kawar, Kanwar, Kaur, Cherwa, Rathia, Tanwar, Chattri	1,65,862	82,226	83,636
Khairwar, Kondar	8,551	4,284	4,267
Kharia	2,793	1,404	1,389
Kondh, Khond, Kandh	161	85	76
Kol	7,818	3,842	3,976
Kolam	1,067	579	488
Korku, Bopchi, Mouasi, Nihal, Nahul, Bondhi, Bondeya	275	147	128
Korwa, Kodaku	2,416	1,164	1,252
Majhi	7,718	3,887	3,831
Majhwar	16,045	7,994	8,051
Mawasi	118	48	70
Munda	1,111	549	562
Nagesia, Nagasia	958	499	459
Oraon, Dhanka, Dhangad	33,738	17,194	16,544
Pao	6,445	3,235	3,210
Pardhan, Pathari Saroti	2,739	1,370	1,369
*Pardhi; Bahelia, Bahellia, Chita Pardhi, ...	2,057	1,033	1,024
Parja	35	19	16
Sahariya, Saharia, Seharia, Sehria, Sosia, Sor	358	164	194
Saonta, Saunta	1,703	841	862
Saur	7,066	3,489	3,577
Sawar, Sawara	10,232	5,115	5,117
Sonr	1,324	643	681
Unclassified	9,096	4,743	4,353

(Contd.)

SKETCH MAP OF DANTEWADA
BASTAR
ORISSA
ANDHRA PRADESH
Dhobie
Paskhara
Lanka
Indrawati
Bandepare
Goti
Barsur
Pamed
Sandra
Mukkabaili
Kutroo
Hirmapaida
Mandem
Bhairamgarh
Tumnar
Baraiguda
Chintapalli
Toynar
Geedam
Patliguda
Nimad
DANTEWADA
Gumda
Bhopalapatnam
Digoli
Padmoor
Karka
Bijapur
Pusnar
Kanakoda
Madare
Paidakorma
Masenar
Kankapal
Mangalore
Mailawara
Kokawara
Katura
Sankanpalli
Mukkapara
Talpalu
Kidanda
Korras
Kukanar
Awapalli
Rokail
Basagmura
Aranpur
Burgam
Usoor
Godpalli
Sabari
Polampalli
Jeerampal
Jagarguda
Nahadi
Sukma
Pujarikaker
Chintalnar
Gogoda
Maitugudiyam
Beeramgarh
Bardepal
Chinta
Dharmaram
Ilmagoda
Penta
Argatta
Palahelama
Kistaram
Golapalli
Konta
LEGEND
District Headquarters
Taluk Headquarters
Other Towns
Railway Line
Major Roads
Other Roads
River
Important Tourist Places

DANTEWARA

LOCATION AND AREA

Latitude : 17.9° North to 18.4° North
Longitude : 80.1 East to 82.1° East

The Dantewara district occupies the southernmost part of Chhattisgarh state. This district is bounded on north and north-east by its parent district, i.e., Bastar district, on east by Koraput district of Orissa state, on south and lower half portion of the western state by Andhra Phadesh state and the remaining western portions by Maharashtra state. The district is named after Danteshwari, the popular tribal deity of the region. The total area of this district is approximately 10827.71 sq kms.

HISTORY

The Dantewara district came into existence on 25 May, 1998. The state government of undivided Madhya Pradesh vide the Gazette notification no. 1010–F–20–8–92–VII–S–8 dated 22-5-1998 modified by jurisdiction of Bastar district. In accordance with the said notification four tehsils namely Bhopalpattnam, Bijapur, Dantewara and Konta of Bastar district were taken out to form the present new district. It is to be pointed out that all these four tehsils were existed at the time of 1991 census as well. These four tehsils were divided into twelve Community Development Blocks *viz.* Darbha, Bhopalpattnam, Usur, Bhairangarh, Bijapur, Geedam, Dantewara, Katekalyan, Kuwakonda, Chhindgarh, Sukma and Konta.

The historical past of Dantewara district is the same as that of its parent district, i.e., Bastar and it has been explained in detail in the note of the said district.

POPULATION (GENERAL, SC/ST)

The total population of Dantewara district according to 2001 census is 719065 persons comprising 356502 males and 362563 females. Rural population of the district is 667074 persons (329228 males and 337846 females) and urban population is 51991 persons (27274 males and 24717 females). Except that of Dantewara tehsil, other three tehsils comprised of rural areas.

The tehsil-wise population breakup, i.e., rural-urban and male-female population distribution is presented according to 2001 census in the following table:

Tehsil	Total/ Rural/Urban	Total Population		
		Persons	Males	Females
Bhopalpattnam	T	98904	49727	49177
	R	98904	49727	49177
	U	—	—	—
Bijapur	T	141738	70827	70911
	R	141738	70827	70911
	U	—	—	—
Dantewara	T	246978	122183	124795
	R	194987	94909	100078
	U	51991	27274	24717
Konta	T	231445	113765	117680
	R	231445	113765	117680
	U	—	—	—

The Scheduled Castes and Scheduled Tribes population in twelve Community Development Blocks of this district as per 1991 census are 28,651 and 4,99,437 persons respectively. The rural-urban breakup of this population is indicated below :

Rural : (i) Scheduled Castes : 24,706
(ii) Scheduled Tribes : 4,92,137
Urban : (i) Scheduled Castes : 3,945
(ii) Scheduled Tribes : 7,300

The decennial growth rate of population of the district as a whole in relation to the state between the period 1991 and 2001 is presented below.

State/ District	Decennial growth rate of population (per cent) 1991–2001		
	Total	Rural	Urban
Chhattisgarh State	18.06	14.23	36.24
Dantewara	15.56	13.05	61.44

LANGUAGES AND RELIGION

Hindi is the main language spoken in this district. Tribal dialects are spoken in the rural areas because this district is dominated by Scheduled Tribes population.

Religionwise breakup of population of this district is indicated below:

Hindus: 612127, Muslims: 4159, Jains: 878, Christians: 3475, Buddhists: 357, Sikhs: 442, other religions and persuasions: 453, Religions not stated: 376.

GEOGRAPHY AND PHYSICAL FEATURES

Most part of the district consists of hills. The loftiest peak of the district is the Bailadila or the 'Bullock's hump'. It is situated to the south of the Indrawati and tilts towards north-south. The highest point of the Tulsidongri range in the eastern part of the district is 3928 feet. The Albaka range of hills of Andhra Pradesh forms part of the western boundary of the district, parallel to the Albaka range and about eight miles to the north-east are the Matimarka hills. Other important hills in the district are that of the Tikhapalli hills, an isolated range of about 2,800 feet in height, covering about 16 sq miles in Konta tehsil and the Kosmi range in the north rising to about 2,600 feet. The district is rich in forest. The forest found in the district falls under the dry region comprising mixed forest range. Here are found trees of a mixed variety viz. Dhawra, Bhirra, Rhoni and others like Char, Tendu, Aonla and Harla. In the rocky regions, the trees are generally stunted and deformed. Common trees in the rocky region are Salai, Hangu, Khair, Harra, Palas, Semas and others. The district is famous for its rich wildlife as it has very thick cover of forest. Tigers and panthers are found throughout the district in the forest. Tigers and panthers have a notoriety for turning man-eaters, evidently because of the scarcity of trees, natural food in the forest and absence of cattle.

RIVERS, CANALS AND WATERWAYS

Indrawati is the main river of this district. On reaching the western border of the district, it turns to the south and forms the district boundary until it joins the Godavari below Sironcha. Other important rivers of the district are the Sabri, the Tel, and the Dantewara. The Sabri forms the boundary of the district with Orissa state in the east. The Tel rises in the district and flows south-west to the Godavari. The Dantewara and its feeders the Sankini and Dankini, join the Indrawati from the south.

TOWNS, VILLAGES AND AMENITIES

The district is comprised of four tehsils namely Bhopalpatnam, Bijapur, Dantewara, Konta. It has four towns, they are Geedam, Dantewada, Bade Bachele, and Kirandul.

COMMUNICATIONS

The district headquarters and also the Kirandul town is linked with broad gauge line from Jagdalpur. The National Highway No. 16 enters in the district from eastern side, intersept the state Highway at Godam, it touches Bhairamgarh which is straight in the west, then it turns in the south west direction and touches Nimed, Digoli, and Bijapur, again the National Highway turns to west and touches the tehsil headquarters of Bhopalapatnam tehsil, after it, this Highwaay enters in Maharashtra state and after 50 km it enters in Andhra Pradesh. In addition, State Highway No. 36 which runs through Jagdalpur connects most of the important places of the district, viz. Bijapur, Dantewara, Kirandul, Bade Kirpal. Another metalled road connects Konta, the tehsil headquarters with Jagdalpur. Thus, the district has satisfactory road network and these provide basic communication facility within the district as well as these cater to the need of local people to travel to neighbouring districts of the state. Interior villages are linked with unmetalled roads.

AGRICULTURE AND IRRIGATION

Inferior millets *viz.* Kodo-Kutki and rice are the main crops of this district. The district being hilly with dense forest, agricultural land are scanty and irrigation facilities are also not satisfactory in the district. As a result, agricultural production is not very much significant. At places local tribals are still seen practising Jhum shifting cultivation.

ANIMAL HUSBANDRY

Cattle are not found in good numbers in the district. Poultry birds are, however, reared in most of the households in rural areas.

INDUSTRY

The district is known for iron ore in the region. The Bailadila iron ore project is well known not only in India, but also in Asia. There is, however, no industry of significance in the district. Kirandul is the mining township.

TRADE, COMMERCE AND EXPORT

The following table provides information on the most important commodities manufactured, exported from and imported in the towns of this district. It also indicates the banking facility available in the town.

Name of town	*Most important commodities*			*Banks*
	Manufactured	*Exported*	*Imported*	
1. Kirandul	Steel furniture	Iron ore	Cloth, Grain, Engineering goods	1
2. Bade Bachelli	—	—	-do-	—

TOURISM

The loftiest peak of Bailadila as the "Bullock's hump' is one of the important tourist attractions in the district. Places of archaeological interest in the district are Barsur and Dantewara. At Barsur, a Shiva temple in a damaged state and also a ruined temple of Ghanesa are found. A temple known as Mama-Bhancha is in the best state of preservation. There is another temple here from which Captain Glasfurd took an inscription in Telugu dating 1109 A.D. Nearby places of tourist interest include Chitrakut which is situated at a distance of 24 miles by road from Jagdalpur.

The district maintains one National Park and two Wild Life Sanctuaries.

Indrawathi

It is a National Park, lies in the northern portion of the district and occupies an area of 1258.37 sq kms. It is around the border area of Maharashtra state: Tiger, panther and different varieties of deer are the main attrocities of this national park.

Pamer

It is a wild life sanctuary, situated in the northern part of the district. Panther, tiger and antilobe are commonly found in this sanctuary.

Bairamgarh

It is a wild life sanctuary localised in the southern part of the district. The sanctuary is spread over an area of 139.00 sq. kms. Commom fauna maintain in this sanctuary are tiger, panther, and different varieties of deer. Migratory birds use to land during winter season here.

FAIR AND FESTIVALS

Important fairs and festivals organised in different parts of the district are Chaitra Poornima, Dashara, Magha Poornima, Shivratri, Kartika Poornima etc.

EDUCATION

According to 2001 censu total literates (excluding the population in the age group of 0–6 years) is 176621 persons. Of these 115499 are males and 61122 are females. In the rural areas of the district 140957 persons (94593 males and 46364 females) are literates and in urban areas 35664 persons (20906 males and 14758 females) are the literates. The rate of literacy of this population to the total population (excluding 0–6 years age group according to 2001 census are shown below.

	Persons	*Males*	*Females*
Total	30.01	39.59	20.59
Rural	25.95	35.33	16.84
Urban	78.37	87.27	68.47

The following table gives information on different types of educational institutions, stadia and public libraries available in the towns of this district.

Name of town	*Educational institutions*	*Stadia*	*Public libraries including reading rooms*
1. Kirandul	Higher Secondary Schools (1) Middle schools (4), Primary Schools (7)	1	2

2. Bade Bachelli	Higher Secondary School (1), Middle School (1), Primary Schools (2)	–	–

COLLEGES 2000

Government Arvind College, Kirandul (Established 1973). Enrolment 479, Teachers 10. (Affiliated College)

Government College, Bhopalapatnam (Established 1988). Enrolment 65. Teachers 5. (Affiliated College)

Government Degree College, Dantewada (Established 1982). Enrolment 162. Teachers 6. (Affiliated College)

Above named Colleges belong to Pt. Ravishankar Shukla University, Raipur, Established 1964).

MEDICAL

The table given below furnishes information regarding availability of medical facility in the towns of this district including that of beds facility:

Name of town	*Medical institution (including beds facility)*
1. Kirandul	Hospital (1), Dispensaries (2) : 48
2. Bade Bachelli	Primary Health centre (1) : –

ADMINISTRATION

(i) Administrative Division: Bastar

Towns and Urban Agglomerations with their Populations, Sex ratio, Decadal growth and Literacy Rate

Town	*Population*	*Percentage decadal growth 1991–2001*	*Sex Ratio*	*Literacy Ratio*
Geedam (CT)	5899		946	75.78
Dantewara (TP)	6632		883	81.51
Bade Bacheli (TP)	20407	62.19	891	74.90
Kirandul (MC)	19053	- 2.90	919	81.81

(ii) Parliamentary Constituencies and Assembly Segments (2001):

No. & Name of Parliamentary Constituency: 20 Bastar

No. & Name of Assembly Segments of Bastar parliamentary Constituency which lies within the Jurisdiction of Dantewara District:

20-BASTAR

154. Dantewara (ST)—Dantewara tehsil (excluding P.Cs. 1 to 9 in Dantewara RIC) and the forest villages in the area.

155. Konta (ST)—Konta tehsil excluding P.Cs. 7 to 9 in Chindgarh RIC and the forest villages in the area.

156. Bijapur (ST)—Bijapur tehsil and the forest villages in the area.

MINERALS AND ORES OCCURRENCES

Passing tests carried out in the Sabari River at Puspal (18.63, 81.9) indicate the presence of monazite.

Bauxite

Bauxite associated with laterite on the Tarali Metta (18.53, 81.23) and at the watershed between Bailadila and Galli nalas. The laterite occur at a height of about 3,000 ft. on the Bailadila range.

Building Materials

Slabs of silicious platy shales are quarried near Devara Pal (18.96, 81.81) and its surroundings for flooring purposes. The sub-arkosic rocks in the area are used as road metal and building material.

Clay

Whitish, buff-stained clay occurs in the Gorali *nadi* section near Sindigar.

Corundum

Crookshank reports the occurrence of small quantity of ruby coloured associated with sellimanate west of Keriapat (18.3, 81.53). Corundum of detrital nature occurs at Bhopalapatnam (18.86, 80.4)

Lead and Silver

Massive galena occurs in vein quartz in a *nala* near Banchi hamlet (18.8, 81.26). A minor occurrence of galena associated with quartz veins has been reported from near Binjam (18.93, 81.31).

Limestone

Grey basinal calcillutite occurs near Bhopalapatnam (18.86, 80.38). The grey limestone occurring near Sargipal is burnt for lime.

Cement grade lime stone occurs at Chinta *vagu* and limed (18.85, 80.35). Limestone suitable for cement manufacture are also found along the Gorali Nadi near Sukma.

Mica

Lepidolite occurs in boulders at surface as well as in *situ* in pegmatites near Mundval (18.65, 81.93). One of the deposits of lepidolite occurs about 400 yards south of Mundaval.

Sillimanite

Small occurrences of sillimanite have been reported from the ridge east of Samsatti (18.3, 81.23) and the hills to the north of Chittaguppa (18.25, 81.25). Sillimanite associated with small amounts of ruby coloured corundum occurs near Keriapal (18.3, 81.53).

DISASTROUS WHEATHER EVENTS

Floods

16 August 1983, several town badly affected, Road communication disrupted. Four villages in Bhopalapatnam tahsil washed away.

August 1986, 2nd to 4th week, there was severe flood in Narmada and Indravati rivers, people reported died, water entered in the low lying areas.

Drought

September 1981, 3rd and 4th week, cattle head perished, standing crops dried.

April and May 1985, acute shortage of water, crops completely damaged

June to August 1987, acute shortage of fodder and drinking water, cattle reported died at several places.

May 1993, 2nd week, livestock and wild animals died due to scarcity of water.

Heavy rains

17–18 July 1993, several houses collapsed, vehicular traffic, railways, air services disrupted telephone service badly affected.

12–13 July 1994, person reported died, large number of cattle head perished.

17–19 June 1996, roads damaged at several places; telecommunication and vehicular traffic disrupted.

Heatwave

17–19 June 1995, at some places the temperature was 7 to 8°C above the normal, standing crops damaged.

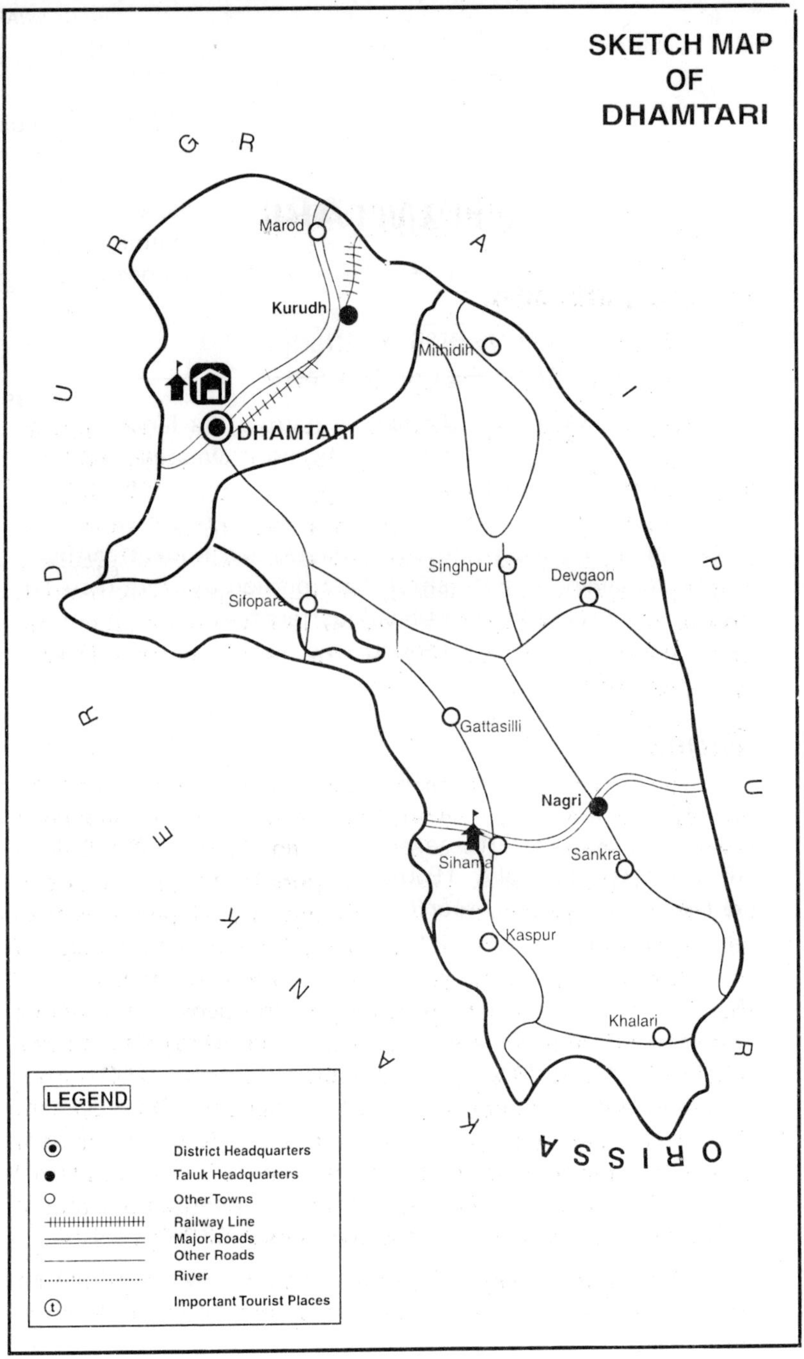
SKETCH MAP
OF
DHAMTARI
DURG
RAIPUR
KANKER
ORISSA
Marod
Kurudh
Mithidih
DHAMTARI
Singhpur
Devgaon
Sifopara
Gattasilli
Nagri
Sihama
Sankra
Kaspur
Khalari
LEGEND
District Headquarters
Taluk Headquarters
Other Towns
Railway Line
Major Roads
Other Roads
River
Important Tourist Places

DHAMTARI

LOCATION AND AREA

Latitude : 20° North to 21° North
Longitude : 81.5° East to 82° East

Dhamtari district, looks likes a narrow flat land with its upper portion tilting little towards the north-western horizon. The district is bounded on the north, east and south-east by Raipur district, on south by Orissa state, on south-west and lower half of the west portion by Bastar and Kanker districts and the remaining upper half of west portion by Durg district. The district is named after its headquarters town, i.e., Dhamtari and it has an area of 2083.94 sq kms (excluding the areas of forest villages).

HISTORY

The district of Dhamtari has been carved out as a separate district on 6 July, 1998 vide the state government of undivided Madhya Pradesh Gazette notification no. 1239–F–20–8–92–VII–S–8 dated 2 July, 1998. In pursuance of the above mentioned notification, four Community Development Blocks namely Dhamtari, Magarlod, Kurud and Nagri (of Raipur district) were taken out from the jurisdiction of Raipur district to form the present new district. According to the census, the above stated four Community Development Blocks were parts of three tehsils *viz.* Kurud, Dhamtari and Nagri. At present (2001) also, Dhamtari district comprises of four Community Development Blocks viz. Dhamtari, Magarlod, Kurud and Nagri. In ancient period, the area comprising of Dhamtari district formed an internal part of Dakshina Koshala. It is further to be pointed out that in 1856, Dhamtari was one of the two tehsils of Raipur district.

The historical part of Dhamtari district is the same as that of its parent district, i.e., Raipur which has been explained in detail in it.

POPULATION (GENERAL, SC/ST)

The total population of Dhamtari district according to 2001 census is 703569 persons comprising 350962 males and 352607 females. Rural population of the district is 610001 persons (303965 males and 306036 females) and urban population is 93568 persons (46997 males and 46571 females).

The tehsilwise population breakup, i.e., rural-urban and male-female population distribution is represented according to 2001 census in the following table.

Tehsil	*Total/ Rural/ Urban*	*Total population*		
		Persons	*Males*	*Females*
Karud	T	294179	146899	147280
	R	282710	141143	141567
	U	11469	5753	5753
Dhamtari	T	248536	124242	124294
	R	166437	83001	83436
	U	82099	41241	40858
Nagri	T	160854	79821	81033
	R	160854	79821	81033
	U	—	—	—

The decennial growth rate of population of the district as a whole in relation to the state between the period 1991 and 2001 is presented below:

State/ District	*Decennial growth rate of population (per cent) 1991–2001*		
	Total	*Rural*	*Urban*
Chhattisgarh	18.06	14.23	36.24
Dhamtari	19.72	20.88	12.70

LANGUAGES AND RELIGIONS

The main language spoken in the district is Hindi. Chhattisgarhi is the dialect generally used by the local people particularly in villages for inter-communication. Religionwise breakup of population of this district is indicated below:

Hindus: 572920, Muslims: 7341, Jains: 2983, Christians: 2223, Buddhists: 194, Sikhs: 955, Other religions and persuasions: 113, Religions not stated: 950.

GEOGRAPHY AND PHYSICAL FEATURES

The district is divided into two physical divisions by the Mahanadi river which flows across the district from its south-western corner to north-eastern corner. The area to the west of the rivers comprises of the open Chhattisgarh plain, thickly populated and closely cultivated. The south and south-eastern part, east of Chhattisgarh plain is hilly. The noteworthy hill features are the Sring-rishi and Angira-rishi of Dhamtari tehsil. The Sihawa group of hills lie on the plateau to the west of Sondur valley in the southern part of Dhamtari tehsil.

RIVERS, CANALS AND WATER WAYS

Mahanadi is the principal river of the district. The general slope of the terrain is towards north. Consequently, the Mahanadi which rises in the Sihawa range, flows north-west throughout its length in the district. Kharun which rises about 13 kms east of Balod in Durg district and flows to the north-east and in this course, it forms western boundary to some distance with Durg district.

TOWNS, VILLAGES AND AMENITIES

During the 2001 census, the district comprised of three tehsils namely Kurud, Dhamtari and Nagri and four Community Development Blocks. It has only two towns.

Details on availability of infrastructural facilities in the villages of this district are not available separately. The combined figures in this regard are provided alongwith its parent district.

COMMUNICATIONS

The district headquarters, i.e., Dhamtari is situated on National Highway No. 43 on Bastar-Kanker-Raipur road. A narrow gauge railway line also connects the Dhamtari with Raipur, the capital of Chhattisgarh state. All the four Community Development Blocks are interlinked by road transport. Both metalled as well as unmetalled roads provide road transport to most parts of the district.

AGRICULTURE AND IRRIGATION

The areas comprising Dhamtari and Kurud Community Development Blocks located in the doab of Mahanadi and Kharun rivers provide good paddy crop. In fact these areas are comparatively better for the agricultural purposes than those in Nagri Community Development Block, Paddy and wheat are the main crops. Pulses and oilseeds are also grown in good quantity in the district. Main crop seasons are *rabi* and *kharif*. Improved agricultural practices are being increasingly used in consumption of fertilizers, pesticides, insecticides. Improved agricultural implements are finding acceptability among the farmers.

ANIMAL HUSBANDRY

Animal husbandry provide power for various agricultural operations. The main livestock of the district include bovine population including buffaloes followed by goats.

INDUSTRY

The district is backward in terms of industrial development. The main industries are those which are engaged in processing of agricultural produce. These are mainly oil, rice, dal mills.

TRADE, COMMERCE AND EXPORT

The table given below provides information on most important commodities manufactured, exported from and imported in the towns of this district. It also indicates the numbers of banks available in these towns.

Name of town	*Most important commodities*			*Banks*
	Manufactured	*Exported*	*Imported*	
1. Kurud	Rice, Bricks, Bidi	Rice, Leather	Iron, wheat cloth	1
2. Dhamtari	Bidi, furniture Sleepers	Rice, Leather Bidi	-do-	–

TOURISM

Dhamtari and Sihama are two places in the district which are of archaeological interest as well as the places of pilgrimages. Sihama is situated near the border of Kanker district while the other located near the border of Durg district.

FAIRS AND FESTIVALS

Important fairs and festivals organised in different parts of the district are Chaitra Poornima, Dashahra, Magha Poornima, Shivratri, Kartika Poornima, etc.

EDUCATION

Information on educational institutions, stadia and public libraries (including reading rooms) available in the towns of this district is provided in the table given below:

Name of town	*Educational institution*	*Stadia*	*Public libraries including reading rooms*
1. Kurud	Higher Secondary School (1) Middle school (1) Primary School (1)	–	–
2. Dhamtari	Higher Secondary Schools (7), Middle Schools (12), Primary Schools (31)	–	1

According to 2001 census total literates (excluding the population in the age group of 0–6 years) is 443298 persons of these 254686 are males and 188612 are females. In the rural areas of the district 379250 persons (218726 males and 160524 females) are literates and in the urban areas 64048 persons (35960 males and 28088 females) are literates. The rate of literacy of this population to the total population (excluding 0–6 years age group according to 2001 census are shown below.

	Persons	*Males*	*Females*
Total	75.16	86.78	63.66
Rural	74.46	86.35	62.82
Urban	79.63	89.5	69.77

COLLEGES 2000

Government College Kurud (Established 1984). Enrolment 414, Teachers 6. (Affiliated College)

Government College, Nagari-sihawa (1984). Enrolment 359, Teachers 7. (Affiliated College)

Government Post Graduate College, Dhamtari (Established 1981). Enrolment 1480, Teachers 44. (Affiliated College)

(Above named colleges belong to Pt. Ravishankar Shukla University, Raipur. Established 1964.

MEDICAL

The following table gives information on medical institutions with beds facility available in the towns of this district:

Name of Town	*Medical institution (including beds facility)*
1. Kurud	Health centre (1), Dispensary (1) : 5
2. Dhamtari	Hospital (2), Family Planning Centre (1) : 64

ADMINISTRATION

(i) Administrative Division: Raipur

Tehsils: Kurud, Dhamtari, Nagri.

Towns and Urban Agglomerations with their Population, Sex Ratio, Decadal Growth and Literacy Rate (2001)

Town	*Population*	*Percentage decadal growth 1991–2001*	*Sex Ratio*	*Literacy Rate*
Kurud (TP)	11469	– 16.09	993	76.31
Dhamtari (MC)	82099	18.37	991	80.08

(ii) Parliamentary Constituencies and Assembly Segments (2001):

No. & Name of Parliamentary Constituency:

18. Mahasamund; 19. Kanker

No. & Name of Assembly segments of Mahasamund Parliamentary Constituency which lies within the jurisdiction of Dhamtari district.

18-MAHASAMUND

144. Kurud—Kurud and Magarlod RICs in Dhamtari tehsil and the forest villages in the area.

145. Dhamtari—Bhothali RIC, Dhamtari town and P.Cs. 50 to 52 in Dhamtari RIC in Dhamtari tehsil.

Number and name of Assembly Segments of Kanker Parliamentary Constituency of Dhamtari district.

19-KANKER

143. Sihawa (ST)—Sihawa RIC and Dhamtari RIC (excluding Dhamtari town and P.Cs 50 to 52) in Dhamtari tehsil and the forest villages in the area.

DISASTROUS WEATHER EVENTS

Squalls

5–6 May 1981, two children died in house collapse, trees and electric poles uprooted, hundreds of hutment collapsed.

Thunderstorm

11 May 1981, electric supply disrupted, several villages affected, person reported killed 31 March 1982, heavy rains, hundred of houses, trees, electric poles uprooted.

Flood

August 1982, 4th week, there was flood in the Mahanadi river, people reported died, thousands of villages affected.

Drought

September 1981, 3rd and 4th week, cattle head perished.

—April and May 1985, acute shortage of drinking water, crops completely damaged.

—June to August 1987, acute shortage of fodder.

—May 2nd week 1993, livestock and wild animals died due to scarcity of water, lakh of people mainly farmers badly affected.

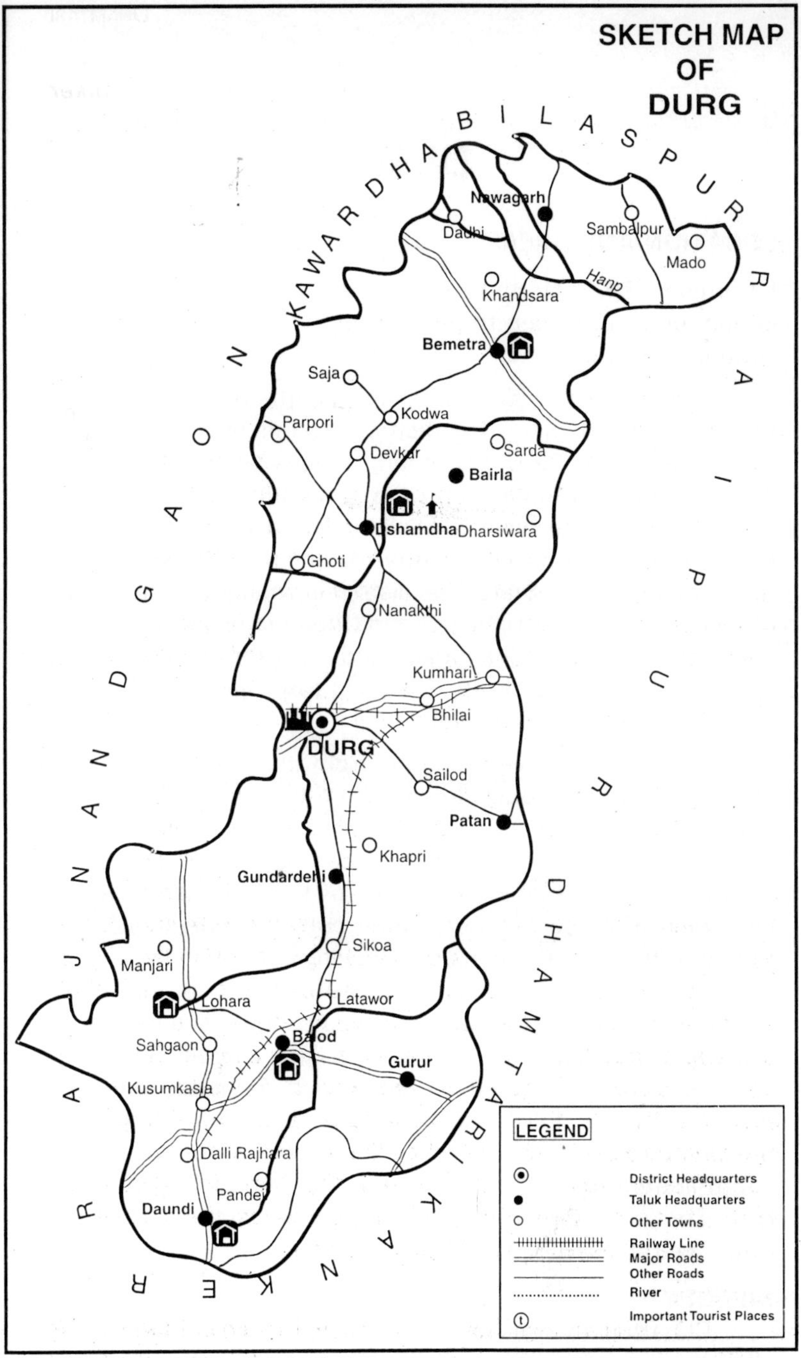
SKETCH MAP
OF
DURG
BILASPUR
KAWARDHA
RAJNANDGAON
RAIPUR
DHAMTARI
KANKER
Nawagarh
Dadhi
Sambalpur
Mado
Hanp
Khandsara
Bemetra
Saja
Kodwa
Parpori
Devkar
Sarda
Bairla
Dhamdha
Dharsiwara
Ghoti
Nanakthi
Kumhari
Bhilai
DURG
Sailod
Patan
Khapri
Gundardehi
Sikoa
Manjari
Lohara
Latawor
Sahgaon
Balod
Gurur
Kusumkasla
Dalli Rajhara
Pandei
Daundi
LEGEND
District Headquarters
Taluk Headquarters
Other Towns
Railway Line
Major Roads
Other Roads
River
Important Tourist Places

DURG

LOCATION AND AREA

Latititude : 20.6° North to 22° North
Longitude : 80.9° East to 81.9° East
Altitude : 293 m

Durg district is situated in the south-eastern part of the rich Chhattisgarh plain. The district extends between latitudes 20.6° North and 22.0° North and longitudes 80.9° to 81.9° East. Its greatest length from north to south is 170 kms and width from east to west is 70 kms The district has 8537 sq kms area and was ranked twenty-fourth among the districts of the Combined M.P., State. The district is bounded by the district of Bilaspur in the north, Raipur and Dhamtari district in the east and in the west by Rajnandgaon and Kawardha district and by Kanker district in the south. The Durg town lies at an elevation of 293 m from the Mean Sea Level.

The district derives its name from the headquarters town of Durg. The name Durg derived from the vernacular word 'a fort' and the headquarters town contains the ruins of a mud fort said to be of great antiquity, now obliterated. Durg is an old town with fort on eastern bank of the Sheonath River, 33 kms west of Raipur. Its very name, which simple means "the fort" would seem to point it out as having once been the principal fortified position in the south of Mahakoshal. In one of the inscriptions, now in the Raipur museum, there is a mention of Shivapura and Shiva Durg and of a king named Shivadeva. Now as Durg is situated on the Seo or Seonath river, it is probable that its full name must have been Shiv-Durg which has been gradually shortened to the simple form of Durg. The south and south-east area falling in the Sanjari Balod tehsil is hilly. The tehsils Bemetara and Durg comprise the plain region. Total area of the district is 8537 sq kms.

HISTORY

Chhattisgarh was known as Daksin Kosala or Maha Kosala to distinguish it from North Kosala. Samudra Gupta of the Gupta

Dynasty conquered this area in the middle of 4th century and the Gupta rule continued till about 6th Century. An inscription found in Arang testifies to the sovereignty of the Guptas in this area. Who were the immediate successors of the Guptas is not known but when famous Chinese traveller Hiuen Tsiang visited Maha Kosala in 639 A.D., a Buddhist king was ruling here. The parent line of this kingdom was probably at Bhandak in Chanda District (Maharashtra) and the headquarters of the Maha Kosala branch was at Sirpur, now a village in Raipur District. The reign of this dynasty seems to have continued upto 8th or 9th century though the later kings changed over from Buddhism to Shaivism as is clear from various records of Maha Shiva who built a number of temples dedicated to Shiva.

At this time a dynasty known as Shailvahini (or mountain dynasty) established itself in the north of Durg district and they extended their rule upto Gandai. An eighth century inscription found at Durg points to the rule of a king Shivadeva of Durg. The intervening period between the rule of this dynasty and the rule of the Haihayas is not historically clear and it can not be said as to when the Haihayas rose to power in Chhattisgarh. The inscription found at Ratanpur and dated 1114 A.D. mentions that the first chief of the Haihayabanshi line conquered Dakshina Kosala about the 10th century powerful chief known as Jagpal ruled the Raipur and Durg areas under the suzerainty of the upper branch of the Haihayas at Ratanpur. Some of the kings of the Raipur branch of the Haihayas lived in the present Durg district. Not much is known, however, of the separate fortunes of the Raipur house until shortly before the invasion of the Marathas.

The southern portions of Durg district were under the Kanker chief who was a tributary of Haihayas and at about the same time another Chief Yasah Karnadeva was ruling in the north in Sahaspur Lohara. Dhamda had been given to Gonds of Sardha and Balod had a separate king who was later overthrown by the Gonds, and a Kalar chief ruled at Sorar. Thus, the district seems to have been divided up into petty principalities the remnants of which flourished upto 1951 in the form of a large number of Zamindaris and Feudatory States.

The invasion of Marathas took place in the 18th century

in 1741. The Maratha general Bhaskar Pant, while on his way to attack Bengal, defeated and annexed the kingdom of Ratanpur but he did not disturb the Haihaya chief ruling at Raipur. The chief, Aman Singh was, however, quietly ousted in 1750. The Maratha rule over this area extended from 1750 to 1818 and no tribute can be paid to their administration, it was of most oppressive kind, having the sole end of extracting the maximum revenue from the people. After the deposition of Appa Sahab this area together with other territories of the Bhonsla kingdom was administered by British (1818-30) and in 1830, it was handed back to the Marathas who continued the administration of the area on the principles laid down by the British. In 1853, Chhattisgarh became British territory by lapse.

For purpose of Suba administration Durg was attached to Bhandara district (now in Maharashtra State) but in 1857 it was separated and made into a tehsil of Raipur district to which it remained attached till 1906.

The political awakening was evident in the Central Provinces from the Provincial Political Conferences that were held at Nagpur, Jabalpur and Raipur but the district does not seem to have been directly associated with the Swadeshi movement till 1906. A real sign of awakening in the district was marked from the year 1919 when Rawlatt Act was passed. Subsequent Jalianwala Bagh massacre the agitation against the British rule started gaining momentum. After the Lahore Congress and declaration of *Purna Swarajya* as the goal, event moved rapidly. The campaign opened in January 1930 which was named as Independence Day. The day was celebrated with great enthusiasm throughout the district. The district also participated in the movement of Civil Disobedience in 1933. These incidents infused new spirit in the people of the district, The struggle for freedom continued unabated in the district reaching wider sections of the people. The elections of early 1937 saw Congress Ministry established in the Central Provinces. It was a phenomenal success for the Congress. Soon after, in 1939 the Second World War broke out and the Congress refused to cooperate in a war which was conducted on imperialistic lines and the ministry resigned in 1939. The end of the Second World War left the British Empire in a weak State. The Labour Government came into power in Britain. Indian Independence Act was passed through the British Parliament on 1st July 1947 and India became Independent on 15th August 1947.

The present boundaries of the district was reconstituted in January 1973. The then Durg district, was bifurcated into Durg and Rajnandgaon districts. The district now comprises three tehsils, viz. Durg, Bemetara and Sanjari Balod tehsils of the erstwhile Durg District. However, 1847.86 sq kms area comprising 496 villages of Chowki, Mohla and Manpur Revenue Inspector's Circles of Sanjari Balod tehsil have been transferred to Rajnandgaon tehsil of newly formed Rajnandgaon district The district was constituted for the first time in 1906 with an area of 9,861.66 sq kms from portions of Raipur and Bilaspur districts. The district comprised of the old Durg tehsil and parts of then Simga and Dhamtari tehsils of Raipur District and a part of Mungeli tehsil of Bilaspur district. In 1907 four Zamindari estates of Panabaras, Koracha, Aundhi and Ambagarh Chowki were transferred from Chanda (now Chandrapur) District of Maharashtra covering an area of 2170.4 sq kms. Consequent upon merging the four feudatory States of Kawardha Khairagarh, Rajnandgaon and Chhuikhadan in 1948, the area of the district was further enlarged. Except Chhuikhadan each State formed a separate tehsil thus raising the number of tehsils from 3 to 6.

POPULATION

Total population of the district according to 2001 census is 2801757 persons, comprising of 1413785 males and 1387972 females. Rural population of the district is 1734388 persons (860027 males and 874361 females) and urban population is 1067369 persons (553758 males and 513611 females).

The tehsil-wise population break-up, i.e., rural-urban and male-female population distribution is represented according to 2001 census in the following table:

Tehsil	Total/ Rural/ Urban	Total Population Persons	Males	Females
Nawagarh	T	127992	63257	64735
	R	127992	63257	64735
	U	—	—	—
Bemetara	T	147615	73101	74514
	R	124388	61295	63093
	U	23227	11806	11121
Saja	T	143828	70496	73332
	R	137030	67047	69983
	U	6798	3449	3349
Brela	T	137252	67563	69689
	R	137252	67563	69689
	U	—	—	—
Dhamaha	T	192591	95804	96787
	R	165273	81959	83314
	U	27318	13845	13473
Durg	T	1108142	573869	534273
	R	184583	93437	91146
	U	923559	480432	443127
Patan	T	195691	98127	97564
	R	186993	93720	93273
	U	8698	4407	4291
Gunderdehi	T	182718	91208	91510
	R	182718	91208	91510
	U	—	—	—
Dondi Luhara	T	166396	81264	85132
	R	166396	81264	85132
	U	—	—	—
Sanjari Bloda	T	268785	134026	134759
	R	191016	94207	96809
	U	77769	39819	37950
Ganur	T	130747	65070	65677
	R	130747	65070	65677
	U	—	—	—

The Scheduled Castes and Scheduled Tribes population of the district as per 1991 census are 305916 persons and 208059 persons respectively. The rural-urban breakup of these population is indicated below :

Rural (i)	Scheduled Castes	:	209665
(ii)	Scheduled Tribes	:	249062
Urban (i)	Scheduled Castes	:	96251
(ii)	Scheduled Tribes	:	48997

The decennial growth rate of population of the district as a whole in relation to the state between the period 1991 and 2001 is presented as below:

State/ District	*Decennial growth rate of population (per cent) 1991–2001)*		
	Total	*Rural*	*Urban*
Chhattisgarh State	18.06	14.23	36.24
Durg	16.88	11.77	26.26

LANGUAGES AND RELIGION

Main languages spoken in the district are Hindi, Bengali, Malayalam, Marathi, Punjabi, Telugu and Urdu.

Religion-wise breakup of population as per 1991 Census (At District Level)

Hindus : 2272955, Muslim : 54979, Christians : 20629, Sikhs : 19367, Buddhists : 12496, Jains 12873, Other religions and persuasions : 547, Religions not stated : 3288.

GEOGRAPHY AND PHYSICAL FEATURES

The district occupies the south western part of the upper Mahanadi-Seonath valley and the bordering hills in the south. Physiographically the district can be divided into two divisions, viz., the Chhattisgarh plain in the north and the southern plateau in the south. The basin is mostly composed of horizontally bedded or very low dipping limestones and Shales, concealed under the capping of alluvial clays and bhata ground. It lies at an elevation of about 300 metres above mean sea level and occupies nearly whole of central and northern part of the district. The principal river Seonath flows across it. The soil cover of the ground is generally shallow but thicker on the banks. Southern and south-eastern part of the district are extension of Bastar plateau interspersed by few hills. It lies at an elevation of about 400 to 700 metres. The Central ridge between Kharkhara and Tandula is important for presence of Rajhara hills of iron ore. The ridge is most prominent in the south, the peaks of Dongar Bor and Kauchar rising about a thousand feet above the surrounding country. East of Tandula the highest peak is 1960 feet high near Markatola while the one above reservoir is only 1402 feet The proportion of cultivated land is small in the southern plateau.

The general slope of the district is towards the north-east in which direction the major streams of the district flow. The major rivers of the district are the Seonath, the Kharun and the Tandula. A large number of streams join these rivers. The Seonath rises near Ambagarh Chowki in Rajnandgaon district. After flowing in the Rajnandgaon district for a considerable distance it enters the district from west. It flows to the north-east in a zig-zag manner and passes through the outskirts of Durg. Dhamdha and Berla. It is joined by Kharkhara and then by Tandula the largest of its tributaries from the south in its course. The Kharun which marks a large portion of eastern boundary also joins the Seonath from the south. After its confluence with Kharun, the Seonath forms the boundary between Durg and Raipur. The western and north-western tributaries of the Seonath are the Sonbarsa, the Amner, the Surhi, the Dota, the Karua ad the Hanp. All these rivers rise from Maikal range.

The Tandula rises from the hills to the north of Bhanupratappur in Bastar district. After flowing for about 3 kms it enters the district from south and flows to the north. The river has been dammed above Balod. The Tandula Reservoir extends into two connected triangular areas along the original streams above the dam. The canal irrigates the eastern part of the plain lying between Seonath and Kharun. It also supplies water to the Bhilai Steel Plant and the township of Bhilainagar. The river joins Sheonath about 13 kms south-west of Durg. The total length of the river is 96.6 kms. Dondi and Gunderdehi are important villages situated on its banks. The Kharun rises in southern part of Sanjari Balod tehsil and flows towards north. It flows due north and joins Seonath and forms the boundary between Durg and Raipur Districts for about 80 kms. The total length of the river is about 120 kms. It passes about 6.5 km west of Raipur town and most of the water supply for Raipur town is from Kharun river.

It is the southern portions of the district that contains

forest. Central and northern portion is almost devoid of forests. The forest is of mixed quality containing Sal (*Shorea robusta*), the other varieties. Other common trees found in these forests are Harra *(Terminala Chebula)*, Tendu *(Diospyros melanoxylon)*. Other common trees found near and in villages sites are Boir *(Zizypus jujaba)*, Neem *(Melia indica)*, Mango *(Magnifera indica)*, Sirsa *(Albizzia lebbrek)* and Karanj *(Pongamia glabra)*.

RIVERS, CANALS AND WATERWAYS

It is the tributaries of Mahanadi that are the important rivers of the district. These are Seonath, the Kharun, TheTandula, the Kharkhara, the Sonbarsa, the Amner, the Sorhi, the Dota, the Kharun. All these rivers are tributaries of the Seonath itself draining its water into Mahanadi. The Seonath river rises in the southern hills near Ambagarh Chowki hills in Rajnandgaon district and flows northwards receiving the waters of the Tandula and Kharkhara flowing past Durg town to the north of which Sonbarsa, Amner, Surhi, Dota join it. About 25 kms south-west of Bemetara it takes a turn towards east where at the boundary of Durg and Raipur districts it joins with its tributary Kharun and Kharkhara, flowing north-east forms the boundary of Durg district with Raipur.

TOWNS, VILLAGES AND AMENITIES

The district, at present comprised of 11 tehsils and 12 Community Development Blocks. It has 18 towns and 1821 villages (1803 inhabited villages and 18 uninhabited villages).

The urban population of the district as percentage of total population in the census 2001 is indicated below. It also shows the sex ratio (females per 1000 males) and density (population per sq km) in the urban population of the district in relation to the state:

State/ District	*Urban population as percentage of total population*	*Sex ratio 1991 (Females per 1000 males)*			*Density (Population per sq km)*
	2001	*Total*	*Rural*	*Urban*	
Chhattisgarh State	20.08	990	1005	932	154
Durg	38.10	982	1017	928	328

Amenities

Number (with percentage) of villages having one or more amenities in the district as per 1991 census is given as follows:

Sl. No.	*Amenities*	*Number of inhabited villages*	*Percentage*
1.	Education	1605	89.02
2.	Medical	196	10.87
3.	Drinking Water	1803	100.00
4.	Post and Telegraph	253	14.03
5.	Market/Hat	420	23.29
6.	Communications	422	23.41
7.	Approach by Pucca Road	569	31.56
8.	Power Supply	1579	87.58

COMMUNICATIONS

Durg district is situated on the Howrah-Bombay main line of south-eastern Railway. National Highway No. 6 also passes through the district.

AGRICULTURE AND IRRIGATION

Gross cropped area in the district is 681500 hectares, net area sown in the district in the year 1989–90 is 543300 hectares. Percentage of total irrigated area to gross cropped is 23.4 per cent. Canal is the main source of irrigation in the district. Paddy is main crop of the District. Wheat and gram are other important crops grown in good quantity in the district.

ANIMAL HUSBANDRY

Cows and buffaloes are common livestock found in the district.

INDUSTRIES

Bhilai steel plant is situated in the district.

HANDICRAFTS

Textiles (woven) works at Balod and Durg.

TRADE, COMMERCE AND EXPORT

The following table provides information on important commodities manufactured in, exported from and imported in the towns of this district.

Name of Town	*Most important Commodities*		
	Imported	*Exported*	*Manufactured*
Khamharia	Cloth	Rice	Utensils
Bemetara	Cloth	Rice	Utensils
Dhamdha	Kirana	Bronze utensils	Bronze utensils
Ahiwara	Cement	Lime stone	Leather shoes
Durg	Bauxite	Steel	Steel
Bhilai Nagar	Engineering Machines	Iron	Rail
Jamul	Jipsum	Cement	Cement
Kumpari	Sulphur	Chemical and fertilizers	Chemical and fertilizers
Patan	Sugar	Handloom cloth	Handloom cloth
Balod	Oil	Rice	Rice

TOURISM

Matri garden is one of the important places of tourist interest within the district apart from the Bhilai steel plant.

Dhamdha is a religious place, where pilgrims from different parts use to come every year.

Durg town and the historical fort is the place of archaeological interest.

FAIRS AND FESTIVALS

Important fairs and festivals organised in different parts of the district are mentioned below:

Kunwar Achhariya Mela, Magha Poornima, Bhhoram Deva ka Mela, Shivratri, Pritampur Mela, Navratri, Dasahra, Berla Mela, Worship of Shiva, Kali Mai, Urs Sayad Baba Atalshah, Urs Hajrat Baba Abdul Rehman Shah Kabali.

EDUCATION

According to 2001 Census, total literates (excluding the population in the age group of 0–6 years) is 1800422 persons. Of these, 1036604 are males and 763818 are females. In the rural areas of the district 1036528 persons (600743 males and 435785 females) are literates and in urban areas 763894 persons (435861 males and 328033 females) are literates.

The rate of literacy of these population to the total population, excluding 0–6 years age group according to 2001 census is shown below:

	Persons	*Males*	*Females*
Total	75.84	86.59	64.91
Rural	71.58	83.87	59.55
Urban	82.51	90.64	73.72

COLLEGES 2000

Bhilai Mahila College, Bhilai Nagar (Established 1979), Enrolment 679. Teachers 19. (Affiliated College)

Bhilai Institute of Technology (Seth Balkrishna Memorial), Bhilai House, Durg (Established 1986). Enrolment 856, Teachers 54. (Affiliated College)

Christian College of Engineering, Bhilai. (Affiliated College)

Government Arts and Science College, Durg (Established 1958). Enrolment 3300, Teachers 89. (Affiliated College)

Chatrapati Shivaji Engineering College, Bhilai.

Government Arts and Commerce College, Bhilai (Established 1983). Enrolment 731, Teachers 16.

Government College, Patan (Established 1989). Enrolment 324. Teachers 9. (Affiliated College)

Government College, Dhamdha (Established 1989). Enrolment 170. (Affiliated College)

Government College, Vaishalinagar, Bhilai (1989). Enrolment 569, Teachers 17. (Affiliated College)

Government College, Nawagarh (Established 1989). Enrolment 115. Teachers 5. (Affiliated College)

B.S. Arya Girls College, Durg (Established 1979). Enrolment 160, Teachers 6. (Affiliated College)

Government Girls College, Durg (Established 1982). Enrolment 1350, Teachers 30. (Affiliated College)

Government Pt. JLN Arts, Commerce and Science College, (Established 1966). Enrolment 729, Techers 20.(Affiliated College)

Government Pt. DP Choubey College, Saja (Established 1989), Enrolment 174, Teachers 9. (Affiliated College)

Kalyan Arts and Commerce College, Bhilainagar (Established 1983). Enrolment 2992. Teachers 43. (Affiliated College)

Kalyan Law College, Bhilainagar (Established 1962). Enrolment 318. Teachers 6. (Affiliated College)

Rashtriya and Vaideshik Bhasha Sansthan, Bhilai (Established 1986). Enrolment 44, Teachers 5.

St. Thomas College, Bhilai (Established 1984). Enrolment 618. Teachers 30. (Affiliated College)

Seth RCS Law College, Durg (Established 1962). Enrolment 563, Techers 10. (Affiliated College)

Seth RCS Arts and Commerce College, Durg (Established 1964). Enrolment 887, Teachers 18. (Affiliated College)

Shankaracharya Engineering College, Durg. (Affiliated College)

(Above named colleges belong to Pt. Ravishankar Shukla University, Established 1963).

MEDICAL

The position of number of beds per 1000 population appears to be far from satisfactory in the towns of the district. Durg, Jamul and Kumhari have more than two beds per one thousand population while in rest of the towns the position is precarious.

MEDIA

Newspaper (Daily), Amar Kiran (Hindi)

ADMINISTRATION

(i) Administrative Division: Raipur

Tehsils. Nawagarh; Bemetara; Saja; Berla; Dhamdha; Durg; Patan; Gunderdihi; Dondilohara; Sanjaribalod and Gurur.

Towns and Urban Agglomerations with their Population, Sex Ratio, Decadal Growth and Literacy Rate (2001)

Town	*Population*	*Percentage Decadal Growth Rate*	*Sex Ratio*	*Literacy Rate*
Khamharia (TP)	6798	9.01	971	73.35
Bemetara (TP)	23227	21.65	967	78.06
Dhamdha (TP)	8574	- 54.15	995	72.61
Ahivara (TP)	18744	150.79	963	77.55
Durg-Bhilaenagar (UA)	923559	30.99	922	83.09
(i) Durg (MC)	231182	38.49	944	82.70
(ii) Bhilai Nagar	553837	20.05	911	83.84
(iii) Bhilai Charoda (M)	87170	82.53	933	80.79
(iv) Jamul (TP)	21633	35.95	926	82.52
(v) Kumhari (TP)	29737	126.60	938	74.86
Patan (TP)	8698	21.79	974	79.28
Baloda (TP)	21044	17.46	969	84.06
Dalli-Rajhara (UA)	56725	1.30	947	78.75
Dalli-Rajhra (M)	50615	- 9.61	937	78.30

(ii) Parliamentary Constituencies and Assembly Segments (2001):

No. & Name of parliamentary Constituencies:

19. Kanker (ST); 21. Durg (SC)

19-KANKER (ST)

Number and Name of Assembly Segments of Kanker Parliamentary Constituency which lies within the jurisdiction of Durg district.

165. Gunderdehi—Bhatagaon and Gunderdehi RICs and P.Cs 95 to 98 in Patan RIC in Durg tehsil.

167. Balod—Gurur and Balod RICs in Balod tehsil and the forest villages in the area.

168. Dondi Lohara (ST)—Kusumkasa and Dondi Lohara RICs in Balod tehsil and the forest villages in the area.

21-DURG (SC)

No. & Name of Assembly Segments of Durg Parliamentary Constituency which lies within the Jurisdiction of Durg District.

158. Maro (SC)—Maro and Nawagarh RICs and P.Cs. 46, 52 and 55 to 57 in Khandsara RIC in Bemetara tehsil.

159. Bemetara (Gen.)—Bemetara and Anandgaon RICs and P.Cs. 47 to 50, 53 and 54 in Khandsara RIC in Bemetara tehsil.

160. Saja (Gen.)—Saja and Deokar RICs and Khandsara RIC and P.Cs. 46 to 48 and 50 to 52 in Bhilai RIC in Durg tehsil.

161. Dhamdha (Gen.)—Dhamda and Nankathi RICs and PCs 46 to 50 to 52 in Bhilai RIC in Durg tehsil.

162. Durg (Gen.)—Durg-I and Durg-II RICs and S.A.F. Colony, Kosa Nala, Supela Bazar West, Supela Bazar, Supela Bazar East and Supela Camp West in Bhilainagar and ex-revenue village Chhaoni lying on the periphery of Bhilainagar in Bhilai RIC in Durg tehsil.

163. Bhilai (Gen.)—Bhilainagar (excluding S.A.F. Colony, Kosa Nala, Supela Bazar West, Supela Bazar, Supela Bazar East, Supela Camp West and ex-revenue village Chhaoni lying on the periphery of Bhilainagar) in Bhilai RIC in Durg tehsil.

164. Patan(Gen.)—Bhilai RIC (excluding P.Cs 46 to 48 and 50 to 52 and Bhilainagar) and Patan RIC (excluding P.Cs. 95 to 98) in Durg tehsil.

166. Khertha(Gen.)—Anda R.C in Durg tehsil; and Khertha RIC in Balod tehsil.

The communitywise breakup (OBE) in Durg is Scheduled Castes (14 per cent), Scheduled Tribes (6 per cent), Telis (20 per cent) and Ahirs (10 per cent), Kurmis, Kewats and Malis are also present in sizable numbers. Satnamis/Chamars (11 per cent) among the Scheduled Castes and Gonds (3 per cent) among the Scheduled Tribes are dominant.

OBSERVATIONAL ORGANISATION

Surface Observatory

The district of Durg lies under meteorological sub-division,

Madhya Pradesh east. This instrument facility is available in Durg headquarters area. The instrument lies in

Latitude	:	21.18° North
Longitude	:	81.28° East
Altitude	:	293 m
Date of starting	:	29-10-1969

MINERALS AND ORES OCCURRENCES

Arsenic

Lenticular deposits rich in arsenopyrite in felsite near its junction with the granite batholith south of Handitola (20.81, 80.35).

Bauxite

Boulders of ferruginous bauxite are seen at several places in the district.

Building Materials

Calcareous shales, associated with limestone are found at Dharia (21.5, 81.1) Silpati (21.5, 81.1) and Kondka (21.51, 81.03) near the border with the former Chhukadasi state. The shales are quarried and easily dressed into slates for using a tiles both for flooring and roofing.

Occurring of flaggy calcareous shale are reported from Anjur (21.01, 80.91), Sonesarar (21.5, 80.96), Sukhri (21.01, 80.96), Ghorda (21.03, 80.95) and Rampur (21.05, 80.96) for use as building stone.

Clay

Occurrence of band of white clay has been reported near Musalijab (21.05, 80.81). The clay is more than 15 ft. in thickness. White clay is also reported along a nalla on the eastern side of the path leading from Charbhata (21.1, 80.56) to Mohanpur (21.11, 80.56). The clay is soft and gritty and has low plasticity. Another small occurrence of greenish clay is recorded in a *nala* bed one mile south of Karelelarh (21.45, 80.8). Another occurrence south of the hill near Dabka (21.4, 80.96) is fairly large. Clay also occurs at Danitola (20.68, 81.13), Sadakchichari (21.08, 80.6), Dhaba (21.1, 80.85) Markatola (20.56, 81.4). At Dhaba (21.08, 80.85) estimated to yield more than twenty lakh tons of clay upto a depth of 15 ft.

Copper

Small quantities of green carbonate of copper noted in a quartz vein containing galena exposed about 5 kms. to the west of Chicholi (21.1, 80.66). Similar traces were found in a quartz vein at Wararband (21.1, 80.83).

Lead and Silver

Occurrene of galena, cerussite and anglesite with subordinate quantities of chalcopyrite, malachite and azurite in quartz veins and associated with a narrow band of steeply dipping slate and green stone, have been reported from west of Muhripar (21.35, 80.86). The percentage of galena, however does not exceed 1.15 of the whole. Galena is also found in small quantities in quartz veins near Telitola (21.1, 80.81) and in the veins occurring between Kotnapani (21.05, 80.61) and Musulijob (21.61, 80.65).

Minor occurrences of galena are also reported from Thelkandan (20.61, 80.75).

Limestone

Lime stone occurs in discontinuous patches at various places in the district.

Mica

A small occurrence of mica has been noted at Tilairwar (21.03, 80.79).

Ochre

The occurrence of red ochre associated with red shales and sand stones along the side of a hill near Khara (21.83, 80.85). The ochre is met with at a depth of about 3 ft. from the surface and is found to extend to about 30 ft. in depth. The ochre is soft and bright red in colour. A large deposit of red ochre is also reported from Dongaria (21.83, 80.86). A small patch of red ochre occurs near Mehera Dhabri (21.33, 80.73). The material is of good quantity. The ferruginous shales of Kankapar (20.68, 80.9) are rich in ochre material. Red ochre of good quality has been obtained from pits in the Gandai (21.66, 81.16) and Thakurtala (21.65, 81.03) areas.

Yellow ochres associated with shales have been found at Garra (21.91, 80.91). A bed of yellow shale at Piparia is locally used for colour washing.

Steatite

Potstone is reported to occur in abundance west of Kalikora (20.68, 81.03) and is worked locally for making utensils. The material is found in pockets and is from 3 to 8 ft. thick. It is dark grey pink in colour.

DISASTROUS WEATHER EVENTS

Lightning

16 July 1982, five children attending classes died and 14 others injured, when lightning struck a school building.

20 July 1984, flowering crops badly affected.

Heavy rains

17–18 August 1985, houses collapsed, rain water entered into low lying areas and in the hutments, short circuit reported at several places. Thousands of labourers of Rajtna labour colony rendered homeless as the rain water entered into the hutment colony. Property worth lakhs of rupees lost.

21–23 August 1990, number of houses damaged, vehicular traffic completely disrupted, people reported died.

Thunder Storm

First June 1994, loud peals of thunnder, with frequent lightning flashes, moderate to heavy rains, electricity supply at several places disrupted.

Heavy rains

12–13 July 1994, standing crops damaged, kachha houses collapsed and people reported killed, water entered into hutments.

19–22 July 1994, people reported died due to house collapse, standing crops affected, vehicular traffic disrupted at various places.

DISTRIBUTION OF *SCHEDULED CASTE* POPULATION BY SEX DISTRICTWISE (1991)

	POPULATION		
	Total	Males	Females
DURG	3,05,916	1,54,356	1,51,560
Audhelia	66	37	29
Bagri, Bagdi	63	34	29
Bahna, Bahana	23	16	7
Balahi, Balai	69	34	35
Banchada	29	12	17
Barahar, Basod	594	294	300
Bargunda	16	7	9
Basor, Burud, Bansor, Bansodi, Bansphor, Basar	540	272	268
Bedia	9	4	5
Beldar, Sunkar	458	206	252
Bhangi, Mehtar, Balmik, Lalbegi, Dharkar	3,064	1,507	1,557
Bhanumati	328	118	210
Chadar	286	149	137
*Chamar, Chamari, Bairwa, Bhambi, Jatav, Mochi, Regar, ...	2,25,648	1,13,858	1,11,790
Chidar	543	297	246
Chikwa, Chikvi	432	240	192
Chitar	292	157	135
Dahait, Dahayat, Dahat	40	21	19
Dewar	1,752	878	874
Dhanuk	155	94	61
Dhed, Dher	24	11	13
Dohor	38	15	23
Dom, Dumar, Dome, Domar, Doris	1,088	551	537
Ganda, Gandi	14,291	7,047	7,244
Ghasi, Ghasia	1,527	749	778
Holiya	9	5	4
Kanjar	39	19	20
Katia, Patharia	174	82	92
Khatik	846	467	379
Koli, Kori	742	423	319
Khangar, Kanera, Mirdha	26	13	13
Kuchbandhia	43	24	19
Mahar, Mehra, Mehar	47,420	23,866	23,554
*Mang, Mang Garodi, Mang Garudi, Dankhni Mang, ...	170	83	87
Meghwal	21	10	11
Moghia	42	26	16
Muskhan	33	15	18
Nat, Kalbelia, Sapera, Navdigar, Kubutar	497	251	246
Pasi	646	361	285
Rujjhar	55	18	37
Sansi, Sansia	15	8	7
Silawat	18	10	8
Zamral	6	1	5
Unclassified	3,739	2,066	1,673

(Contd.)

DISTRIBUTION OF *SCHEDULED TRIBE* POPULATION BY SEX DISTRICTWISE (1991)

	POPULATION		
	Total	Males	Females
DURG	2,98,059	1,47,768	1,50,291
Agariya	72	38	34
Andh	44	20	24
Baiga	25	13	12
Bhaina	27	16	11
*Bharia Bhumia, Bhuinhar Bhumia, Bhumiya, Bharia, ...	83	46	37
Bhattra	15	10	5
Bhil, Bhilala, Barela, Patelia	227	119	108
Bhil Mina	16	11	5
Bhunjia	45	23	22
Biar, Biyar	80	44	36
Binjhwar	325	179	146
Birhul, Birhor	61	26	35
Damor, Damaria	24	12	12
Dhanwar	269	152	117
Gadaba, Gadba	70	38	32
*Gond; Arakh, Arrakh, Agaria, Asur, ...	1,65,617	82,434	83,183
Halba, Halbi	1,16,327	56,957	59,370
Kamar	70	39	31
Karku	116	63	53
Kawar, Kanwar, Kaur, Cherwa, Rathia, Tanwar, Chattri	5,093	2,515	2,578
Khairwar, Kondar	334	164	170
Kharia	65	31	34

(Contd.)

	POPULATION		
	Total	Males	Females
Kondh, Khond, Kandh	72	37	35
Kol	172	87	85
Kolam	37	25	12
Korku, Bopchi, Mouasi, Nihal, Nahul, Bondhi, Bondeya	74	34	40
Korwa, Kodaku	32	18	14
Majhi	1,864	1,045	819
Majhwar	36	20	16
Mawasi	2	2	0
Munda	332	185	147
Nagesia, Nagasia	46	28	18
Oraon, Dhanka, Dhangad	1,337	718	619
Pao	8	4	4
Pardhan, Pathari Saroti	92	47	45
*Pardhi; Bahelia, Bahellia, Chita Pardhi, ...	1,653	837	816
Parja	12	3	9
Sahariya, Saharia, Seharia, Sehria, Sosia, Sor	36	16	20
Saonta, Saunta	21	12	9
Saur	18	10	8
Sawar, Sawara	113	61	52
Sonr	1,011	493	518
Unclassified	2,086	1,136	950

SKETCH MAP OF JANJGIR CHAMPA

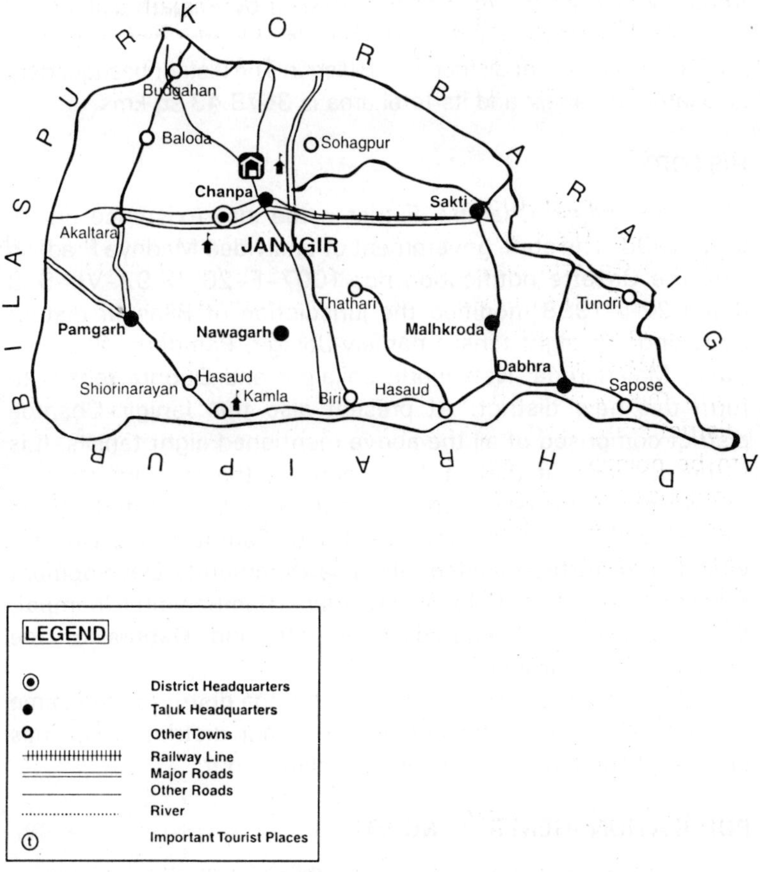

JANJGIR–CHAMPA

LOCATION AND AREA

Latitude : 20.8° North to 21.1 North
Longitude : 81.5° East to 83.2° East
Attitude : 245 m

Janjgir–Champa district occupies the upper central region of Chhattisgarh state. It is bounded on the north by newly created Korba district, on the east and south east by Raigarh district, on the south by Bilaigarh and Kasdol tehsils of Raipur district and on the west by its parent district, i.e., Bilaspur. The district headquarters is located at Janjgir and its total area is 3678.43 sq kms.

HISTORY

The Janjgir–Champa district came into existence on 25 May, 1998. The state government of undivided Madhya Pradesh vide the Gazette notification no. 1007–F–20–8–92–VII–S–8 dated 22-5-1998 modified the jurisdiction of Bilaspur district by taking out eight tehsils namely Janjgir, Pamgarh, Champa, Sakti, Malkharoda, Nawagarh, Jaijaipur and Dabhra tehsils to form this new district. At present also the Janjgir–Champa district comprised of all the above mentioned eight tehsils. It is to be pointed out that at 1991 census, the area which now comprised of Janjgir–Champa district was constituted of five tehsils namely Janjgir, Champa, Sakti, Pamgarh and Dabhra, which were further divided into nine Community Development Blocks *viz.* Akaltara, Baloda, Nawagarh, Bamhanidih (Champa), Sakti, Jaijaipur, Malkharoda, Pamgarh and Dabhra of the erstwhile Bilaspur district.

The historical past of Janjgir–Champa district is the same as that of its parent district, i.e., Bilaspur district which has been explained in detail in section related to it.

POPULATION (GENERAL, SC/ST)

The total population of Janjgir–Champa district, according

to 2001 census is 1316140 persons comprising 658377 males and 657763 females. Rural population of the district is 1170826 persons (583540 males and 587286 females) and urban population is 145314 persons (74837 males and 70477 females).

The tehsil-wise population break-up, i.e., rural-urban and male-female population distribution is represented according to 2001 census in the following table:

Tehsil	*Total/ Rural/ Urban*	*Total Population*		
		Persons	*Males*	*Females*
Janjgir	T	360671	182267	178404
	R	288365	144940	143425
	U	72306	37327	34979
Nawagarh	T	128644	64627	64017
	R	128644	64627	64017
	U	—	—	—
Champa	T	169788	85422	84366
	R	131839	65807	66032
	U	37949	19615	18334
Sakti	T	142068	70892	71176
	R	115615	57341	58274
	U	26453	13551	12902
Pamgarh	T	137609	69023	68586
	R	129003	64679	64324
	U	8606	4344	4262
Dabhra	T	136855	67894	68961
	R	136855	67894	68961
	U	—	—	—
Malkhroda	T	114634	56433	58201
	R	114634	56433	58201
	U	—	—	—
Jaijepur	T	125871	61819	65052
	R	125871	61819	64052
	U	—	—	—

The Scheduled Castes and the Scheduled Tribes population in nine Community Development Blocks of this district as per 1991 census are 2,48,097 and 1,35,302 persons respectively. The rural-urban breakup of this population is indicated below :

Rural : (i) Scheduled Castes : 2,30,046
(ii) Scheduled Tribes : 1,30,248

Urban : (i) Scheduled Castes : 8,051
(ii) Scheduled Tribes : 5,054

The decennial growth rate of population of the district as a lot whole in relation to the state between the period 1991 and 2001 is presented below:

State/ District	*Decennial growth rate of population (per cent) 1991–2001*		
	Total	*Rural*	*Urban*
Chhattisgarh	18.06	14.23	36.24
Janjgir Champa	18.55	18.08	22.48

LANGUAGES AND RELIGION

The main language spoken in the district is Hindi. Chhattisgarhi is the dialect generally used by all the people for intra-communication. Religionwise breakup of population of this district is indicated below:

Hindus: 10,92,142, Muslims: 9,613, Jains: 673, Christians: 2138, Buddhists: 1277, Sikhs: 567, Other religions and persuasions: 134, Religion not stated: 3656.

GEOGRAPHY AND PHYSICAL FEATURES

In its physical features, the district is open and the great part marked by the Mahanadi river. In the central plain region there are two isolated ridges the Sontri and the Dalha and the latter rises abruptly from near Akaltara and is visible from long distances. The general slope of the district is from north-west to south-east. The climate of the district is characterised by a hot dry summer and well distributed rainfall in the south-west monsoon season.

RIVERS, CANALS AND WATERWAYS

The river Mahanadi flows throughout the southern border of the district dividing it from Raipur district in south direction and is the main river of this district. The river Hasdev which runs through the Surjguja district via newly created Korba district is another principal river in this district which flows in the plains of Champa dividing the district into two parts longitudinally and ultimately drains into the Mahanadi, 8 miles from Seorinarayan.

The Lilagar rising in the Korba hills flows to the south between BIlaspur and Janjgir tehsils and falls into the Seonath just before the latter joins the Mahanadi.

TOWNS, VILLAGES AND AMENITIES

The district is basically formed of five tehsils 1991 census, which were divided into eight tehsils in the later period (2001). At the 1991 census, the area comprising this district was divided into nine Community Development Blocks. It has eight towns.

Details on availability of infrastructural facilities/amenities in the villages of this district is not available separately, as it was part of Bilaspur district at the time of 1991 census. The combined data in this regard is provided in the note of Bilaspur district.

COMMUNICATIONS

The district is well placed in terms of rail transport. Its four towns namely Akalthra, Naila–Janjgir, Champa and Sakti are connected with broad gauge line from Bilaspur, an important junction in Chhattisgarh state in western side and to Raigarh, yet another district headquarters in eastern side. There is a good network of State Highways as well in the district. Most of the towns are interlinked by roads. Important State Highways which pass through the district are SH–26 and SH–22.

AGRICULTURE AND IRRIGATION

Agriculture provides sustenance to the bulk of the population of this district. The main crop seasons are kharif and rabi. The most important crops are paddy and wheat followed by maize. The irrigation network include canals, tube-wells, wells and other miscellaneous sources.

ANIMAL HUSBANDRY

Animals provide traditional drought power for cultivation and transportation for agricultural produce. In addition, they also provide fruitful vocation to the farmers for supplementing their incomes by sale and purchase of these animals. Cattle, buffaloes, and goats are the main livestock. However, the quality of these are generally poor. To look after the welfare of animal wealth, several veterinary institutions like hospitals, development centres are working in the district.

INDUSTRY

Champa town is famous for tussar (kosa) silk and thus the important items of manufacture in this town is Kosa. In addition, Naila–Janjgir and Champa are also considered as coal mine areas. The Cement Corporation of India has established a cement industry at Akaltara. Thus, the industrial development has already been in progress in the district.

TRADE, COMMERCE AND EXPORT

The following table gives details on the most important commodities manufactured, exported from and imported in the towns of this district. It also indicates the number of banks available in these towns.

Name of town	*Most important commodities*			*Banks*
	Manufactured	*Exported*	*Imported*	
1. Akaltara	Rice, Cement, Readymade Cloth	Rice, Cement, Tiles	Kirana, Clothes, Sugar	4
2. Champa	Kosa cloth, Utensils, Gold and Silver ornaments	Kosa cloth, Utensils, Gold and Silver ornaments	Fruits, Kosa, Gold and Silver Spices	3
3. Naila Janjgir	Soap, Sawn timber, Bidi	Rice, Soap, Kosa	Cloth, Pulses, sugar	2
4. Naya Baradwar	Rice, Sawn timber	Paddy, Dolomite stone, Rice	Cloth, Pulses, sugar	2
5. Sakti	Kosa cloth, Gur, Bidi	Vegetable, Brass Utensils, Kosa cloth	Cloth, Kirana, Sugar	2
6. Baloda	Bidi, Timber	Bidi, Timber	Cloth, Sugar, Medicine	1
7. Shivri Narayan	Bidi, Timber, Vegetable	Bidi, Timber, Vegetable	Cloth, Sugar, Kirana	1
8. Kharod	Bidi	Bidi	Salt, Sugar, Cloth	1

TOURISM

The district has no major place of tourist interest.

Shivrinarayan temple is famous in this region and a mela is organised once in a year which is attended by a large number of the people of this region.

Janjgir and Champa are places of pilgrimage where devotees come every year. Rest houses and Dharamshala facilities available at both the places

FAIRS AND FESTIVALS

Important fairs and festivals organised in different parts of the district are Maghapurnima, Shivratri, Christian Mela Kabir Panthi Mela, Republic Day, Chaitra Purnima.

EDUCATION

The following table gives information on different types of educational institutions including stadia and public libraries available in the towns of this district.

Name of town	*Educational institutions*	*Stadia*	*Public libraries including reading rooms*
1. Akaltara	Higher Secondary Schools (2), Middle Schools (2), Primary Schools (2)	–	1
2. Champa Bachelli	Higher Secondary Schools (2), Middle Schools (5), Primary Schools (5)	–	1
3. Naila Janjgir	Higher Secndary Schools (3), Middle Schools (3), Primary Schools (10)	–	2
4. Naya Baradwas	Higher Secondary School (1), Middle School (2), Primary Schools (3)	–	–
5. Sakti	Higher Secondary Schools (4), Middle Schools (4), Primary Schools (5)	–	1
6. Baloda	Higher Secondary School (1), Middle School (1), Primary School (1)	–	1
7. Shiv-Narayan	Higher Secondary School (1), Middle School (1), Primary School (1)	–	–
8. Kharod	Higher Secondary School (1) Middle school (1), Primary School (1)	–	–

According to 2001census total literates (excluding the population in the age group of 0-6 years) is 726739 persons of these 449415 are males and 277324 are females. In the rural areas of the district 628406 persons (391446 males and 236960 females) are literates and in urban areas 98333 persons (57969 males and 40364 females) are literates. The rate of literacy of this population to the total population (excluding 0-6 years age group according to 2001 census are shown below.

	Persons	Males	Females
Total	66.26	82.21	50.41
Rural	64.64	81.1	48.42
Urban	78.86	90.54	66.54

COLLEGES 2000

Government College, Malkharouda (Established 1989). Enrolment 200. (Affiliated College)

Government Degree College, Akaltara (Established 1983). Enrolment 379. Techers 7. (Affiliated College)

Government Degree College, Champa (Established 1974). Enrolment 383. Teachers 17. (Affiliated College)

Government Degree College, Dabhra (Established 1983). Enrolment 496, Teachers 6. (Affiliated College)

(Above named colleges belong to Guru Ghasidas University, Established 1983.)

LANGUAGE

Hindi is the main language spoken in this district. Chhattisgarhi is the dialect used by the rural people for inter-communications, particulary in the rural areas.

MEDICAL

The table given below furnishes information regarding availability of medical facilities in the towns of this district including that of the beds facility.

Name of town	*Medical institution (including beds facility)*	
1. Akaltara	Health centre (1) :	6
2. Champa	Hospital (4) :	280
3. Naila-Janjgir	Dispensary (1)	
	Health centre (1) :	38

4. Naya Baradwar	Hospital (1) :	6
5. Sakti	Health centre (1) :	6
6. Baloda	PHC (1),	
	FPC Dispensary (1):	5
7. Shivrinarayan	Hospital (1) :	3
8. Kharad	PHC (1),	
	FPC (1) :	5

ADMINISTRATION

(i) Administrative Division : Bilaspur

Tehsils: Janjgir, Nawagarh, Champa, Sakti, Pamgarh, Dabhra, Malkhroda, Jaijaipur

Towns and Urban Agglomerations with their Population, Sex ratio, Decadal growth and Literacy rate (2001)

Town	*Population*	*Percentage decadal growth 1991–2001*	*Sex Ratio*	*Literacy*
Baloda (TP)	11331	79.91	965	76.44
Sakti (TP)	20225	19.72	948	80.76
Champa (M)	37949	26.14	935	77.69
Naila—Janjgir (M)	32495	82.00	930	81.61
Akaltara (TP)	20373	- 17.70	932	79.77
Naya Baradwar (TP)	6228	13.92	966	77.31
Kharod (TP)	8606	11.23	981	72.72
Shivrinarayan	8107	- 15.14	941	77.00

(ii) Parliamentary Constituencies and Assembly Segments (2001):

No. & Name of Parliamentary Constituency : 14. Janjgir; 16. Sarangarh (SC)

No. & Name of Assembly Segments of Janjgir Parliamentary Constituency which lies within the Jurisdiction of Janjgir-Champa district:

14-JANJGIR

120. Akaltara (Gen.)—Baloda RIC and Akaltara RIC (excluding P.Cs. 58 and 60) in Janjgir tehsil and the forest villages in the area.

122. Champa (Gen.)—Champa RIC and Janjgir RIC (excluding P.Cs. 50, 52 and 53) in Janjgir tehsil.

123. Sakti (Gen.)—Sakti RIC in Sakti tehsil and P.Cs. 73 to 80 in Rampur RIC in Katghora tehsil.

Number and Name of Assembly Segments of Sarangarh Parliamentary Constituency which lies within the Jurisdiction of Janjgir-Champa district.

16-SARANGARH (SC)

121. Pamgarh (Gen.)—Pamgarh and Nawagarh RICs, P.Cs 58 and 60 in Akaltara RIC and P.Cs. 50, 52 and 53 in Janjgir RIC in Janjgir tehsil.

124. Malkharoda (SC)—Jaijaipur RIC and Malkharoda RIC (excluding P.Cs. 51, 52, 57, 59 and 60) in Sakti tehsil.

125. Chandrapur (Gen.)—Chandrapur RIC and P.Cs. 51, 52, 57, 59 and 60 in Malkharoda RIC in Sakti tehsil.

MINERALS AND ORES OCCURRENCES

Limestone

Grey, medium-grained, well bedded dolomitic limestone in the *nala* section north of Chitapandaria (21.95, 82.86) near Akaltara (21.91, 82.85), Bhutdih (21.9, 82.86).

SKETCH MAP OF JASHPUR

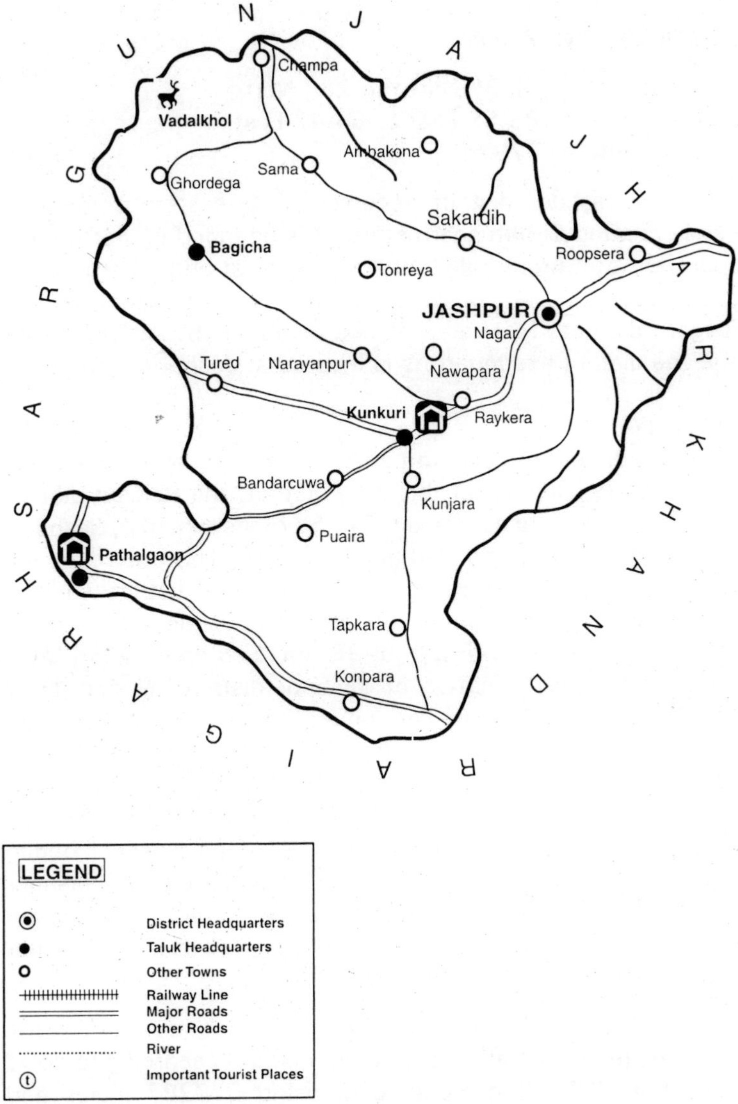

JASHPUR

LOCATION AND AREA

Latitude : 22.3° North to 23° North
Longitude : 83.5° East to 84.4° East
Altitude : 779 m

The Jashpur district occupies north-eastern corners of newly created Chhattisgarh state. It is bounded on north-west and west by Surguja, district on north-east and east by Bihar and Orissa states and on the south by its parent district, i.e., by Raigarh district. Total area of this district is 5322.67 sq kms and the district headquarters is located at Jashpurnagar.

HISTORY

The district of Jashpur came into existence on 25th May, 1998. While carving out this new district, the Raigarh district was bifurcated; and as a result of it, four tehsils namely Jashpur, Bageecha, Kunkuri and Patholgaon were taken out (from the Raigarh district) to form the present Jashpur district vide the Government of Madhya Pradesh, Revenue department notification no. 1006–F–20–8–92–VII–5–8 dated 22nd May, 1998. After the formation of Jashpur district, all the above mentioned four tehsils are kept under the administrative control of this new district. This district broadly corresponds to the territory comprising the Jashpur feudatory state alongwith adjoining villages. The Jashpur state was under the commissionner of Chhotanagpur till 1905 and was included in the erstwhile Bengal Province. The historical past of Jashpur district is the same as that of its parent district, i.e., Raigarh which has been explained in detail in it as well as in the chapter on Introduction.

POPULATION (GENERAL, SC/ST)

The total population of Jashpur district, according to 2001 census is 739780 persons, comprising 370287 males and 369493 females. Rural population of the district is 705536 persons (352106 males and 353430 females) and urban population is 34244 persons (18181 males and 16063 females). Tehsilwise population breakup, i.e., rural–urban and male-female population details are presented below:

Tehsil	*Total/ Rural/ Urban*	*Total Population*		
		Persons	*Males*	*Females*
Bageecha	T	217009	108482	108527
	R	217009	108482	108527
	U	—	—	—
Jashpur	T	135427	68713	66714
	R	115237	57693	57544
	U	20190	11020	9170
Kunkuri	T	222499	111008	111491
	R	222499	111008	111491
	U	—	—	—
Pathalgaon	T	164845	82084	82761
	R	150791	74923	75868
	U	14054	7161	6893

The decennial growth rate of population of the district as a whole in relation to the state between the period 1991 and 2001 is presented.

State/ District	*Decennial growth rate of population (per cent) 1991–01*		
	Total	*Rural*	*Urban*
Chhattisgarh	18.06	14.23	36.24
Jashpur	12.71	11.87	33.22

LANGUAGES AND RELIGIONS

The main language spoken in the district is Hindi. Local people, particularly in rural areas speak Chhattisgarhi, a dialect for inter-communications.

Religionwise breakup of the population of the district is indicated below:

The Scheduled Castes and the Scheduled Tribes population of this district based on 1991 census are given below:

Total : (i) Scheduled Castes : 46,902
(ii) Scheduled Tribes : 4,27,174

Rural : (i) Scheduled Castes : 44,223
(ii) Scheduled Tribes : 4,18,312
Urban : (i) Scheduled Castes : 2,679
(ii) Scheduled Tribes : 8,862

Religions	*Bageecha tehsil*	*Jashpur tehsil*	*Kunkuri tehsil*	*Pathalgaon tehsil*
1. Hindus	147500	78711	144393	128126
2. Muslims	1600	2736	2532	557
3. Jains	169	257	154	17
4. Christians	42509	34350	54658	17095
5. Buddhists	—	16	4	6
6. Sikhs	14	50	58	272
7. Other religions & persuasions	23	40	55	28
8. Religion not stated	261	24	8	129

GEOGRAPHY AND PHYSICAL FEATURES

The northern-most portion of the district consists almost equal proportion of high and low land. On the north-eastern part lies the prominent table-land of Uparghat. It rises abruptly in a scarped fortress like wall of granite from west to east. The ascent is about 200 to 400 metres to the north of Bagicha, Narayanpur and Serdanr. The general elevation of the tract varies from 600 metres to 750 metres on the Jashpur plateau in the east and 750 metres to 1000 metres on the Khuria plateau in the west. The whole of Jashpur tehsil and adjoining area to the south of the scrap making the Uparghat are known as the Nichghat. The greater part consists of a narrow and gently rolling country along Ib and its tributaries, in the centre of the area. The northern hills are mostly aligned from north to south, e.g., the Marwel and Kosango hills whereas the southern hills of Pathalgaon and Kasil Dongas seek a south-easterly alignment. The table-land of Marwel forms the watershed between Maini and Ib. The Pathalgaon–Lailunga plateau occupies the central and west-central part of the district. This is the widest part of the hill range which runs along the west bank of the Mahanadi river in the north and further, along the east bank of Kurket nala in the south.

RIVERS, CANALS AND WATERWAYS

The rivers of the district come under the Mahanadi drainage

system. The important rivers in the district are Ib and Kanhas. The Ib rises from the Khuriya hills in the Pandrapat plateau in Jashpur tehsil. The Kanhas rises from the Bankhona peak flows north for a short distance and then turns north west running parallel to the northern boundary of the district for a small part of the length. Sakh is another river which divides the district on the north-east corner from Bihar state.

TOWNS, VILLAGES AND AMENITIES

The district is at present comprised of four tehsils and eight Community Development Blocks. Total number of towns in the district are only two of which one each is in Jashpur and Pathalgaon tehsils.

COMMUNICATIONS

The district is deprived of a railway line. Due to the absence of rail transport, one has to travel by bus upto Raigarh. Road transport is the main mode of communications in the district. The state Highway No. 14 connects the district headquarters, Jashpurnagar to Ambikapur in east and to Ranchi in west directions. The state Highway No. 22 interlinks Pathalgaon, Kunkuri with Jashpurnagar which run through from Korba via Dharamjaigarh. Similarly state Highway No. 1 connects Pathalgaon tehsil headquarters from Raigarh via Gharghoda and Dharamjaigarh. Apart from these state Highways, there is a good network of both metalled as well as non-metalled roads.

AGRICULTURE AND IRRIGATION

Rice, maize and wheat are the main crops of this district. Pulses and oilseeds are the other crops. Groundnut forms an important oilseed crop in the district. The percentage of irrigated area to total cultivable area is insignificantly low.

ANIMAL HUSBANDRY

Main livestock of the district is cattle (cows and bullocks), buffaloes and goats apart from poultry birds. The quantity of livestock is poor.

INDUSTRY

The district is backward in terms of industry. Economy of the district is based on forests. Sal is the most predominant species and in Jashpur tehsil these forests occur in Narainpur Kunjara and Tapkaha.

TRADE, COMMERCE AND EXPORT

The following table provides information on most important commodities manufactured, exported from and imported in the towns of this district. It also indicates the number of banks available in these towns.

Name of Town	*Most Important Commodities*			*Banks*
	Manufactured	*Exported*	*Imported*	
1. Pathalgaon	Groundnut oil, Shoes, Note Books	Shoes, Urad, Rice	Cloth, Salt, Sugar	2
2. Jaspurnagar	Groundnut oil Lime, Soap	Rice, Bidi leaves, Timberwood	Kerosene oil, Cloth.	2

Among the agricultural produce, groundnut forms an important oilseed crop grown in Jashpur district and hence groundnut oil is the important manufactured item.

TOURISM

The rock paintings of Singhanpur, Kobra, Pahar, Khairpur and Karmagarh available nearby the district are main places of tourist interest.

The district is famous for the Badalkhol Wild Life Sanctuary which is spread in 104.35 sq km. Tiger, Panther, varieties of deer, and Blue Bull are the main fauna of this sanctuary. Migratory bird use to land in good numbers during winter.

EDUCATION

The following table gives information on different types of educational institutions including Stadia and public Libraries available in the towns of this district.

Name of Town	*Educational Institution*	*Stadia*	*Public Libraries including reading rooms*
1. Pathalgaon	Higher Secondary School (1), Middle Schools (2), Primary Schools (4)	—	—

2. Jashpur-nagar	Higher Secondary Schools (2), Middle Schools (3), Primary Schools (5)	–	1

According to 2001 census total literates (excluding the population in the age group of 0–6 years) is 404817 persons of these 236950 are males and 167867 are females. In the rural areas of the district 380614 persons (223214 males and 157400 females) are literates and in urban areas 24203 persons (13736 males and 10467 females) are literates. The rate of literacy of this population to the total population (excluding 0–6 years age group according to 2001 census are shown below.

	Persons	*Males*	*Females*
Total	65.37	76.7	54.09
Rural	64.55	76.14	53.09
Urban	81.71	87.11	75.56

COLLEGES 2000

Government Arts College, Pathalgaon (Established 1984). Enrolment 102, Teacher 6. (Affiliated College)

Government Girls College, Jashpurnagar (Established 1987). Enrolment 162, Teachers 7. (Affiliated College)

Govt. NES College, Jashpurnagar (Established 1963). Enrolment 1147. Teachers 23. (Affiliated College)

(Above named colleges belong to Guru Ghasidas university, Bilaspur, Established 1983.)

MEDICAL

The table given below furnishes information regarding availability of medical facility in the towns of this district including that of bed facility.

Name of town	*Medical institution (including beds facility)*
1. Pathalgaon	Hospital (1), Heart Centre (1) : 48
2. Jashpurnagar	Hospital (3), TB clinic (1), Dispensary (Hom-1) : 68

ADMINISTRATION

(i) Administrative Divisions: Bilaspur

Tehsils: Bageecha; Jashpur; Kunkuri; Pathalgaon.

Towns and Urban Agglomerations with their Population, Sex Ratio, Decadal Growth and Literacy Rate (2001)

Town	*Population*	*Percentage decadal growth 1991–2001*	*Sex Ratio*	*Literacy Rate*
Jashpur Nagar (TP)	20190	36.53	832	82.14
Pathalgaon (TP)	14054	28.74	963	81.08

(ii) Parliamentary Constituencies and Assembly Segments 2001:
No. & Name of Parliamentary Constituency

13. RAIGARH (ST)

No. & Name of Assembly Segments of Raigarh Parliamentary Constituency which lies within the Jurisdiction of Jashpur District.

RAIGARH (ST)–

97. Bagicha (ST)–Bagicha and Sanna RICs in Jashpur tehsil and the forest villages in the area.

98. Jashpur (ST)–Jashpur and Kastura RICs and P.Cs. 78 to 82 and 98 in Kunkuri RIC in Jashpur tehsil and the forest villages in the area.

99. Tapkara (ST)–Tapkara RIC and Kunkuri RIC (excluding P.Cs. 78 to 82 and 98) in Jashpur tehsil and the forest villages in the area.

100. Pathalgaon (ST)–Pathalgaon RIC and Kapu RIC (excluding P.Cs 1 to 6 and 36) in Udaipur (Dharamjaigarh) tehsil.

MINERALS AND ORES OCCURRENCES

Bauxite

Primary laterite resulting from the alternations of Deccan of trap *in situ* is found extensively in N.W. Jashpur in the Khuria highlands, forming cappings on flat tapped hills locally known as *Pats* rising over 3,000 ft. above sea level. These laterite cappings locally contain segregation of bauxite. A.K. Dey in

Jashpur *tahsil* found two areas of laterite where segregations of bauxite are rich. One is located N.W. of Patia (22.96, 84.01) and the other lies S.W. of Daunapat (23.01, 84.1).

He also noticed some nodular segregation of bauxite on the low laterite hill to the S.W. of Paika (23.0, 84.2) and on small hills to the east and S.E. of Pakritol (22.91, 84.33).

Bauxite is also reported from the following localities: Rauni (23.03, 83.65) Garhpahar (23.1, 84.1), Murhi (20.08, 83.58), Daitunpari (23.01, 83.7), Thutapani Pahar (23.0, 83.98), Jarhapat (23.1, 84.08), Chichli (23.05, 83.63) Bijaghat (23.1, 83.55), Busha Hill (22.8, 83.76) on the *pats* south of Arakona (23.01, 84.0), S.W. of Saraidih (23.08, 84.1) east of Madwa (23.03, 84.11), S.W. of Pandrapet (23.1, 84.7) and a mile S.W. of Jalepat (23.08, 83.65).

Copper

Thin films and small stringers of malachite in an aplite vein occur on an hill about a km. SW of Simirkacha (22.58, 83.85).

Limestone

A large deposit of capolino, a variety of crystalline limestone containing layers of a micaceous mineral, occur in the valley of a tributary *nala* of the Dorki *nadi* near Khuriarani cave and a few bands of grey crystalline limestone occur in the Archaean rocks near Dharaughag (23.10, 83.58)

Mica

Occurrence of muscovite in pegmatite veins around Rengola (22.8, 84.11) and near Keondpani (22.75, 84.2). Bartoli (22.7, 84.15) etc. Books of muscovite measuring about 4 ins. across have also been found in pegmalite veins near Kinkachaar (22.8, 84.16), Jhuti Amba (22.8, 84.26).

Deposits of light yellow ochre from near Baherna (23.31, 83.96) and several others of brick and red ochre at Kukuria (23.26, 83.61), Nopanipahar (23.13, 83.56) and Giabura (23.03, 83.56).

Building Materials

The granitegenesis occurring near Pathalgaon (22.55, 83.46). It is quarried for use as real metal.

DISASTROUS WEATHER EVENST

Hailstorm

April 1st 1982, crops worth Rs one crore damaged.

Thunderstorm

6 June 1982, tin roof tops of many houses blown away, large number of trees and electric poles uprooted, disrupting vehicular traffic.

—14 June 1992, crops damaged, electricity supply badly affected.

—18 October 1993, there was continuous rain, thunder and lightning, wind speed was more than 75 km per hour.

Drought

September 1981, 3rd and 4th week, acute shortage of water, standing crop dried.

—April and May 1985, cattle head perished due to scarcity of water and fodder.

—June to August 1987, livestock and wild animals reported died at several places.

—May 1993, 2nd week, standing crops damaged, farmers badly affected.

Heavy Rains

On 22nd August 1984, there was raining cats and dogs, caused damage to the property and standing crops.

—21-24 August 1996, two persons died, cattle head perished.

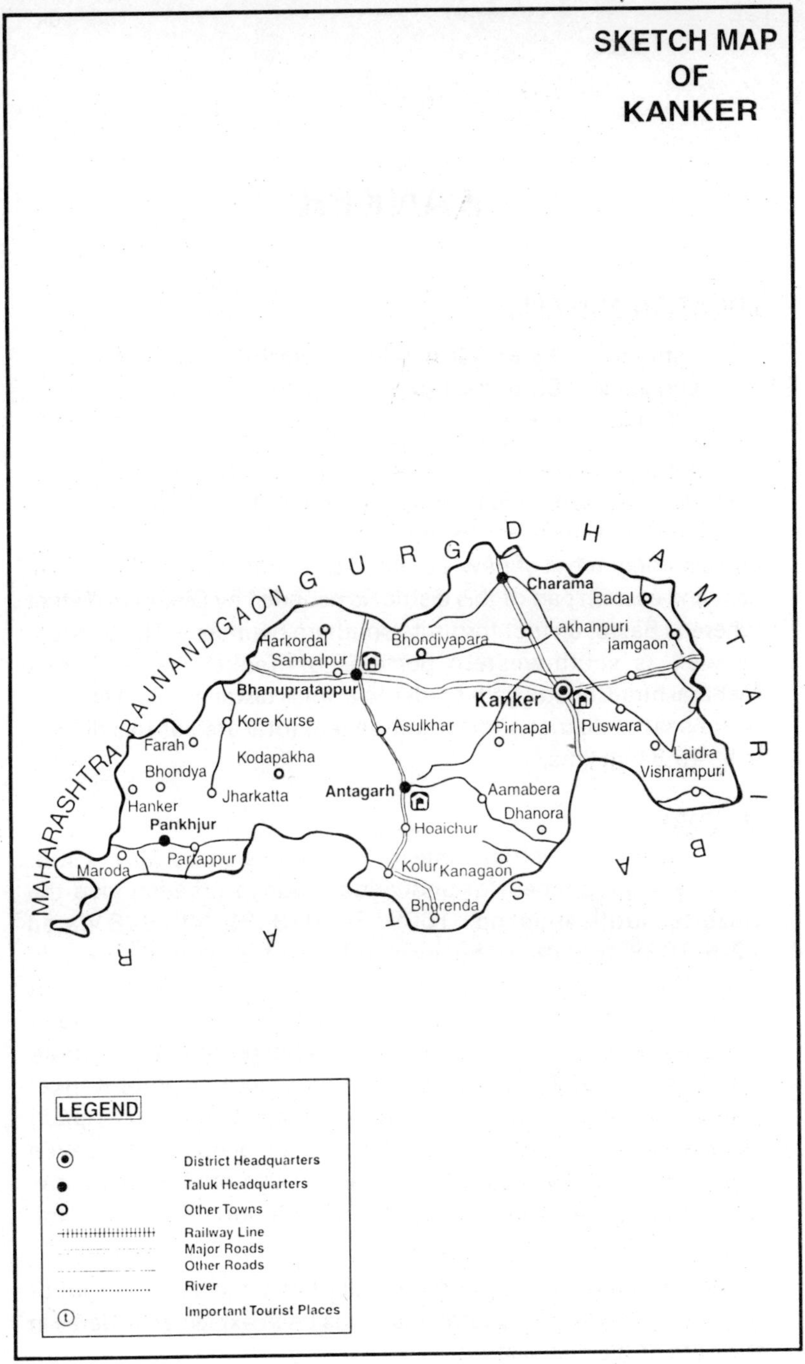
SKETCH MAP OF KANKER
MAHARASHTRA
RAJNANDGAON
DURG
DHAMTARI
BASTAR
Charama
Badal
Lakhanpuri
jamgaon
Harkordal
Bhondiyapara
Sambalpur
Bhanupratappur
Kanker
Kore Kurse
Asulkhar
Pirhapal
Puswara
Laidra
Vishrampuri
Farah
Kodapakha
Bhondya
Hanker
Jharkatta
Antagarh
Aamabera
Dhanora
Pankhjur
Hoaichur
Partappur
Maroda
Kolur
Kanagaon
Bhorenda
LEGEND
District Headquarters
Taluk Headquarters
Other Towns
Railway Line
Major Roads
Other Roads
River
Important Tourist Places

KANKER

LOCATION AND AREA

Latitude : 19.9° North to 20.6° North
Longitude : 80.5° East to 81.9° East
Altitude : 402 m

Kanker district lies in the upper southern portion of Chhattisgarh state. It is bounded on the north by Mohla tehsil of Rajnandgaon district, Sanjasibalod and Gurur tehsils of Durg district and Dhamtari tehsil of newly created Dhamtari district. The north-east and eastern part of this district is bounded by Dhamtari district whereas Baster district forms its southern boundary. The western as well as south-western portions of Kanker district forms Maharashtra-Chhattisgarh border to a small distance. Kanker town is the seat of district administration and total area of this district is 5146.84 sq kms.

HISTORY

The Kanker district came into existence on 25 May, 1998. The state government of undivided Madhya Pradesh vide the Gazette notification no. 1009–F–20–8–92–VII–S–8 dated 22-5-1998 modified the jurisdiction of Bastar district. In accordance with the said notification, six tehsils namely Kanker, Bhanupratappur, Charama, Antagarh, Narharpur and Pakhanjur of Bastar district were taken out to form the present new district. It is to be pointed out that the area now comprised of Kanker district consisted of five tehsils namely Charama, Bhanupratappur, Kanker, Antagarh and Pakhanjur further divided into seven Community Development Blocks namely Charama, Durgkondal, Bhanupratappur, Kanker, Sarana (Narharpur), Antagarh and Koyalibeda at the 1991 census.

The historical past of Kanker district is the same as that of its parent district, i.e., Bastar and it has been explained in detail in the note of the said district.

POPULATION (GENERAL, SC/ST)

The total population of Kanker district, according to 2001 census is 651333 persons, comprising 324678 males and 326655 females. Rural population of the district is 619239 persons (308426 males and 310813 females) and urban population is 32094 persons (16252 males and 15842 females). Except that of Kanker tehsil, other five tehsils of the district comprise of rural area.

The tehsil-wise population breakup, i.e., rural-urban and male-female population distribution is represented according to 2001 census in the following table:

Tehsil	*Total Rural Urban*	*Persons*	*Total population Males*	*Females*
Chrama	T	96983	47617	49366
	R	96983	47617	49366
	U	—	—	—
Bhanu-Pratappur	T	137192	68308	68884
	R	137192	68308	68884
	U	—	—	—
Kanker	T	108761	53921	54840
	R	76667	37669	38998
	U	32094	16252	15842
Narharpur	T	100451	49155	51296
	R	100451	49155	51296
	U	—	—	—
Antagarh	T	65517	32759	32758
	R	65517	32759	32758
	U	—	—	—
Pakhanjur	T	142429	72918	69511
	R	142429	72918	69511
	U	—	—	—

The Scheduled Castes and Scheduled Tribes population of the district as per 1991 census are 24,880 and 3,06,123 persons respectively. The rural-urban breakup of this population is indicated below:

Rural :	(i)	Scheduled Castes	:	23,397
	(ii)	Scheduled Tribes	:	3,02,538
Urban :	(i)	Scheduled Castes	:	1,483
	(ii)	Scheduled Tribes	:	3,585

The decennial growth rate of population of the district as a whole in relation to the state between the period 1991 and 2001 is presented below.

State/ District	*Decennial growth rate of population (per cent) 1991–01*		
	Total	*Rural*	*Urban*
Chhattisgarh	18.06	14.23	36.24
Bastar	18.84	17.42	55.03

LANGUAGES AND RELIGION

Hindi is the main language spoken in this district. Tribal dialects are spoken in the rural areas as this district is dominated by Scheduled Tribes population.

The religionwise breakup of population of this district is indicated below:

Hindus: 523472, Muslims: 3646, Jains: 675, Christians: 980, Buddhists: 1024, Sikhs 340, Other religions and persuasions: 1311, Religion not stated: 703.

GEOGRAPHY AND PHYSICAL FEATURES

Though most of Kanker and Bhanupratappur tehsils, except in the eastern part along the valley of the Mahanadi consist of hills, the general level of these tehsils is much lower than that of the plateau of Bastar. In Kanker and Bhanupratappur tehsils, the altitude is some 900 feet above the sea. In the southern parts of these tehsils, the ground rises until it reaches the height of the plateau, i.e., 2000 feet. The district is rich in forests and the forests of this area belonged to northern mixed belt. The important forest trees are Teak, Sal, Sirsa, Bijasal, Kusum, Palas, Mahua, Tendu, Harra, Aonla, Saja, Kanta, Salai and Thar. This region is important for collection of forest produce. The climate on the plateau is pleasantly cool. The district receives both the south-west and north-east monsoons and falls in the heavy rainfall region of the state.

RIVERS, CANALS AND WATERWAYS

Important rivers of the district are the Dudh and the Mahanadi. The latter rises in the Sihawa hills of the neighbouring district and enters Kanker tehsil after traversing only a short distance from its origin. It flows through eastern part of this tehsil and turning northwards from about 18 miles north-east of Kanker. The Dudh rises about 15 miles west of Keskal and flowing north-east Kanker town joins the Mahanadi. Other important rivers of the district are Kotri, Sillari, and Buri.

TOWNS, VILLAGES AND AMENITIES

The district is comprised of five tehsils. It has only one Urban Agglomeration viz. Kanker (U.A.)

COMMUNICATIONS

The district headquarters i.e., Kanker is interlinked by National Highway No. 43 from Dhamtari district in the north and Jagdalpur in the south. The Kanker town is connected with Bhanupratappur tehsil headquarters by state highway no. 32. Apart from these, there are a few metalled as well as non metalled roads which pass through villages and Community Development Blocks headquarters. The district is deprived of rail transport.

AGRICULTURE AND IRRIGATION

Rice and Kodo-Kutki are the important crops grown in the district, maize being the important crop in some areas. The percentage of irrigated area to total cultivable area is abysmally low.

ANIMAL HUSBANDRY

Common livestock of the region viz. cows, bullocks, buffaloes and goats are found in this district as well. Poultry birds are reared in good numbers, particularly in villages of this district.

INDUSTRY

Kanker district is backward in terms of industrialisation. Forest is the main resource for economic development in this district. But being a tribal area and also due to lack of communication facility no significant efforts have been made by the district administration as well as state government for industrial development.

TRADE, COMMERCE AND EXPORT

The following table provides information on most important commodities manufactured, exported from and imported in the town of this district. It also indicates the banking facility available in the town.

Name of town	Most important commodities			Banks
	Manufactured	Exported	Imported	
1. Kanker	Cement, Pipe Aluminium, Utensils, Bidi	Bidi, Wood Charcoal	Cloth, Gur, Salt	4

TOURISM

At Kanker, the chief archaeological remains are found on a hill to the south of the town where the early ruler lived. There are ruins of old buildings of stone and bricks, a temple of Shiva, a stone gateway, two tanks and two caves. On the eastern portion of the hill there is a tank and a cave known as Jogigupta. Two copper plate inscriptions were discovered at village Tahnkapur in Kankes sub-division. Mudpur contains some remains of old temples and statues.

FAIRS AND FESTIVALS

Important fairs and festivals organised in different parts of the district are Chaitra Poornima, Dashahra, Magha Poornima, Shivratri, Kartika Poornima, etc.

EDUCATION

Kanker is known for its Higher Secondary level education in its surrounding. The following table gives information on different types of educational institutions, stadia and public libraries available in the town of this district.

Name of town	Educational institution	Stadia	Public libraries including reading rooms
1. Kanker	Arts and Commerce College (1) Higher Secondary Schools (3) Middle School (4), Primary Schools (8)	1	1

According to 2001 census total literates (excluding the population in the age group of 0–6 years) is 400709 persons. Of these 225598 are males and 175111 are females. In the rural areas of this district 376581 persons (212309 males and 164272 females) are literates and in urban areas 24128 persons (13289 males and 10839 females) are literates. The rate of literacy of this population to the total population (excluding 0–6 yeas age group according to 2001 census are shown below.

	Persons	*Males*	*Females*
Total	73.31	83.03	63.69
Rural	72.65	82.51	62.94
Urban	85.32	92.45	77.95

COLLEGES 2000

Bhanupratap Deo Government PG College, (Established 1962). Enrolment 1560. Teachers 38. (Affiliated College)

Government College, Bhanupratap pur (Established 1983). Enrolment 417. Teachers 8. (Affiliated College)

Government College, Pakhanjur (1988). Enrolment 161. Teachers 6.

Government College, Charama (Established 1989). Enrolment 310, Teachers 7. (Affiliated College)

Government Girls College, Kanker (Established 1989). Enrolment 285. Teachers 7. (Affiliated College)

(Above named colleges belong to Pt. Ravishankar Shukla University, Established 1964.)

MEDICAL

The table given below furnishes information regarding availability of medical facilities in the town of this district including that of beds facility.

Name of town	*Medical institution (including beds facility)*
Kanker	Hospital (1) : 34

ADMINISTRATION

(i) Administrative Division: Bastar

Tehsils: Charama, Bhanupratappur, Kanker, Narharpur, Antagarh, Pakhanjur

Community Development Blocks: Charama, Durg Kondal, Bhanupratappur, Kanker, Sarana (Narharpur), Antagarh, Koyalibeda

Towns and Urban Agglomerations with their Population, Sex Ratio, Decadal Growth and Literacy Rate (2001)

Town	*Population*	*Percentage decadal growth 1991–2001*	*Sex Ratio*	*Literacy Rate*
Kanker (UA)	32094	55.03	975	85.32
Kanker (MC)	24485	21.18	1001	87.00

(ii) Parliamentary Constituency and Assembly Segments (2001)

No. & Name of Parliamentary Constituency: 19 Kanker

No. & Name of Assembly Segments of Kanker Parliamentary Constituency which lies within the jurisdiction of Kanker District:

19-KANKER

146. Bhanupratappur (ST)—Bhanupratappur tehsil; and Charama RIC (excluding P.Cs. 2 and 13 to 16) and P.Cs. 20 to 24 and 26 in Kanker RIC in Kanker tehsil.

147. Kanker (ST)—Narharpur RIC, P.Cs. 2 and 13 to 16 inj Charama RIC and Kanker RIC (excluding PCs. 20 to 24 and 26) in Kanker tehsil.

MINERALS AND ORES OCCURRENCES

Copper

Malachite occurs as small impregnations in cleaved cuddapah shales near Guripal in North Kanker Range.

DISASTROUS WEATHER EVENTS

Floods

16 August 1983, more than 100 houses damaged do to flood in the Godvari river, several towns badly affected, road communication disrupted.

—August 1986, there was flood in the Narmada and Indravati river. Houses collapsed or severely damaged.

Heavy Rains

12–13 July 1994, persons reported died, large number of cattle head perished.

17–19 June 1996, roads damaged at several places, telecommunication and vehicular traffic disrupted.

Drought

September 1981, 3rd and 4th week, cattle head perished, standing crops dried.

April and May 1985, acute shortage of drinking water.

June to August 1987, actue shortage of fodder and drinking water.

May 1993, 2nd week, wild animals and livestock reported died in the district.

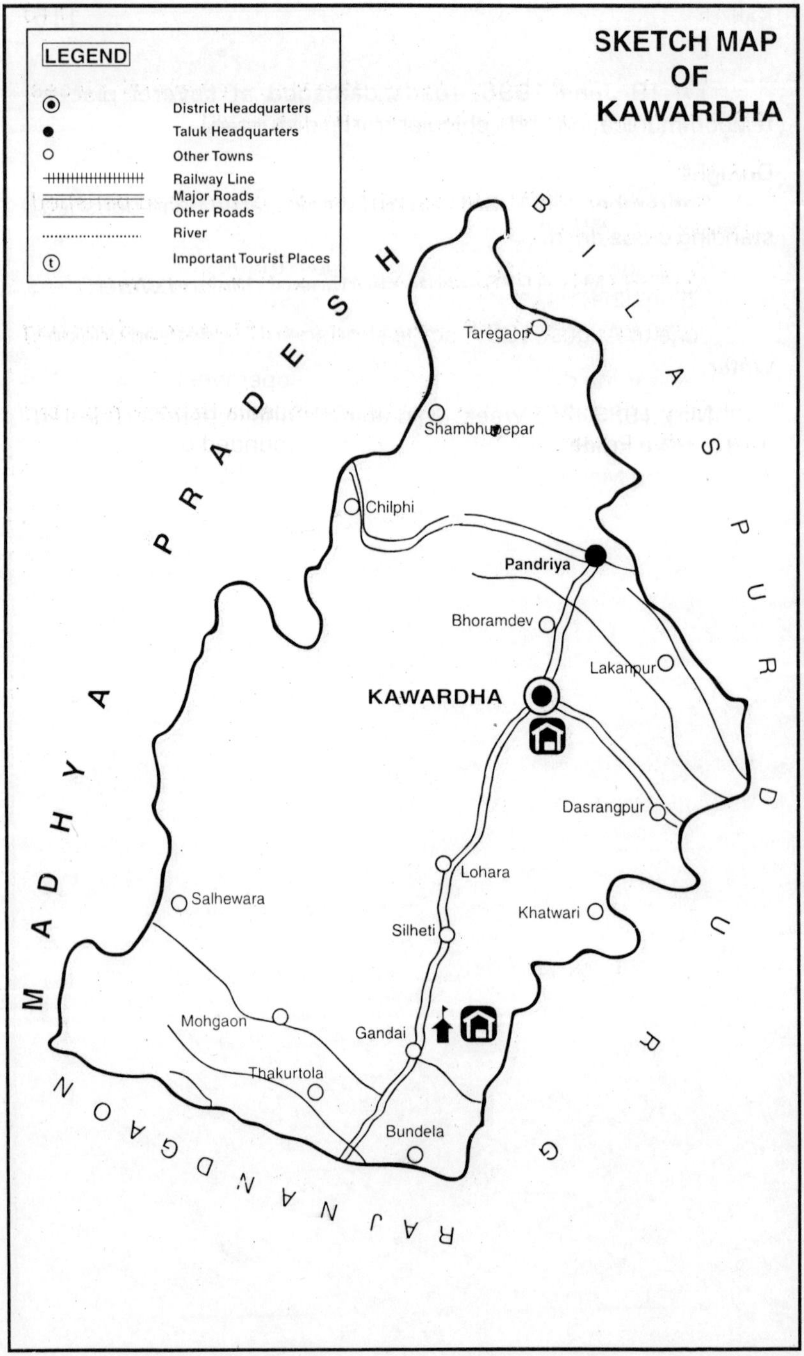

SKETCH MAP OF KAWARDHA
LEGEND
District Headquarters
Taluk Headquarters
Other Towns
Railway Line
Major Roads
Other Roads
River
Important Tourist Places
MADHYA PRADESH
BILASPUR
DURG
RAJNANDGAON
Taregaon
Shambhupepar
Chilphi
Pandriya
Bhoramdev
Lakanpur
KAWARDHA
Dasrangpur
Lohara
Salhewara
Khatwari
Silheti
Mohgaon
Gandai
Thakurtola
Bundela

KAWARDHA

LOCATION AND AREA

Latitude : 21.5 North to 22.5°North
Longitude : 80.85 East to 81.5° East
Altitude : 625 m

Kawardha district is located in the upper western portion of Chhattisgarh state adjoining to Dindori–Mandla-Balaghat districts of Madhya Pradesh state. The district is bounded on the north by Dindori and Mandla districts and on the west by Balaghat district of Madhya Pradesh whereas the eastern portion is surrounded by Lormi and Mungeli tehsils of Bilaspur district and also Nawagarh and Bemetara tehsils of Durg district, both in Chhattisgarh state. The southern portion of the district is adjacent to Chhuikhadan tehsil of its parent district, i.e., Rajnandgaon and Saja tehsil of Durg district. Total area of this district is 2772.83 sq kms and Kawardha is the headquarters of district administration.

HISTORY

The Kawardha district came into existence on 6th July, 1998. In exercise of the powers conferred under sub-section (2) of section 13 of the Madhya Pradesh Land Revenue Code, 1959 (No. 20 of 1959), the state government of undivided Madhya Pradesh vide the Gazette notification no. 1241–F–20–8–92–VII–S–8 dated 2 July, 1998 altered the limits of Rajnandgaon district by excluding therefrom the whole of Kawardha, Sahaspur–Lohara and Bodla Blocks and alter the limits of Bilaspur district by excluding therefrom the whole of Pandariya Block and created a new district of Kawardha comprising of the whole of Kawardha, Sahaspur–Lohara, Bodla and Pandariya Blocks. At the time of 1991 census, three C.D. Blocks namely Kawardha, Sahaspur, Lohara and Bodla were under the jurisdiction of Kawardha tehsil of Rajnandgaon district and Pandaria C.D. Block constituted on Pandria tehsil of Bilaspur district.

The historical past of Kawardha district is the same as that of its parent districts viz. Rajnandgaon and Bilaspur which have been explained in the note of the respective districts.

The name Kawardha has originated from the ward Kabirdham, i.e., residence of Kabir, a religious reformer and Kawardha is still the headquarters of the Kabirpanthi sect. The state was given to Mahabali Singh, a brother of the zamindar of Pandariya by the Bhonsalas for military services rendered in putting down the revolt by the king of Sagar.

POPULATION (GENERAL, SC/ST)

The total population of Kawardha district according to 2001 census is 584667 persons comprising 292054 males and 292613 females. Rural population of the district is 539799 persons (268869 males and 270930 females) and urban population is 44868 persons (23185 males and 21683 females).

The tehsil wise rural-urban and also male-female population distribution is represented according to 2001 in the following table:

Tehsil	*Total/ Rural/ Urban*	*Total Population*		
		Persons	*Males*	*Females*
Kawardha	T	4,02,819	2,00,659	2,02,160
	R	3,70,404	1,83,872	1,86,532
	U	32,415	16,787	15,628
Pandriya	T	1,81,848	91,395	90,453
	R	1,69,395	84,997	84,398
	U	12453	6398	6055

The Scheduled Castes and Scheduled Tribes population in this district as per 1991 census are 71,186 and 1,02,407 persons respectively. The rural-urban breakup of this population is indicated below:

Rural :	(i)	Scheduled Castes	:	65,428
	(ii)	Scheduled Tribes	:	1,00,460
Urban :	(i)	Scheduled Castes	:	5,758
	(ii)	Scheduled Tribes	:	1,947

The decennial growth rate of population of the district as a whole in relation to the state between the period 1991 and 2001 is presented below:

State/ District	Decennial growth rate of population 1991–01		
	Total	Rural	Urban
Chhattisgarh	18.06	14.23	36.24
Kawardha	13.86	12.64	30.87

LANGUAGES AND RELIGION

Hindi is the main language spoken in this district. Local people, particularly in villages use Chhattisgarhi, a dialect for inter-communications.

Religionwise breakup of population of this district is indicated below:

Hindus: 5,01,291, Muslims: 7,927, Jains: 783, Christians: 369, Buddhists: 143, Sikhs: 846, Other religions and persuasions: 736, Religion not stated: 1,401.

GEOGRAPHY AND PHYSICAL FEATURES

Physiographically the district can be divided into two distinct parts (i) Hilly part of the west and (2) plain region of eastern part. The ranges of Maikal and Mangata are spread in western part of the district. The ranges in the west are the highest in the region. The Maikal ranges in the district are known by different names viz. Kilish, Raniguda, Khalahi, Keshmarda, Bizapani and Chilpi. The area is thickly covered with forest. The general slope of the district is towards east. Sal, Teak, Saja, Dhawda, Harra, Tendu and Mahua are the species of trees commonly found within the forests of the district. The district receives its rainfall from the south-west monsoon, and the district receives less than 120 centimetres rainfall.

RIVERS, CANALS AND WATERWAYS

Sheonath is the most important river of the district. It rises from Kotgul in the Banbaras plateau and follows north-west in the district. Sheonath is the tributary of Mahanadi. The important tributaries of the Sheonath are Amner, Jonk, Ghumriya, Palri, Zura, Hanf and Fox. The Agar is tributary of the Maniai river which rises in the Pandaria hills at the border of the district and flows between Pandaria and Lohmi which is Bilaspur district.

TOWN, VILLAGES AND AMENITIES

The district is comprised by four Community Development Block, of which three CD Blocks constituted of part of Kawardha district whereas the remaining one C.D. Block (i.e., Pandaria) was part of neighbouring Bilaspur district at the 1991 census. The district has two towns.

COMMUNICATIONS

The district is deprived of rail facility and, therefore, the local people have to visit neighbouring districts like Durg for transport. The district headquarters Kawardha is linked with Rajanandgaon via Chhuikhadhan and Khairagarh in south direction and also in the north-east side to Pandaria CD Block by state Highway No. 9. The Pandaria CD Block is linked with Bilaspur via Mungeli and Takhatpur by state Highway No 26. Yet another Highway No. 37 connects the Kawardha from Mandla in north-west direction and to Bemetara in Durg district in south-east direction. In addition the district has a good network of both metalled and non-metalled roads within its jurisdiction.

AGRICULTURE AND IRRIGATION

Agriculture is the main occupation of the people of this district as majority of the working force is engaged in cultivation. Since, the area comprising Kawardha district constitutes part of Chhattisgarh region, it is known for paddy production. There are two main harvests viz. kharif and rabi. Non-cereal crops are also grown in the district. The irrigation facilities are meagre and, therefore, the cultivators are required to depend on rain as the irrigation to their field.

ANIMAL HUSBANDRY

Animal husbandry provides draught power for cultivation and therefore it has an important place in the agricultural economy of the district. Cattle (both bulls and cows), buffaloes and goats are the main livestock.

INDUSTRY

In the field of industrial activity, position of this district is not at all satisfactory even at present day. There is no large or medium scale industry.

TRADE, COMMERCE AND EXPORT

The table given below provides detail on most important

commodities manufactured, exported from and imported in the towns of this district. It also indicates the banking facility (number of banks) available in these towns:

Name of town	Most important commodities			Banks
	Manufactured	Exported	Imported	
Kawardha	Poha, Furniture Groundnut oil	Grains, Wheat Groundnut oil	Cloth, Kerosene, Medicine	2
Pandaria	Soap, Sawn Timber, Bidi	Grain, Wheat	Cloth, Salt, Sugar	1

TOURISM

Gandai: It is a religious point, situated in the northern part of the district. Dharamshala and hotel facilities are available for the pilgrims.

The district has no place of tourist interest within its limits. However, in nearby Khairagarh and Dongargarh both in Rajnandgaon district have certain places of tourist interest. The well known temple of Dongargarh is located in Hill top of Dongargarh town. Sangeet Mahavidyalaya is located at Khairagarh.

FAIRS AND FESTIVALS

Important fairs and festivals organised in different parts of the district are Maghapurnima, Shivratri, Christian Mela Kabir Panthi Mela, Republic Day, Chaitra Purnima.

EDUCATION

The following table gives information on different types of educational institutions, stadia and public libraries available in the district.

Name of town	Educational institution	Stadia	Public libraries including reading rooms
1. Kawardha	Higher Secondary Schools (2) Middle Schools (4), Primary Schools (7)	–	1
2. Pandaria	Higher Secondary School (1), Middle School (1)	–	–

According to 2001 census total literates (excluding the population in the age group of 0–6 years) is 263749 persons of these 168950 are males and 94799 are females. In the rural areas of the district 234974 persons (151748 males and 83226 females) are literates and in urban areas 28775 persons 17202 males and

11573 females) are literates. The rate of literacy of this population to the total population (excluding 0–6 years age group according to 2001 census are shown below.

	Persons	*Males*	*Females*
Total	55.39	71.35	39.6
Rural	53.64	69.92	37.66
Urban	75.46	87.16	62.9

COLLEGES 2000

Government Degree College, Kawardha (1983). Enrolment 730, Teachers 14.

MEDICAL

The table given below furnishes information regarding availability of medical facility available in the towns of this district including that of beds facility.

Name of town	*Medical institution (including beds facility)*
1. Kawardha	Health Centre (1) : 30
2. Pandaria	Hospital (1), Health Centre (1), Family Planning Centre (1) : 10

ADMINISTRATION

(i) Administrative Division: *Bastar*

Tehsil: *Kawardha Pandariya*

Community Development Blocks: Kawardha, Sahaspur-Lohara, Bodla, Pandariya.

Towns and Urban Agglomerations with their Population, Sex Ratio, Decadal Growth and Literacy Rate (2001)

Town	*Population*	*Percentage decadal growth 1991–2001*	*Sex Ratio*	*Literacy*
Kawardha (UA)	32415	35.54	931	77.44
Kawardha (M)	31788	32.92	933	77.51
Pandriya (TP)	12453	20.10	946	70.25

(ii) Parliamentary Constituency and assembly segments:

No. & Name of Parliamentary Constituency:

22. RAJNANDGAON

No. & Name of Assembly Segments of Rajnandgaon Parliamentary Constituency which lies within the Jurisdictions of Kawardha district

176. Kawardha—Dasrangpur and Bodla RICs and Kawardha Towns and P.Cs. 28, 29, 34 and 35 in Kawardha RIC in Kawardha tehsil and the forest villages in the area.

MINERALS AND ORES OCCURRENCES

Bauxite

Boulders of ferruginous bauxite are seen at several places within the Kawardah tahsil along the footpath between Daldal (22.4, 81.16) and Kukrapani (22.36, 81.2).

Bauxite occurring in bands and irregular segregations in the laterite covering an area of about 2 kms. on a hill, one mile east of Bhave (21.5, 80.75).

Important occurrences of bauxite have been reported from Moranda (22.5, 81.2), Kurki (22.45, 81.16), Kesmarda (22.45, 81.2), Rabda (22.43, 81.16), Daldal (22.4, 81.16), Bangora (22.45, 81.13), Chandra (22.4, 81.13), Dhauwahi (22.35, 81.11), Bahera Dongar (22.35, 81.11), Rajdhar (22.23, 81.05), Raigarh Benda (22.2, 81.03), Soradhaghat (22.2, 81.1) Bothidih (22.15, 81.06), Akalbaria (22.2, 81.03), Bahnakhodra (22.1, 81.03), Parjujhota (22.06, 81.03).

Other occurrences of bauxite are reported from (22.46, 81.18), Pakri Dadar (22.43, 81.15).

Limestone

An occurrence of dark grey limestone is recorded in the bed of a *nala* near Maheli (22.21, 81.3). Just west of Maheli is a hill about 200 ft. high called Ponda Dungri, which consists wholly of this lime stone, the total area being about 800 acres. Another ridge composed of lime stone is also noticed nearby. Another occurrence of dark grey bedded limestone is recorded in the bed of the Surkhi *nala* just north of the Kawardha town. Occurrences of limestone and calcareous shale have been reported from Dharia (21.5, 81.01).

An occurrence of dolomite has been reported from near Kodwa (21.61, 81.36). The deposit extends towards north and east with occasional gaps of several kms. of cultivated fields.

Mica

Mica occurs in a pegmatite vein about one km. east of Kukrupani (22.35, 81.31). The pegmatite vein is 5 ft. thick and the maximum size of mica found is 2 sq. inches.

Ochre

Occurrence of red ochre associated with red shales and sandstones along the sides of a hill near Khara (21.83, 80835) village. The ochre is met with at a depth of about 3 ft from the surface and is found to extend to about 30 ft in depth. The ochre is soft and bright red in colour. A large deposit of red ochre is also reported from Dongaria (21.83, 80.6) yellow ochres associated with shales have been found about a km. of Garra (21.91, 80.91). A bed of yellow shale at Piparia about 3 km. North of Khairagarh town is locally used for colour washing.

Pyrites

Speeks of pyrites are common in the shales near Silpari (21.5, 81.03) and Kondka (21.51, 81.03).

DISASTROUS WEATHER EVENTS

Drought

September 1981, 3rd and 4th week, Kharif crop badly affected, aridity was less than 25 per cent.

April and May 1985, acute shortage of drinking water, crops completely damaged,

June to August 1987, Acute shortage of drinking water, and fodder.

May 1993, 2nd week, forest animal and livestock reported died the scarcity of water, acute shortage of drinking water, farmers were the main sufferers.

Heatwave

17–19 June 1995, people reported died, cases of sun stroke reported, standing crop damaged, temperature was more than 7 to 8 °C above the normal temperature.

Heavy rains

Several kachha houses collapsed, vehicular traffic, railways, air services disrupted, telecommunication services badly affected.

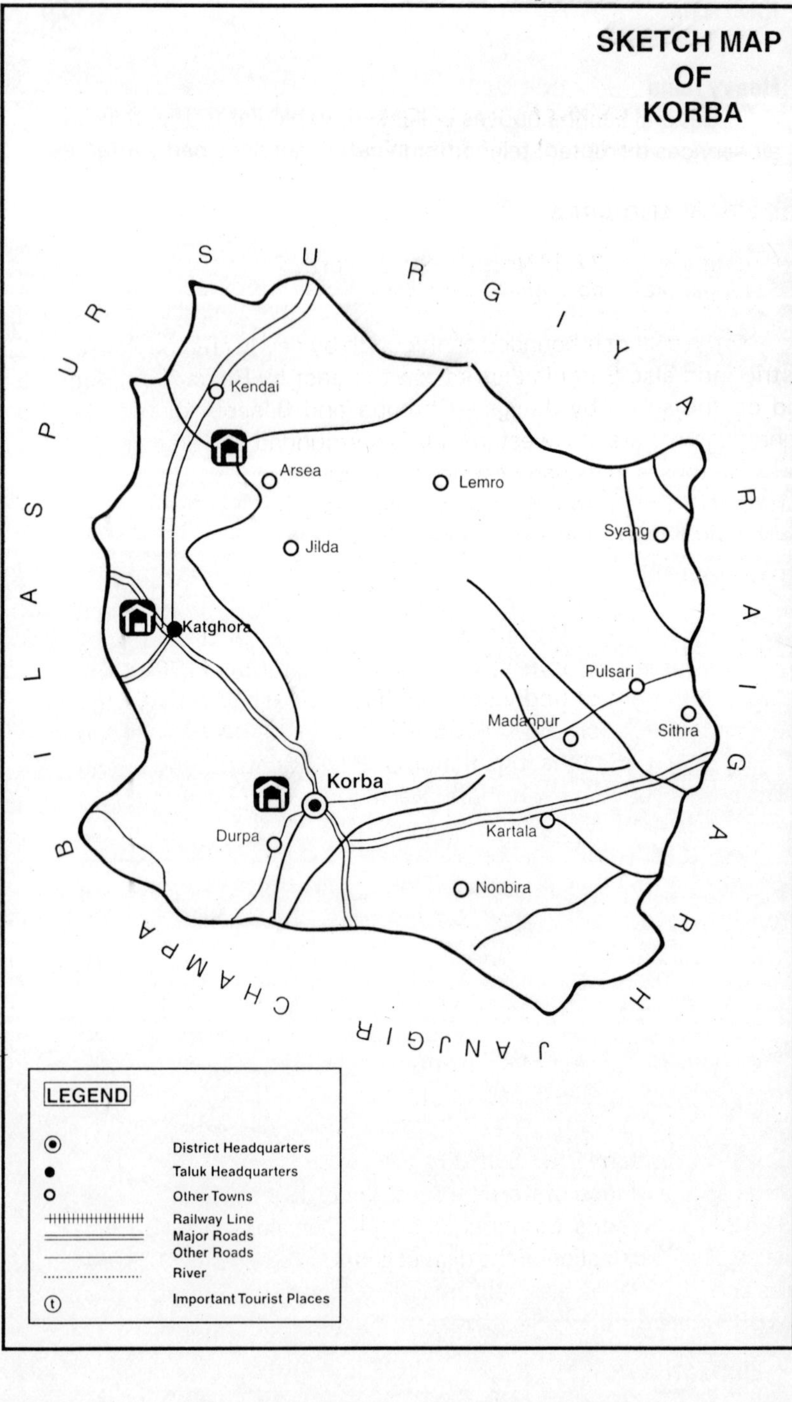
SKETCH MAP OF KORBA
SURGIYA
RAIGARH
JANJGIR CHAMPA
BILASPUR
Kendai
Arsea
Lemro
Syang
Jilda
Katghora
Pulsari
Madanpur
Sithra
Korba
Kartala
Durpa
Nonbira
LEGEND
District Headquarters
Taluk Headquarters
Other Towns
Railway Line
Major Roads
Other Roads
River
Important Tourist Places

KORBA

LOCATION AND AREA

Latitude : 22.1° North to 22.9° North
Longitude : 82.5°East to 83.1°East

Korba district is bounded on the north by newly created Koriya district and also Surguja district, on the east by Raigarh district and on the south by Janjgir—Champa and Bilaspur district of Chhattisgarh state. Its western side is sorrounded by Pendra Road and Kota tehsils of its parent district, i.e., Bilaspur. The district has assumed its name from the town tehsil and now, also the seat of district administration viz. Korba. Total area of this district is 4240.17 sq kms.

HISTORY

Korba district came into existence on 25 May, 1998. The state government of undivided Madhya Pradesh state vide the Gazette notification no. 1008–F–20-8–92–VII–S–8 dated 22-5-1998 modified the jurisdiction of Bilaspur district by taking out four tehsils namely Katghora, Kartala, Pali and Korba to form the present new district. At present also, the Korba district constitutes all these four tehsils. It is to be pointed out that at 1991 census, the area comprising Korba district was constituted of two tehsils namely Katghora and Korba of the erstwhile Bilaspur district which was further divided into five Community Development Blocks namely Pondiupraura, Pali, Katghora, Korba and Kartala.

The historical past of Korba district is the same as that of its parent district, i.e., Bilaspur district.

POPULATION (GENERAL, SC/ST)

Total population of Korba district according to 2001 census is 1012121 persons comprising 515467 males and 496654 females. Rural population of the district is 645115 persons (323784 males and 321331 females) and urban population is 367006 persons (191683 males and 175323 females).

The tehsil-wise population breakup, i.e., rural-urban and male-female population distribution is represented according to 2001 census in the following table.

Tehsil	Total Rural Urban	Persons	Total population Males	Females
Katghora	T	292154	148166	143988
	R	253438	127996	125442
	U	38716	20170	18546
Pali	T	158989	79638	79351
	R	158989	79638	79351
	U	–	–	–
Korba	T	439717	227290	212427
	R	111427	55777	55650
	U	328290	171513	156777
Kartala	T	121261	60373	60888
	R	121261	60373	60888
	U	–	–	–

The decennial growth rate of population of the district as a whole in relation to the state between the period 1991 and 2001 is presented below:

State/	Decennial growth rate of population 1991–01		
District	Total	Rural	Urban
Chhattisgarh	18.06	14.23	36.24
Korba	22.55	- 2.90	127.27

LANGUAGE AND RELIGIONS

Hindi is the main language spoken in this district. Chhattisgarhi is the dialect used by the rural people for inter-communications, particulary in the rural areas.

Religionwise breakup of population of this district is indicated below:

Hindus: 7,81,013, Muslims: 15,683, Jains: 676, Christians: 13,125, Buddhists: 665, Sikhs: 3,178, Other religions and persuasions: 9280, Religion not stated: 2265.

GEOGRAPHY AND PHYSICAL FEATURES

The district is surrounded on north by ranges of hills. The eastern outer wall of the Satpuras known as the Maikal range, runs from north-east to south-west. Irregular ranges of hills alternating with small elevated plateaus stretch, most parts of the district. The thick forests constitute important characteristics of this district. It could be classified into three distinct types on the basis of topography, soils and rainfall. These three types are: (i) the forests of the plains where generally the soil is heavy and rainfall is comparatively less, then are characterised generally by rank growth of grass stunted and deformed trees consisting mostly of fuel species and inferior timber trees, (ii) the forest of the valleys and plateaus and very gentle slopes of the hills consist of valuable timber trees and bamboos. Here, the soil is light and rainfall is good and (iii) the forests on bad hill-slopes and in the valleys with a warmer southerly aspect are principally characterised by an inferior growth of bamboos, the rugged tops of hills and sometimes only growing the hill grasses. The common species of trees found in the forests are Mahua, Saja, Bija, Char, Tendu, Palas, Harra and Bamboo. The climate of the district is characterised by a hot dry summer and well distinguished rainfall in the south-west monsoon season.

RIVERS, CANALS AND WATERWAYS

The district comes under the drainage system of Mahanadi though this river does not flow within it. Infact the rivers Hasdev and Mand, the tributaries of the Mahanadi, pass through this district. The river enters the district from Surguja district and flows through the rocky and wooded grounds of Matin-Uprala and ultimately drains into the Mahanadi after passing through neighbouring district. The Mand river runs alongwith eastern boundary to some distance bordering Raigarh district. Another river, Lilager rises from the Korba hills and flows to the south between Bilaspur and Janjgir and falls into the Seonath just before the latter joins the Mahanadi.

TOWNS, VILLAGES AND AMENITIES

The district comprises of two tehsils at the 1991 census which was divided into four tehsils thereon. According to 2001 census, there are four tehsils, namely, Katghora, Pali, Korba and Kartala. The district has 4 towns, namely Katghora, Rajgamar, Korba and Dipka.

COMMUNICATIONS

Korba district is deprived of rail facility. The nearest railway station is Champa which is located on Bilaspur-Raigarh broad gauge line, State Highway no. 5 connects Korba as well as Katghora from Champa in south and Gaurilla (of Bilaspur district) on north-western direction. The State Highway no. 5 interlinks Katghora with Ambikapur in Surguja district. There are a good number of metalled as well as unmetalled roads connecting both rural and urban areas of the district.

AGRICULTURE AND IRRIGATION

The district having small industrial potential, mainly depends on agricultural economy. The terrain and uneven distribution of soil results in uncertainty of out-turn. Kharif and rabi are the two harvests of the district. The most important crop is paddy followed by wheat and maize. Irrigation facility is not considered satisfactory and, therefore, the cultivators are required to depend on rain for irrigation purpose.

ANIMAL HUSBANDRY

Cattle, comprising cows and bullocks, buffaloes and goats are the main livestock of this district apart from poultry. They provide traditional draught power for cultivation.

INDUSTRY

Korba town is known for its industrial activities in the region. Bharat Aluminium Corporation Limited and National Thermal Power Corporation (NTPC) are the two main and Central Government concerns located in the town. In February 2001, the Union Government announced its decision to sell 51 per cent stake in BALCO to Sterlite Industries, a non-ferrous metal company for Rs 551.5 crore. This triggered a massive protest by the state government, its workers in addition to the opposition parties of Lok Sabha and Rajya Sabha. The district has good forests and as such sawing of timber is an important activity of manufacture in Korba town.

TRADE, COMMERCE AND EXPORT

The following table gives details on most important commodities manufactured, exported from and imported in the towns of this district. It also indicates the number of banks available in the towns.

Name of town	Most important commodities			Banks
	Manufactured	Exported	Imported	
1. Korba	Sawn Timber, Khoba	Coal, Aluminium, Lac.	Cloth, Wheat, Sugar	7
2. Katghora	—	Timber	Salt, Cloth, Spices	1

TOURISM

The district has no place of tourist interest within its jurisdiction.

FAIRS AND FESTIVALS

Important fairs and festivals organised in different parts of the district are Maghapurnima, Shivratri, Christian Mela Kabi & Panthi Mela, Republic Day, Chaitra Purnima.

EDUCATION

Information on educational institutions, stadia and public libraries including reading rooms available in the towns of this district is provided in the table given below:

Name of town	Educational institution	Stadia	Public libraries including reading rooms
1. Korba	Higher Secondary Schools (4) Middle Schools (4), Primary Schools (8)	—	1
2. Katghora	Higher Secondary Schools (1), Middle Schools (4), Primary Schools (4)		

According to 2001 census total literates (excluding the population in the age group of 0–6 years) is 534376 persons of these 332910 are males and 201446 are females. In the rural areas of the district 283404 persons (185382 males and 98022 females) are literates and in urban areas 250972 persons (147528 males and 103444 females) are literates. The rate of literacy of this population to the total population (excluding 0–6 age group according to 2001 census are shown below.

	Persons	Males	Females
Total	63.24	77.27	48.65
Rural	53.47	69.72	37.11
Urban	79.7	89.43	68.99

COLLEGES 2000

Government Arts College, Katghora (Established 1986). Enrolment 467. (Affiliated College)

Government Degree College, Korba (Established 1981). Enrolment 1951, Teachers 45. (Affiliated College)

Government Girls College, Korba, (Established 1989). Enrolment 436. (Affiliated College)

Kamla Nehru Mahavidyalaya, Korba, (Established 1971). Enrolment 683. Teachers 10. (Affiliated College)

(Above named colleges belong to Guru Ghasidas University, Bilaspur, Established 1983.)

MEDICAL

The following table gives information on medical institutions (alongwith beds facility) available in the towns of this district:

Name of town	Medical institution (including beds facility)
1. Korba	Hospital (4), Health centre (1) : 106
2. Katghora	PHC (1), : – FPC (1) : –

ADMINISTRATION

(i) ***Administrative division:*** Bilaspur

Tehsils: Katghora, Korba (1991 census). Now divided into four tehsils viz. Katghora, Kartala, Pali, Korba.

Community Development Blocks: Pondiupraura, Pali, Katghora, Korba, Kartala.

Towns and Urban Agglomerations with their Population, Sex Ratio, Decadal Growth and Literacy Rate (2001)

Town	*Population*	*Percentage decadal growth 1991–2001*	*Sex Ratio*	*Literacy Rate*
Katghora (TP)	18534	25.56	951	73.30
Rajgamar (CT)	12595		942	76.73
Korba (M)	315695	115.16	913	79.67
Dipka	20182		981	88.08

(ii) Parliamentary Constituency and Assembly Segments:

No. & Name of Parliamentary Constituency: 14. Janjgir.

No. & Name of Assembly Segments of Janjgir Parliamentary Constituency which lies within the Korba district.

14-JANJGIR

107. Rampur (ST)—Korba RIC (excluding Korba Town and P.C. 21), Rampur RIC (excluding P.Cs.73 to 80) and P.Cs. 14, 20, 22 and 30 in Tanakhar RIC in Katghora tehsil.

108. Katghora—Korba Town and P.C. 21 in Korba RIC, Katghora RIC and Pali RIC (excluding P.Cs. 34 and 36 to 46) in Katghora tehsil.

109. Tanakhar (ST)—Pasan RIC, Tanakhar RIC (excluding P.Cs. 14. 20, 22 and 30) and P.Cs. 34 and 36 to 46 in Pali RIC in Katghora tehsil.

MINERALS AND ORES OCCURRENCES

Bauxite

Majority of the high hills in the Korba and Uprora area are capped by primary or high-level laterite formed *in situ* from the underlying rocks. The bauxite deposits in this area have segregated from laterite and occur on the summits of flat topped high hills and their scarps.

Good quality pesolithic and massive grey bauxite occurs at many places on the Phutka Pahar (23.56, 82.76), Local segregations and boulders of bauxite occur in Laddi Pahar (23.53, 82.76), Mahadeo Pahar (22.61, 82.8) and Janta Pahar (22.6, 82.81).

Presence of good quality, massive and pirolithic bauxite is also recorded at different places on the summits of the following hills: Paunakhra Pahar (22.46, 82.91), Rannikhet Pahar (22.5, 82.93), Gurduari Pahar (22.5, 82.95), Karela Pahar (22.53, 82.95) and Satpathri Khar Pahar (22.66, 83.01).

Coal

At Korba (22.35, 82.7). This field is situated in the valley of the Hosdo River and occupies an area of more than 300 sq. kms. At Korba a 70 ft. thick coal seam occurs. One 150 ft. thick coal seams of attractive quality occurs near Ghordeva (22.4, 82.63) and another 20 ft. seam is recorded near Ghordewa. An important seam 6 ft. in thickness occurs near Rajgamar (22.4, 82.85) east of the Hasdo River.

DISASTROUS WEATHER EVENTS

Thunderstorm

1st June 1994, loud peals of thunder, with frequent lightning flashes, moderate to heavy rains, electricity supply disrupted, vehicular traffic and telephone system badly affected.

SKETCH MAP OF KOREA

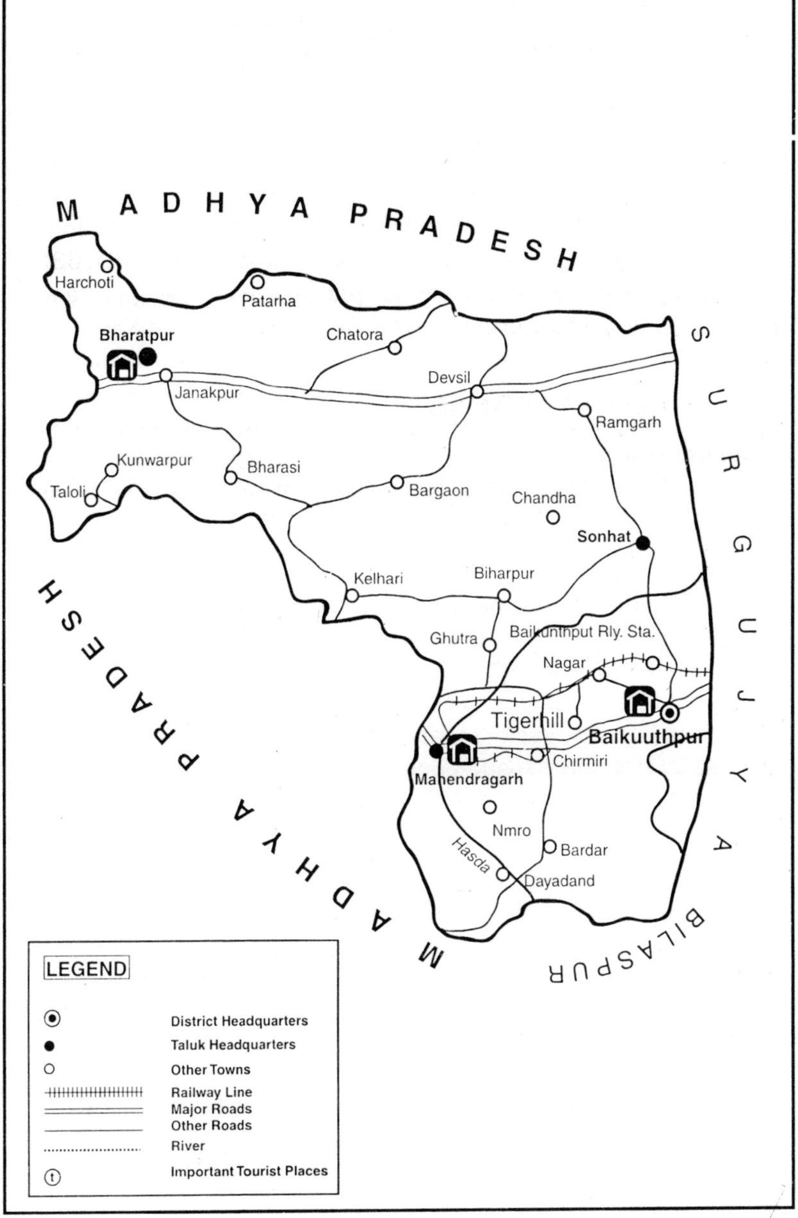

KORIYA

LOCATION AND AREA

Latitude : 22.9° North to 23.9° North
Longitiude : 81.5° East to 82.5° East

The Koriya district occupies North-western corner of newly created Chhattisgarh state. It is bounded on the north by Kusmi and Singrauli tehsils of Sidhi district, on west by Jaisingh Nagar, Sohagpur and Katma tehsils of Shahdol district, both of Madhya Pradesh and on south-west by Pendra Road tehsil of Bilaspur district, in the south by Korba district and on east by Surajpur tehsil of its parent Surguja district which are now parts of Chhattisgarh state. The district headquarters located at Baikunthpur and its total area is 4320.11 sq kms.

HISTORY

The district Koriya has been carved out as a separate district on 25 May, 1998 vide the Government of Madhya Pradesh, Revenue department notification no. 1005–F–20–8–92–VII–S–8 dated 22 May, 1998. In pursuance of the said notification the district of Surguja was bifurcated and as a result, its four tahsils namely Bharatpur, Manendragarh, Sonhat and Baikunthpur were taken out to form this new district. At present also the district of Koriya constitutes the above mentioned four tehsils.

The area now constituting Koriya district basically comprised of two feudatory states namely Chang Bhakhar and Koriya which were merged in 1951 with Surguja feudatory state to form Surguja district. While Bharatpur tehsil was taken from the feudatory state of Chang–Bhakhar, the remaining tehsils were taken from the Koria state. The erstwhile Koriya state is said to have originally belonged to a Kol chief who lived in Koriyagarh, a hill 9.6 kms (6 miles) to the west of Chirmiri on which ruins of a tank and blocks of stones may still be seen. This Kol chief was ousted by Raja Dhasmal Shah who was passing through the state on his return from Jagannathpuri.

POPULATION (GENERAL, SC/ST)

Total population of Koriya district, according to 2001 census is 585455 persons, comprising 300723 males and 284732 females. Rural population of the district is 410534 persons (208282 males and 202252 females) and urban population is 174921 persons (92441 males and 82480 females).

The tehsil-wise population break-up, i.e., rural-urban and male-female population distribution is represented according to 2001 census in the following table:

Tehsil	*Total Rural Urban*	*Persons*	*Total population Males*	*Females*
Bharatpur	T	72028	36387	35641
	R	72028	36387	35641
	U	—	—	—
Baikunthpur	T	161234	82550	78684
	R	135806	68866	66940
	U	25428	13684	11744
Sonhat	T	39678	20122	19556
	R	39678	20122	19556
	U	—	—	—
Manendragarh	T	312515	161664	150851
	R	163022	82907	80115
	U	149493	78757	70736

The Scheduled Castes and the Scheduled Tribes population in four Tehsil of the district viz. Bharatpur (Janakpur), Sonhat, Baikunthpur, Manendragarh as per 1991 census, are presented below:

Total :	(i)	Scheduled Castes	:	35,194
	(ii)	Scheduled Tribes	:	2,12,203
Rural :	(i)	Scheduled Castes	:	21,476
	(ii)	Scheduled Tribes	:	1,95,234
Urban :	(i)	Scheduled Castes	:	13,718
	(ii)	Scheduled Tribes	:	16,969

The decennial growth rate of population of the district as a whole in relation to the state between the period 1991 and 2001 is presented as follows:

State/ District	Decennial growth rate of population of the 1991–01 (per cent)		
	Total	Rural	Urban
Chhattisgarh	18.06	14.23	36.24
Koriya	16.91	22.54	5.54

LANGUAGES AND RELIGIONS

The main language spoken in the district is Hindi. Local people use Chhattisgarhi, a dialect for inter-communications.

Religionwise breakup of population of this district is indicated as follows (1991 census):

Religions	Bharatpur Tehsil	Baikunthpur (including Sonhat tehsil)	Manendragarh tehsil
1. Hindus	59212	174831	239010
2. Muslims	419	6218	10854
3. Jains	15	170	802
4. Christians	118	2075	3315
5. Buddhists	8	21	91
6. Sikhs	20	354	1176
7. Other religions and Persuasions	22	254	485
8. Religion not stated	227	420	641

GEOGRAPHY AND PHYSICAL FEATURES

The district is in the belt of Sal forest and the Sal trees are the predominant species. As per Gazettes of erstwhile Chang Bakhar state the ravages of wild elephants were at one time so serious as to cause the entire abandonment of village sites, till a large number were captured but at the present date no wild elephants are to be found in the state. Likewise the Gazettee of erstwhile Koriya state mentions : "Tigers and wild elephants at one time were numerous and committed serious depredations. They caused the desertion of many small villages, but their numbers have now been considerably reduced." Nowadays in the region not a single wild elephant is found.

The district has local variation of soil called Mair. It is a blackish soil suitable for paddy and wheat. This may be equated with Kunhas soil. Dudia is a greyish soil. This is inferior and gives poor yield. The district is rich in respect of minerals with a sizeable population engaged in mining and quarrying.

The district being a high table-land with numerous hills and plateaus, the climate of the district is generally moderate.

RIVERS, CANALS AND WATERWAYS

The principal rivers of the district are Gopad, Banas and Hardev. The Gopad rises in the Sonhat plateau and flows north till it reaches the boundary of the district. The News is its principal tributary. The Banas rises from central hilly region of Bharatpur tehsil and forms the western boundary of the district flowing towards west and north-west. The Hardev river rises in the eastern part of Sonhat plateau, flows southwards into the neighbour district. Its main tributaries are Crej, Jink and Atem.

TOWNS, VILLAGES AND AMENITIES

The district is comprised of four tehsils, namely Bharatpur, Baikunthpur, Sonhat, Manendragarh. It has six towns and one urban agglomeration (viz. Chirimiri UA).

COMMUNICATIONS

A broad guage line, i.e., Chirmiri-Anuppur via Manendragarh and Bishrampur caters to the need of train passengers of the district. Another railway track in the district is mainly utilised for transportation of coal from coal fields to other places. The district has, however, a good network of road transport. There are many inter and intra-district bus services.

AGRICULTURE AND IRRIGATION

Kharif is the main crop season in the district. Paddy, wheat, jowar, maize and Kodokutki are the main cereal crops, whereas Urad and Arhar constitute main pulse crops. Til, linseed and groundnut are also sown. Area under irrigation is not quite satisfactory and not much development in this regard seems to have taken place in the recent time.

ANIMAL HUSBANDRY

Cattle constitutes the wealth of the cultivators. Cows, bullocks, buffaloes and goats are common animals found in the district.

INDUSTRY

Coal plays the major role in the district's economy. There are many major coal mines in the district, some of which are Kurasia, Chirmiri, North Jhagarakhand, South Jhagarakhand, Baikunthpur, Daman Hill, Chherchha and NCPH colliery. Stone and morams quarrying also play equally important role in the district's economy. Important minerals found in the district are bauxite, uranium, fireclay, mica, cement stones and limestones.

TRADE, COMMERCE AND EXPORT

The following table provides information on most important commodities manufactured, exported from and imported in the towns of this district. It also indicates the banking facility (number of banks) available in these towns:

Name of town	*Most important commodities*			*Banks*
	Manufactured	*Exported*	*Imported*	
1. Baikunthpur	Bidi, Groundnut oil	Tilhan, Rice Country liquor	Soap, Cloth, Kerosene	4
2. Jhagrakhand	Poles	Poles	Wheat, Cloth Kirana	1
3. Chirmiri	—	Coal, Coun try liquors, Wood	Rice, Cloth, Kirana	3
4. Manendragarh	Paper	Rice, Coal, Lac.	Sugar, Cloth Kirana	4

TOURISM

Important places of tourist interest in the district are given below:

Amrit Dhara: It is in Baikunthpur tehsil on the bank of Hardeo river, which appears in the summer season and disappears in the rainy season.

Sitamarhi Cave: A cave known as Sitamarhi is located near Ghogra village situated on the bank of Dauna river. The cave contains two monoliths, said to be Mahadeo, similar Sitamarhis are found in the jungles of Kanjia and Chhataunda

On the Moreagarh hill, 6 miles west of Chirmiri, remains of a tank and some stone blocks which probably once formed dwellings, are seen.

FAIRS AND FESTIVALS

Important fairs and festivals organised in different parts of the district are Chaitra Poornima, Dashahra, Magha Poornima, Shivratri, Kartika Poornima, etc.

EDUCATION

The following table gives information on different type of educational institutions, stadia and public libraries available in the towns of this district.

Name of town	*Educational institution*	*Stadia*	*Public libraries including reading rooms*
1. Baikunthpur	Higher Secondary Schools (2) Middle Schools (3), Primary Schools (5),	–	1
2. Jhagrakhand	Middle Schools (3) Primary Schools (8)	–	–
3. Chirmiri	Higher secondary Schools (2), Middle Schools (5), Primary Schools (8)	–	1
4. Manendra-garh	HigherSecondary Schools (2), Middle Schools (4), Primary schools (10)	1	–

According to 2001 census total literates (excluding the population in the age group of 0–6 years) is 309312 persons of these 190899 are males and 118413 are females. In the rural areas of the district 191994 persons (121216 males and 70778 females) are literates and in urban areas 117318 persons (69683 males and 47635 females) are literates. The rate of literacy of the population to the total population (excluding 0–6 years age group according to 2001 census are shown below:

	Persons	*Males*	*Females*
Total	63.44	76.01	50.08
Rural	57.07	70.92	42.77
Urban	77.61	86.87	67.14

COLLEGES 2000

Government Degree College, Baikunthpur (Established 1982). Enrolment 259, Teachers 6. (Affiliated College)

Government Lahiri College Chirimiri (Established 1953). Enrolment 619. Teachers 14. (Affiliated College)

Government Vivekanand College, (Established 1973). Enrolment 535. Teachers 12. (Affiliated College)

(Above named colleges belong to Guru Ghasidas University, Bilaspur, Established 1983).

MEDICAL

The table given below furnishes information regarding availability of medical facility in the towns of this district including that of beds facility:

Name of town	*Medical institution (including beds facility)*
1. Baikunthpur	Health centre (1): 14
2. Jhagrakhand	Health centre (1): 5
	Dispensary (2) : –
3. Chirmiri	Hospital (1) : 31
	Dispensary (1) : –
4. Manendragarh	Hospital (1),
	Health Centre (1) : 212

ADMINISTRATION

(i) Administrative Division: Bilaspur

Tehsils: Bharatpur, Manendragarh, Sonhat, Baikunthpur.

Community Development Blocks: Bharatpur, Sonhat, Baikunthpur, Manendragarh

Towns and Urban Agglomerations with their Population, Sex Ratio, Decadal Growth and Literacy Rate (2001)

Town	*Population*	*Percentage decadal growth 1991–2001*	*Sex Ratio*	*Literacy Rate*
Charcha (CT)	15352	14.53	864	79.31
Chirimiri (UA)	93366	4.37	900	76
Chirimiri (M)	91312	6.97	899	76.37
Baikunthpur (TP)	10076	21.16	850	89.41

Manendragarh (M)	30755	16.82	889	83.12
Khongapani (CT)	17865	24.96	889	70.13
Jhagrakhand (TP)	7507	- 46.12	927	73.18

(ii) Parliamentary Constituency and Assembly Segments (2001)

No. and Name of Parliamentary Constituency. 10– Sidhi.

No. and Name of Assembly Segments of Sidhi Parliamentry Constituency which lies within the jurisdiction of Koriya district: Sidhi.

10-SIDHI

137. Saraipali—Saraipali and Khamharpali RICs in Mahasamund tehsil.

138. Basna—Basna RIC and Pithora RIC (excluding P.C.s 25 to 28) in Mahasamund tehsil and the forest villages in the area.

139. Khallari (Gen.)—Khallari and Komakhan RICs and P.C.s 25 to 28 in Pithora RIC in Mahasamund tehsil and the forest villages in the area.

140. Mahasamund (Gen.—Mahasamund and Patewa RICs in Mahasamund tehsil and the forest villages in the area.

DISASTROUS WEATHER EVENTS

Drought

September 3rd and 4th week 1981, cattle head perished standing crops dried, aridity was less than 25 per cent.

April and May 1985, acute shortage of drinking water, crops completely damaged.

June to August 1987, acute shortage of fodder, cattle reported died at several places, shortage of drinking water.

May 2nd week 1993, livestock and wild animals died due to scarcity of water, laks of people, mainly farmers, badly affected.

Heat wave

17–19 June 1995, standing paddy crops damaged, temperature was 7 to 8 degree celcius above the normal temperature.

Heavy Rains

17 and 18 July 1993, several houses collapsed, vehicular traffic, railways, air services disrupted, telecommunication services badly affected.

SKETCH MAP OF MAHASAMUND

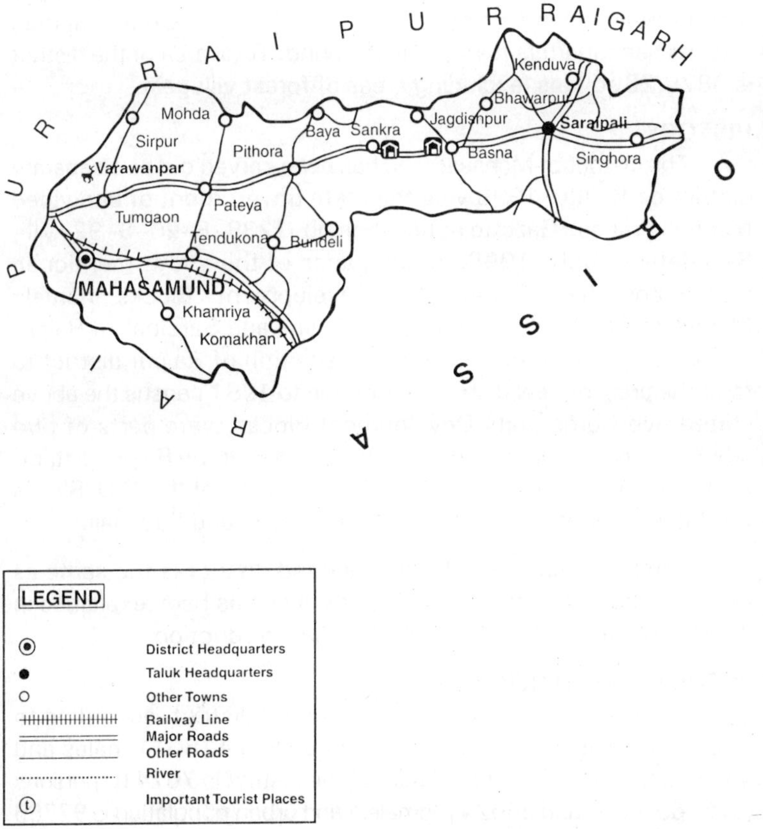

MAHASAMUND

LOCATION AND AREA

Latitude : 20.8° North to 21.3° North
Longitude : 82.1° East to 83.30° East

Mahasamund district is situated on the middle eastern periphery of Chhattisgarh state, bordering Orissa. Except the north-eastern portion and its eastern periphery which are bounded by Sarangarh tehsil of Raigarh district and Orissa state respectively, the rest of the area of this new district is surrounded by Raipur district which is in fact its parent district. The district is named after its headquarters town, Mahasamund. Total area of the district is 3876.26 sq kms (excluding areas of forest villages).

HISTORY

The district of Mahasamund has been carved out as a separate district on 6 July, 1998 vide the state government of undivided Madhya Pradesh Gazette notification no. 1238–F–20–8–92–VII–S–8 dated 2 July, 1998. In pursuance of the above mentioned notification five Community Development Blocks namely Mahasamund, Bagbahara, Pithora, Basna and Saraipali of Raipur district were taken out from the jurisdiction of Raipur district to form the present new district. According to 1991 census the above stated five Community Development Blocks were parts of two tehsils viz. Mahasamund and Saraipali tehsils of the Raipur district. At present also, Mahasamund district comprises of five C.D. Blocks viz. Mahasamund, Bagbahara, Pithora, Basna and Saraipali.

The historical past of Mahasamund district is the same as that of its parent district, i.e., Raipur which has been explained in detail in related section as well as in the introduction.

POPULATION (GENERAL, SC/ST)

The total population of Mahasamund district, according to 2001 census is 860176 persons comprising 426011 males and 434165 females. Rural population of the district is 762410 persons (376169 males and 386241 females) and urban population is 97766 persons (49842 males and 47924 females).

Tehsil	Total/ Rural/ Urban	Persons	Males	Females
1. Basna	T	139356	68670	70686
	R	130543	64147	66396
	U	8813	4523	4290
2. Saraipali	T	170759	85032	85727
	R	153684	76190	77494
	U	17075	8842	8233
3. Mahasamund	T	550061	272309	277752
	R	478183	235832	242851
	U	71878	36477	35401

The decennial growth rate of population of the district as a whole in relation to the state between the period 1991 and 2001 is presented below.

State/ District	Decennial growth rate of population (per cent) 1991–2001		
	Total	Rural	Urban
Chhattisgarh	18.06	14.23	36.24
Mahasamund	8.72	6.70	27.50

LANGUAGES AND RELIGION

The main language spoken in the district is Hindi. Chhattisgarhi is the dialect generally used by the local people particularly in villages for inter-communication. Religionwise breakup of population of this district is indicated below:

Hindus: 772720, Muslims: 8467, Jains: 1265, Christians: 4504, Buddhists: 1171, Sikhs: 2249, Other religions and persuasions: 30, Religion not stated: 791.

GEOGRAPHY AND PHYSICAL FEATURES

Physiographically, the bulk of Mahasamund district is hilly. The western boundary of the district runs along the Mahanadi river. Whereas yet another river known as Jok divides the district in the middle as it passes from south to north direction. The climate of the district is not so hot because of the presence of Sal forests. The other species found alongwith Sal are Saja, Kathua, Bija, Dharwa, Bahera, Harra, Lendia, Salai and Tinsa. Other common varieties found in the forest are Mahua, Tendu, Chaos, Haldu and Aonla.

RIVERS, CANALS AND WATERWAYS

Mahanadi is the principal river of the district which run from south to north-eastern direction. The Jonk is an important tributary in this district. Chirar Mala runs in southern boundary for short length.

TOWNS, VILLAGES AND AMENITIES

The district is comprised of three tehsils and five Community Development Blocks. It has five towns.

Details of availability of infrastructured facilities in the villages of this district is not available separately as this district was not existing at the time of 1991 census.

COMMUNICATIONS

The district headquarters i.e., Mahasamund is connected with broad gauge line which runs through Bhilai–Raipur to Khariar road–Vijaynagaram. However, to visit Calcutta or Mumbai, the local people have to go to Raipur either by road transport or rail transport. The bus transport is considered as convenient because of the good number of bus services between Raipur and Mahasamund. The National Highway 6 passes through the district and connects Pithora, Barna and Saraipali tehsils. Mahasamund and Bagbahara are interlinked with Raipur by State Highway No. 37. Apart from these important Highways, there are a good network of metalled and un-metalled roads in the district.

AGRICULTURE AND IRRIGATION

The district falls in the rice belt of the Chhattisgarh region. Paddy and wheat are the main crops. Oilseeds particularly groundnut are grown in larger area in addition to pulses. Mahasamund and canal project is one of the oldest irrigation system of the state.

ANIMAL HUSBANDRY

Cows and buffaloes constitute the main source of milk supply and also of the valuable farmyard manure. Bullocks and the buffaloes are used for agricultural operations. Pigs, goats and poultry birds are other livestock found in this district.

INDUSTRY

Mahasamund district is deprived of any major industry. Rice mills and oil mills are in plenty. Manufacture of Bidi is the main item in Saraipali town.

TRADE, COMMERCE AND EXPORT

The following table provides information on important commodities manufactured in, exported from and imported in the towns of this district. It also gives information on number of banks available in these towns.

Name of town	*Most important commodities*			*Banks*
	Manufactured	*Exported*	*Imported*	
1. Bagbahara	Gudakhu	Rice, Bidi leaves, Mahua	Wheat, Cloth, Sugar	2
2. Mahasamund	Groundnut oil, Soap, Bidi	Groundnut oil, Wood, Rice	Kerosene, Cloth	4
3. Saraipali	Bidi, Bricks	Rice, Ground-nut oil, Tendu leaves	Cloth, Kirana, Medicine	3
4. Pithora	Bidi	Wood, Tendu leaves	Wheat, Cloth Medicine	2

TOURISM

Baranwapar: It is a wild life sanctuary which lies within the jurisdiction of the district, at the border area of Mahasmund and Raipur district. Spread over an area of 244.66 sq. km, this sanctuary is famous for tiger, panther, different varieties of deer and wild hog. Migratory birds use to land here in winter season.

FAIR AND FESTIVALS

Important fairs and festivals organised in different parts of the district are Chaitra Poornima, Dashahra, Magha Poornima, Shivratri, Kartika Poornima, etc.

EDUCATION

The following table presents information on types of educational institutions available in the towns of this district, apart from the number of stadia and public libraries; if available:

Name of town	*Educational institution*	*Stadia*	*Public libraries including reading rooms*
1. Bagbahara	Higher secondary school (1), Middle schools, (2) Primary Schools (12)	–	1
2. Mahasamund	Higher Secondary Schools (3) Middle Schools (5), Primary Schools (15)	–	2

3. Saraipali	Higher Secondary schools (2), Middle schools (3), Primary Schools (7)	—	1
4. Pithrora	Higher Secondary schools (2) Middle Schools (3), Primary schools (4)	—	1

According to 2001 census total literates (excluding the population in the age group of 0–6 years) is 491886 persons of these 292988 are males and 198898 are females. In the rural areas of the district 425822 persons (254955 males and 170867 females) are literates and in urban areas 66064 persons (38033 males and 28031 females) are literates. The rate of literacy of this population to the total population (excluding 0–6 years age group according to 2001 census are shown below.

	Persons	*Males*	*Females*
Total	67.64	81.58	54.04
Rural	66.2	80.58	52.28
Urban	78.63	88.96	67.93

COLLEGES 2000

Government KL Arts and Commerce College, Bagbahara, (Established 1963). Enrolment 375. Teachers 9. (Affiliated College)

Government Mahasamund College, Mahasamund. Enrolment 1046. Teachers 16. (Affiliated College)

Shantri Bai Arts Commerce and Science College, Mahasamund (Established 1993). Enrolment 180. Teachers 14. (Affiliated College)

Yatan Girls College, Mahasamund (Established 1985). Enrolment 139. (Affiliated College)

(Above named colleges belong to Pt. Ravi Shankar University, Established 1964.)

MEDICAL

The following table provides information on types of medical facilities available in the towns of this district including the number of beds facility available therein:

Name of town	Medical institution (including beds facility)	
1. Bagbahara	Health Centre (1):	20
2. Mahasamund	Hospital (1), Health centre (1), Dispensary (1) :	32
3. Saraipali	Health Centre (1) :	6
4. Pithora	Health Centre (1) :	10

ADMINISTRATION

(i) Administrative Division: Raipur

Tehsil: Basna, Mahasamund, Saraipali

Community Development Blocks: Mahasamund, Bagbahara, Pithora, Basna and Saraipali

Towns and urban Agglomerations with their Population, Sex ratio, Decadal growth and Literacy Rate (2001).

Town	*Population*	*Percentage decadal growth 1991–2001*	*Sex Ratio*	*Literacy*
Saraipali (TP)	17075	23.12	931	79.94
Pithora (TP)	7929	- 10.22	980	79.13
Busna (CT)	8813	–	948	80.60
Mahasamund	47203	20.49	965	80.88
Bagbahara	16746	13.14	981	69.58

(ii) Parliamentary Constituencies and Assembly Segments (2001):

No. & Name of Parliamentary Constituency: 18. Mahasamund.

No. & Name of Assembly Segments of Mahasamund Parliamentary Constituency which lies within the jurisdiction of Mahasamund district.

18-MAHASAMUND

137. Saraipali—Saraipali and Khamharpali RICs in Mahasamund tehsil.

138. Basna—Basna RIC and Pithora RIC (excluding P.C.s 25 to 28) in Mahasamund tehsil and the forest villages in the area.

139. Khallari—Khallari and Komakhan RICs and P.C.s 25 to 28 in Pithora RIC in Mahasamud tehsil and the forest villages in the area.

140. Mahasamund—Mahasamund and Patewa RICs in Mahasamund tehsil and the forest villages in the area.

Mahasamund was in Baloda Lok Sabha seat in 1957 the community wise break up (OBE) in Mahasamund is: Scheduled Castes 13 per cent; Scheduled Tribes 29 per cent; and Telis 10 per cent. Others in sizable numbers are Ahirs, Malis, Kewats, and Kurmis, satnamis/chamars 9 per cent and Gondas 2 per cent among the scheduled castes and Gonds 19 per cent and Kawars 4 per cent among the scheduled tribes are dominant.

MINERALS AND ORES OCCURRENCES

Lead and Silver

Traces of galena have been recorded in a quartz vein near Khashpahar (21.26, 82.76).

DISASTROUS WEATHER EVENTS

Drought

September 1981, 3rd and 4th week, aridity was less than 25 per cent, Kharif crop badly affected.

April and May 1985, acute shortage of drinking water, crops completely damaged.

June to August, 1987, acute shortage of drinking water and fodder.

—May 1993, 2nd week, forest animals reported died in the shortage of water, acute shortage of drinking water reported, lakhs of people badly affected.

Heatwave

17–19 June 1995, at some places the temperature was 5 to 6 degree above normal and at some places it was 7 to 8°C above the normal temperature.

Heavy rains

17 and 18 July 1993, several houses collapsed, vehicular traffic, railways, air services, disrupted, telecommunication services badly affected.

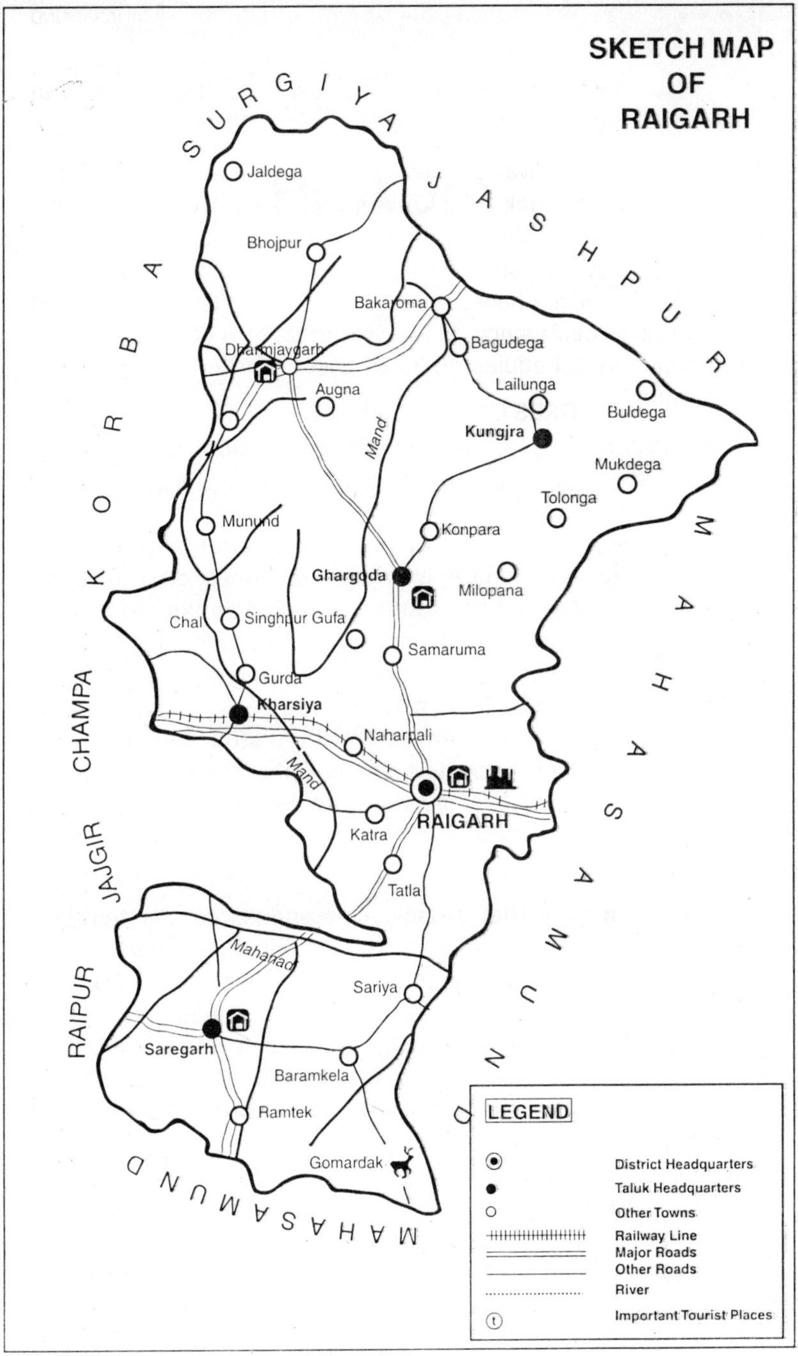
SKETCH MAP
OF
RAIGARH
SURGIYA
JASHPUR
KORBA
CHAMPA
JAJGIR
RAIPUR
MAHASAMUND
MAHASAMUND
Jaldega
Bhojpur
Bakaroma
Bagudega
Dharmjaygarh
Augna
Lailunga
Buldega
Kungjra
Mand
Mukdega
Tolonga
Munund
Konpara
Ghargoda
Milopana
Chal
Singhpur Gufa
Samaruma
Gurda
Kharsiya
Naharpali
Mand
RAIGARH
Katra
Tatla
Mahanadi
Sariya
Saregarh
Baramkela
Ramtek
Gomardak
LEGEND
District Headquarters
Taluk Headquarters
Other Towns
Railway Line
Major Roads
Other Roads
River
Important Tourist Places

RAIGARH

LOCATION AND AREA

Latitude: 21.2° North to 22.5° North
Longitude: 83.1° East to 83.9° East
Altitude: 220 m

Raigarh district, in Bilaspur Revenue Division, is situated on easternmost part of Chhattisgarh State and lies between 21.2° and 22.5° north latitude 83.1° and 83.9° east longitude. The district is bounded by Surguja and Jashpurnagar district on the north, Sundergarh and Sambalpur districts of Orissa on the east, Mahasamund district on the south, Korba and Janjgir district on the west. The district varies from the lofty forest clad plateau of Pandrapat and Khuria in the north to the treeless dreary, dusty plains of Raigarh and Sarangarh in the south.

The district gets its name from the district headquarters town, Raigarh which according to the Chhattisgarh Feudatory States Gazetteer (1909), is derived from the world *rai* meaning a species of thorny tree and *garh* a fort.

HISTORY

The present district broadly corresponds to the territory comprising the feudatory States of Raigarh, Sarangarh, Jashpur and Udaipur with some adjustments of villages. Jashpur and Udaipur States were till 1905 under the commissioner of Chhota Nagpur and were included in the erstwhile Bengal Province. It was in 1905 that these territories were transferred to the erstwhile Central Provinces as a result of the territorial adjustments between Orissa and erstwhile Central Provinces. Consequent upon the merger of princely States in 1948, Raigarh district was constituted then by including the territories of the four feudatory States of Raigarh, Sarangarh, Jashpur and Udaipur. Then it had seven tehsils, viz., Udaipur, Jashpur, Ghar-ghoda, Raigarh, Sarangarh, Kharsia and Sakti. Consequent upon the Reorganisation of States on linguistic basis in 1956 some inter district transfers took place. The whole of Sakti tehsil and 52 villages of of Sakti tehsil and 52 villages of Kharsia tehsil of Raigarh district were transferred to Bilaspur district. Raigarh tehsil was expanded by the transfer of 148 villages and one town of Kharsia tehsil and 2 villages from Janjgir tehsil of Bilaspur district. Sarangarh tehsil was also expanded by the transfer of 25 villages from Janjgir tehsil of Bilaspur district. This resulted in the abolition of Kharsia tehsil. Thus Raigarh district which emerged on 1st November, 1956 in the new State of Madhya Pradesh constituted of five tehsils, *viz.,* Udaipur, Jashpur, Gharghoda, Raigarh and Sarangarh, continued unchanged since then. The tehsils are situated in an order from north to south with Dharamjaigarh tehsil on the extreme north followed by, Gharghoda, Raigarh and then Sarangarh on the extreme south of the district boundary.

POPULATION

Total population of the district according to 2001 census is 1265084 persons, comprising 633993 males and 631891 females, Rural population of the district is 1095793 persons (546883 males and 548910 females) and urban population is 169291 persons (87110 males and 82181 females).

The tehsil-wise population break-up, i.e., rural-urban and male-female population distribution is represented according to 2001 census in the following table.

Tehsil	*Total Rural Urban*	*Persons*	*Total population* *Males*	*Females*
Udaipur	T	179718	89656	90062
	R	166115	82794	83321
	U	13603	6862	6741
Lailunga	T	113527	56756	56771
	R	113527	56756	56771
	U	—	—	—
Ghargoda	T	148832	74134	74698
	R	140729	70042	70687
	U	8103	4092	4011
Raigarh	T	364278	185614	178664
	R	248538	125698	122840
	U	115740	59916	55824
Kharsia	T	129429	64583	64846
	R	112042	55700	56342
	U	17387	8883	8504

Sarangarh	T	329300	163250	166050
	R	314842	155893	158949
	U	14458	7357	7101

The decennial growth rate of population of the district as a whole in relation to the State between the period 1991 and 2001 is presented below:

State/ District	*Decennial growth rate of population (per cent) 1991–2001*		
	Total	*Rural*	*Urban*
Chhattisgarh State	18.06	14.23	36.24
Raigarh	18.68	18.01	23.25

LANGUAGES AND RELIGION

Main languages spoken in the district are Hindi, Oriya and Urdu. Main religion of the district are Hindus, Christians, Muslims, Sikhs, Buddhists and Jains.

GEOGRAPHY AND PHYSICAL FEATURES

Physiographically the lattitude 23.25' North divides the district into two broad divisions. The northern being predominantly hilly religion and the southern predominantly plain country. Above this lattitude, the ground goes on increasing in a series of steps till it reaches the lofty plateau of Mainpat and Khuria in the north. Mahanadi river can also be taken to be dividing the district into two regions. The northern region having a general slope towards the south and the southern region having a general slope towards the north.

The Mainpat is a high plateau along the great Central Water Parting line of India, on the Chhota-Nagpur group of plateau. The high land of *pat* extends mostly in Surguja district along the northern and north-western boundary of Udaipur tehsil. The highest peak of Mainpat in Surguja is 1158 metres.

The Pathalgaon-Lailunga plateau occupies the central and west central part of the district. This is the widest part of hill range which runs along the west bank of the Mahanadi river in the north, and further, along the east bank of Kurket *nala* in the south. The Mahanadi Valley extends in Raigarh and Sarangarh tehsils between Chanwardhal and Sarangarh hills. The general width of the plain is about 24 kms on both sides of the river. The general elevation of the plain in Raigarh district is about 1248 kms.

The area comprises one of the most fertile tract and thickly populated region of the state. A line of low hills range known as the Chanwardhal hills runs from north-west to south west along the northern limits of Mahanadi valley.

A main line of hills known as the Sarangarh hills in Sarangarh tehsil extends in a west to east direction from the Sonakhan hills of Raipur district. They scarp towards Raipur along the southern boundary and disturb the plain topography of Sarangarh tehsil.

The district occupies a big forest area. The flora of the district has been cleared off from all even and culturable tracts. The forests of the district are classed into four major types, viz., Sal, Mixed, Bamboo and Teak.

RIVERS, CANALS AND WATERWAYS

The rivers of the district come under two distinct drainage systems, Mahanadi and the Son. Of these, it is the Mahanadi that really commands the drainage of this district, except the two rivers, the Geor and the Kanhar which rising in the table lands in the north flow northwards to join the Son. The important rivers of the district are as under:

The Mahanadi—It rises at 20°20' north and 82°0' east in Sihawa hills a few kilometres east of Nagri village in Raipur district. The Mahanadi flows towards the west up to Kanhar, towards the north-east upto the Raipur-Bilaspur boundary, and to the eastern limit crosses Rajgrh district. The principal tributaries of the Mahanadi from the north are Mand, the Kelo and the Ib.

The Geor—This is another principal river of the district which comes under the drainage system of the Son. The Geor also rises in the plateau near Chichli.

TOWNS, VILLAGES AND AMENITIES

The district at present comprises 6 tehsils. It has 5 towns.

The urban population of the district as percentage of total population in the census year 2001is indicated below. It also shows the sex ratio (females per 1000 males) and density (population per sq km) in the urban population of the district in relation to the State:

State/ District	Urban population as percentage of total population	Sex ratio 2001 (Females per 1000 males)			Density (Population per sq. km.)
	2001	Total	Rural	Urban	
Chhattisgarh	20.08	990	1005	932	154
Raigarh	13.38	995	1004	943	179

Amenities

Number of villages having one or more amenities in the district are Education, Medical, Drinking Water, Post and Telegraph, Market and Hat, Communications, Approach by Pucca Road, Power Supply.

COMMUNICATIONS

Raigarh is one of the most important railway stations of south-eastern railway on Bombay-Hawrah route. It is also connected by road with important and big towns of the State.

AGRICULTURE AND IRRIGATION

Cultivation is the mainstay of the people of Raigarh district. Main crops are paddy, wheat, gram, mustard and groundnut. The main source of irrigation in the district is canals. The percentage of irrigated area to total cultivable area is insignificantly low.

ANIMAL HUSBANDRY

Livestock is a chief wealth next to agriculture. In order to improve the overall standard of living, the Animal Husbandry Department has been focussing on this district.

INDUSTRIES

Kosa silk of Raigarh district is famous in Chhattisgarh state. There are 14 kosa cloth weaving small scale industries, apart from 21 weaving cooperative societies. Approximately, 11.57 lakh metres, worth Rs 5.78 crore, kosa cloth was manufactured by these industries/societies. Apart from the Kosa silk work, the district has a number of Industries, these are M/s Jindal Strips Ltd., Patarapali, M/s Standard Charome, jorapali, M/s. Mohan Jute Mill, Raigarh, M/s. Ganesh Ferro Alloys, Joropali, M/s. Raigarh Solvent, Raigarh, M/s. Savithe Rice Mills, Raigarh, M/s Mahamia Ferro Alloys and M/s. Srichem Resin, Raigarh, Rice, High Carbon Ferro Magnese, Hasiyn clothes, Kosa silk and sponge Iron were manufactured in the district.

HANDICRAFTS

Textiles (woven) at Raigarh

HOTELS

Riverview Hotel, (Government Approved) 2 star at Raigarh; Room: 31

TRADE, COMMERCE AND EXPORT

The following table provides information on important commodities manufactured in, exported from and imported in the towns of this district.

Name of town	*Most important commodities*		
	Imported	*Exported*	*Manufactured*
Dharam Jaigarh	Cloth	Jute	Jute
Gharghora	Iron	Rice	Rice
Kharsia	Paddy	Rice	Jaggery
Raigarh	Jute	Iron almirah	Jute articles

The district is rich in limestone reserve and as such a cement factory has come up near Kharsia town. The Kaseras of this district have been engaged in the manufacture of brass utensils till the recent past but the metal being scarce, they seem to have switched to the manufacture of aluminium utensils. Kosa *saris* are exported from Kharsia town. Rice is surplus in the district and therefore it is exported outside.

TOURISM

Historical buildings in and around the district are Pujaripali Temple, Shiv Mandir Kertin Deol, Raj Mahal (Giri Vilas), Sarangarh and Sambeshwari Devi Mandir, Sarangarh. Places of tourist interest include Kailash caves, Singhanpur caves, Butalda caves, Deorkona. Waterfalls are Ranidah, Rajpuri, Bene, Ramjharna, Nandan Jhiria. The district is famous among wild life lovers. The Gomardah Wild Life sanctuary, which occupy an area of 277.82 sq. km lies in this district. The important fauna of this sanctuary are, Tiger, Panther, different varieties of Deer, Bear, Blue Bull and Birds.

FAIRS AND FESTIVALS

In urban area the social life is progressive. In rural area the life is governed by tribal customs and traditions. Prominent *melas* of the district include Janmansthami mela, Shivratri mela, Devi mela, Gohira Mela, Dussehra mela, Rath yatra, Asthayathra, Vyapari Yatra. Prominent tribal festivals of the district are Karma, Chhere-Chhera, Sarhul, etc.

Important fairs and festivals organised in different parts of the district are mentioned below:

Vyapari Yatra, Shivratri, Ramrekha Yatra, Magha Poornima, Gahira Mela, Janmashtami, Gopashtami, Ratha Yatra, Dasahra, Sankrant, Vishnu Yagnya, Urs.

EDUCATION

According to 2001 census, total literates (excluding the population in the age group of 0-6 years) is 753189 persons. Of these, 443932 are males and 309257 are females. In the rural areas of the district 635219 persons (376060 males and 259159 females) are literates and in urban areas 117970 persons (67872 males and 50098 females) are literates. The rate of literacy of this population to the total population, excluding 0–6 years age group according to 2001 census is shown below:

	Persons	*Males*	*Females*
Total	70.5	83.1	57.9
Rural	68.9	81.94	55.98
Urban	80.57	90.18	70.4

There are 2644 schools and 6 colleges in the district. In terms of the number of institutions per ten thousand population Dharamjaigarh town has the highest average in respect of all types of institutions. Raigarh town has relatively low averages but it has to be noted that it is the size of the institutions and not the mere number which counts so far as spread of education is concerned.

Libraries:

Government

The Govt. Library, Raigarh

Non-Government

1. Municipal Library, Kharsia
2. Municipal Library, Sarangarh
3. Club Library, Dharamjaigarh
4. Mahatma Gandhi Municipal Library, Raigarh

COLLEGES 2000:

Government Arts and Commerce College, Kharsia (Established 1964), Enrolment 598, Teachers 16. (Affiliated College)

Government Degree College, Sarangarh (Established 1983), Enrolment 750. (Affiliated College)

Government Girls College, Raigarh (Established 1983), Enrolment 319, Teachers 6. (Affiliated College)

K.G. Arts and Science College, Raigarh (Established 1958), Enrolment 2174, Teachers 51. (Affiliated College)

P.D. Arts and Commerce College, Raigarh Established (1965), Enrolment 568, Teachers 17.

Swami Balkrishna Puri Law College (Established 1972), Enrolment 220, Teachers 8. (Affiliated College)

(Above named Colleges belong to Guru Ghasidas University, Established 1983)

MEDICAL

Medical Institutions in the district:

Hospitals (district and civil)	:	4
Dispensaries	:	88
Auyrvedic Dispensaries	:	37
Homoepathic Dispensaries	:	6

MEDIA

Media. All India Radio, Raigarh.

Newspaper

Kelo Prawah, Hindi daily, published from Raigarh, circulation is 25761.

ADMINISTRATION

(i) Administrative Division: Bilaspur

Tehsils: Udaipur (Dharamjaigarh), Gharghoda, Raigarh, Kharsia, Sarangarh and Lailunga.

Towns and Urban Agglomerations with their Population, Sex Ratio, Decadal Growth and Literacy Rate

Town	*Population*	*Percentage decadal growth 1991–2001*	*Sex Ratio*	*Literacy*
Dharamjaigarh (TP)	13603	23.66	982	74.56
Gharghora (TP)	8103	15.10	980	75.45
Kharsia (TP)	17387	14.95	957	82.25
Raigarh (UA)	115740	28.22	932	81.33
Raigarh (M)	110987	27.91	931	81.56
Sarangarh	14458	3.84	965	80.85

(ii) Parliamentary Constituencies and Assembly Segments (2001):

No. & Name of Parliamentary Constituencies:

13-RAIGARH (ST), 16-SARANGARH (SC).

No. & Name of Assembly Segments of Raigarh Parliamentary Constituencies which lies within the jurisdiction of Raigarh district.

RAIGARH (ST)

101. Dharamjaigarh (ST)—Dharamjaigarh RIC and P.Cs. 1 to 6 and 36 in Kapu RIC in Udaipur (Dharamjaigarh) tehsil; and Gharghoda RIC in Gharghoda tehsil and the forest villages in the area.

102. Lailunga (ST)—Lailunga and Tamnar RICs in Gharghoda tehsil and the forest villages in the area.

103. Raigarh—Raigarh I and Raigarh II RICs and P.Cs. 44 to 52 in Pussour RIC in Raigarh tehsil.

104. Kharsia—Kharsia and Bhupdeopur RICs in Raigarh tehsil.

Rajgarh was in Surguja Lok Sabha seat in 1957. The communitywise breakup (OBE) in Raigarh is Christians (10 per cent), Scheduled Castes (6 per cent), Scheduled Tribes (58 per cent) and Ahirs (9 per cent). Telis are also present in numbers. Gandas and Satnamis/Chamars around 3 per cent each among the Scheduled Castes and Oraons (21 per cent), Kawars (14 per cent) and Gonds (6 per cent) among the Scheduled Tribes are dominant.

Number and Name of Assembly Segments of Sarangarh Parliamentary Constituency which has within the jurisdiction of Raigarh district.

SARANGARH (SC):

105. Saria—Pussour RIC (excluding P.Cs. 44 to 52) in Raigarh tehsil; and Saria and Baramkela RICs in Sarangarh tehsil and the forest villages in the area.

106. Sarangarh (SC)—Sarangarh and Hardi RICs in Sarangarh tehsil and the forest villages in the area.

Sarangarh was in Baloda Bazar Lok Sabha seat in 1957 and 1962. The communitywise breakup (OBE) in Sarangarh is Scheduled Castes (23 per cent), Scheduled Tribes (8 per cent), Ahirs (9 per cent) and Telis, Kewats, Malis and Sunars around 5 per cent each. Satnamis/Chamars (13 per cent) and Gandas (4 per cent) among the Scheduled Castes and Gonds (4 per cent) among the Scheduled Tribes are dominant.

PLANNED DEVELOPMENT

The whole district will be made fully literate. All the requisite primary education facilities will be provided under Rajiv Gandhi Education Mission. Development of communication network, exploitation of mineral resources, establishment of 1000 MW power plant and activities under different Rajiv Gandhi Missions will definitely make the district rich and prosperous.

OBSERVATIONAL ORGANISATION

Surface Observatories

The district Raigarh lies in meterological sub-division, Madhya Pradsh, East. This facility is available at Raigarh. The instrument lies in

Latitude	:	21.88°
Longitude	:	83.35° East
Altitude	:	220 m
Date of starting	:	10-8-1950

Hydrometerological Station for Climatological Purposes

This facility is available at Gharghode. The instrument lies in

Latitude	:	22.16° North
Longitude	:	83.35° East

Altitude : 271 m
Date of starting : 21-1-1948

MINERALS AND ORES OCCURRENCES

Building Materials

Flaggy limestones are quarried near Churela (221.6, 83.2), Dhaurabhata (21.66, 83.19), Manbadora (21.6, 83.15) and Ghorghati (21.5, 83.13) for use as building material and road metal.

The sandstones occurring in the hills to the North of Raigarh town (21.9, 83.4) are quarried for road metal.

Clay

Terracotta clay deposits occur between Biaora and Raigarh.

Coal

Occasional coal seams (5 to 19 ft. thick) are met with in the nalla cuttings in Gharghoda Tahsil Analyses show that the coal is high in ash and low in colorific value. Coal bearing Barakar rocks occur in the area between Gharghoda (22.16, 83.35) and Dharamjaygarh (22.46, 83.21). Coal seams 5 ft. thick occur near Amghat (22.1, 83.4) and Kusumghat (22.3, 83.26).

Limestone

Several deposits of low grade limestone, locally used for lime burning and as road metal have been reported from Saraipali (22.01, 83.13), Banipathar (22.00, 83.2), Basughar (21.93, 83.16) and Jharidih (22.00, 83.05). The deposit at Jharidih yields lime stone for metallurgical purposes. An occurrence of lime stone is reported from (21.98, 82.86). There are also bands of lime stone each about 3 ft. thick. Limestone occurs interbebbed with shales near porath (21.66, 83.41), Ruchida (26.6, 83.4) and Kanthipali (21.5, 83.33).

DISASTROUS WEATHER EVENTS

Hailstorm

April 1st 1982, crops worth Rs one crore in 37 villages damaged.

Flood

August 4th weak 1982, people reported died in the low lying areas, thousands of villages affected due to Mahanadi river.

Heavy rains

On 22nd August 1984, there was raining cats and dogs, kachha houses collapsed at several places and people reported killed.

Drought

September 3rd and 4th week 1981, Kharif crop badly affected, aridity was less than 25 per cent, shortage of water.

April and May 1985, acute shortage of water, crops completely damaged.

Thunderstorm

6 June 1992, Tin roof tops of many houses blown away, large number of trees, electric poles uprooted, disrupting vehicular traffic.

14 June 1992, it was severe, crops damaged. electric supply badly affected, road communications at several points disrupted due to falling of electric poles and trees.

18 October 1993, there was continuous rain, thunder and lightning, wind speed was more than 75 km per hour, 3 person reported died and more than hundred huts destroyed.

Heavy rains

21–24 August 1996, two persons died, cattle head perished, low lying aea flooded, kachha house collapsed, road rail links affected.

Lightning

Two persons died in the district at Pali and Unhere.

DISTRIBUTION OF *SCHEDULED CASTE* POPULATION BY SEX DISTRICTWISE (1991)

	Total	Males	Females
RAIGARH	1,95,913	97,944	97,969
Audhelia	53	30	23
Bagri, Bagdi	575	271	304
Bahna, Bahana	12	6	6
Balahi, Balai	449	233	216
Banchada	124	65	59
Barahar, Basod	2,363	1,239	1,124
Bargunda	1	1	0
Basor, Burud, Bansor, Bansodi, Bansphor, Basar	3,563	1,758	1,805
Bedia	20	6	14
Beldar, Sunkar	90	50	40
Bhangi, Mehtar, Balmik, Lalbegi, Dharkar	991	484	507
Bhanumati	85	41	44
Chadar	35	16	19
*Chamar, Chamari, Bairwa, Bhambi, Jatav, Mochi, Regar, ...	67,087	33,950	33,137
Chidar	835	405	430
Chikwa, Chikvi	20,263	9,952	10,311
Chitar	47	18	29
Dahait, Dahayat, Dahat	9	7	2
Dewar	912	458	454
Dhanuk	149	76	73
Dhed, Dher	14	13	1
Dohor	242	109	133
Dom, Dumar, Dome, Domar, Doris	6,161	3,103	3,058
Ganda, Gandi	57,878	28,786	29,092
Ghasi, Ghasia	24,420	12,039	12,381
Holiya	14	9	5
Kanjar	150	78	72
Katia, Patharia	273	152	121
Khatik	89	45	44
Koli, Kori	326	159	167
Khangar, Kanera, Mirdha	1,635	801	834
Kuchbandhia	48	26	22
Mahar, Mehra, Mehar	1,409	733	676
*Mang, Mang Garodi, Mang Garudi, Dankhni Mang, ...	276	134	142
Meghwal	28	12	16
Moghia	9	4	5
Muskhan	26	14	12
Nat, Kalbelia, Sapera, Navdigar, Kubutar	465	232	233
Pasi	83	45	38
Rujjhar	55	23	32
Sansi, Sansia	303	161	142
Silawat	35	18	17
Zamral	2	2	0
Unclassified	4,309	2,180	2,129

(Contd.)

DISTRIBUTION OF *SCHEDULED TRIBE* POPULATION BY SEX DISTRICTWISE (1991)

	POPULATION		
	Total	Males	Females
RAIGARH	8,21,477	4,07,056	4,14,421
Agariya	5,442	2,658	2,784
Andh	96	59	37
Baiga	64	32	32
Bhaina	6,167	3,043	3,124
*Bharia Bhumia, Bhuinhar Bhumia, Bhumiya, Bharia, ...	22,035	10,910	11,125
Bhattra	45	26	19
Bhil, Bhilala, Barela, Patelia	130	58	72
Bhil Mina	45	19	26
Bhunjia	230	104	126
Biar, Biyar	86	43	43
Binjhwar	10,744	5,266	5,478
Birhul, Birhor	683	345	338
Damor, Damaria	39	16	23
Dhanwar	4,422	2,201	2,221
Gadaba, Gadba	127	75	52
*Gond; Arakh, Arrakh, Agaria, Asur, ...	1,14,364	56,780	57,584
Halba, Halbi	77	34	43
Kamar	27	12	15
Karku	156	87	69
Kawar, Kanwar, Kaur, Cherwa, Rathia, Tanwar, Chattri	1,93,821	96,965	96,856
Khairwar, Kondar	3,711	1,818	1,893
Kharia	25,532	12,390	13,142
Kondh, Khond, Kandh	3,525	1,758	1,767
Kol	1,972	993	979
Kolam	1,262	694	568
Korku, Bopchi, Mouasi, Nihal, Nahul, Bondhi, Bondeya	106	46	60
Korwa, Kodaku	27,763	13,625	14,138
Majhi	26,989	13,643	13,346
Majhwar	9,944	4,954	4,990
Mawasi	144	81	63
Munda	5,632	2,751	2,881
Nagesia, Nagasia	28,404	14,037	14,367
Oraon, Dhanka, Dhangad	2,81,510	1,38,744	1,42,766
Pao	2,808	1,358	1,450
Pardhan, Pathari Saroti	471	254	217
*Pardhi; Bahelia, Bahellia, Chita Pardhi, ...	340	163	177
Parja	725	365	360
Sahariya, Saharia, Seharia, Sehria, Sosia, Sor	508	242	266
Saonta, Saunta	263	139	124
Saur	6,040	2,995	3,045
Sawar, Sawara	26,039	12,722	13,317
Sonr	1,683	826	857
Unclassified	7,306	3,725	3,581

(Contd.)

SKETCH MAP
OF
RAIPUR
BILASPUR
DURG
MAHASAMUND
DHANTARI
ORISSA
Shivnath
Mahanadi
Nipniya
Bhatapara
Vishrampur
Arjuni
Baloda Bazar
Simga
Tilda
Datan
Palori
Chicholi
Sihri
Khrora
Bangoli
RAIPUR
Samonda
Arang
Bhatgaon
Chapaghar
Kendra
Phingeshwar
Rajim
Khadma
Chura
Kopra
Devreya
Kamraj
Parseli
Rasela
Garyaband
Litipara
Bindra
Navagarh
Kusumi
Sitanadi
Udante
Dhavalpur
Mainpur Khurd
Bardula
Tawrenga
Risgaon
Indagaon
Gohrapadar
Devbhog
Katgi
Pawani
Bhatgaon
Kasdol
Bilaigarh
Sarsiwa
Dhansir
Arjuni
Madhuban
Nawagaon
Devri
Nawapara
Tala
LEGEND
District Headquarters
Taluk Headquarters
Other Towns
Railway Line
Major Roads
Other Roads
River
Important Tourist Places

RAIPUR

LOCATION AND AREA

Latitude: 19.9° North to 21.9° North
Longitude: 81.5° East to 83.0° East
Altitude: 298 m (at Raipur)

Raipur District is situated in the Chhattisgarh region of the State and occupies the south-eastern part of upper Mahanadi basin and a large belt of hilly areas to the south and east.

The district is bounded on the north by Bilaspur and Janjgir-Champa district, in the south by Koraput district of Orissa State and in the east by Koraput and Kalahandi districts of the same State. Sarangarh tehsil of Raigarh district and Kanker tehsil of Kanker district respectively form the north-east and south-west boundaries of the district. The Kharun river in the west forms the western boundary of the district and Seonath and Mahandadi mark the northern boundary with Bilaspur and Janjgir champa district. The greatest length of the district from north to south is about 227 kms. and the greatest width is about 114 kms.

The district headquarters is located at Raipur.

HISTORY

In ancient period, Raipur District formed an integral part of Dakshina Koshala. What is known as Chhattisgarh was known in early history as Dakshina Koshala. From Hiuen Tsang's account, it seems probable that some portions of the present Raipur district formed part of the dominion of Satvahana rulers. Samudra Gupta of Gupta Dynasty conquered this area in the middle of the 4th century and the Gupta ruled continued till about 6th century. Very little is known of the dynasty of kings who ousted the Guptas. The Haihayas rose to power in this area in the 10th century.

In 1741, the Maratha General, Bhaskar Pant while on his way to attack Bengal, defeated and annexed the kingdom of Ratanpur but Amar Singh, the Haihaya chief of Raipur was not disturbed by the Marathas immediately. He was quietly ousted in 1750 and the *parganas* of Raipur, Rajim and Patan were given to him for maintenance for which he paid a yearly tribute of Rs. 7000. These too were annexed by Marathas on the death of Amarsingh in 1753. From this date to 1818 the territory in which the present Raipur district is situated, was under the Government of the Marathas. In 1757, Bimbaji assumed control of the Maratha administration in Nagpur and restored some order and tranquility in this area by strong military rule. After his death in 1787, his widow Anandi Bai managed the affairs of the State with the help of one Vitthal Deokar. It was this officer who introduced the system of *pargana* accounts on the village system.

On the assumption of control of this area by the British, Captain Edmonds was the first officer to be in charge. He, however, died a few months after his arrival and was succeeded by Colonel Agnew. He ruled the country justly and firmly, established law and order in the area and introduced many reforms in the land revenue system.

The British protectorate continued from 1818 till 1830 when Chhattisgarh along with other territories was handed back to the Marathas as the Raja had attained majority. On the lapse of the Nagpur province in 1854, Chhattisgarh with the rest of Bhonsala territories came under British rule. At this Raipur was big district in area and in 1856 was divided into two tehsils, viz., Raipur and Dhamtari. In 1856, Durg was made a tehsil and in 1861 Bilaspur was separated from Raipur. In 1863 a fourth tehsil, Simga was added to Raipur. This continued till 1906 when Durg was constituted a separate district by taking away Durg tehsil and portions of Dhamtari and Simga. The remaining area was divided into 4 tehsils as before by creating a new tehsil Mahasamund and at the same time Simga. Tehsil was abolished from portions of old Simga and tracts from Bilaspur district transferred to Raipur district.

POPULATION

Total population of the district according to 2001 census is 3009042 persons, comprising 1520024 males and 1489018 females. Rural population of the district is 2092567 persons (1044238 males and 1048329 females) and urban population is 916475 persons (475786 males and 440689 females).

The Tehsil-wise population break-up, rural-urban and male female population distribution is represented according to 2001 census in the following table.

Tehsil	Total Rural Urban	Total population		
		Persons	Males	Females
Simga	T	136655	68033	68622
	R	123518	61420	62098
	U	13137	66113	6524
Bhatapara	T	140136	70098	70038
	R	90056	44577	45479
	U	50080	25521	24559
Balodabazar	T	149131	74413	74718
	U	126278	62676	63602
	R	22853	11737	11116
Plari	T	119610	58447	61163
	R	119610	58447	61163
	U	—	—	—
Kasdol	T	160055	79275	80780
	R	160055	79275	80780
	U	—	—	—
Belaigaon	T	165245	80952	84293
	R	157024	76836	80188
	U	8221	4116	4105
Arang	T	242513	122012	120501
	R	225920	113614	112306
	U	16593	9398	8195
Abhanpur	T	175995	88729	87266
	R	175995	88729	87266
	U	—	—	—
Raipur	T	1037509	538526	498983
	R	258829	132755	126074
	U	778680	405771	372909
Rajim	T	145526	72790	72736
	R	145526	72790	72736
	U	—	—	—
Tilda	T	176114	88287	87827
	R	149203	74657	74546
	U	26911	13630	13281
Bindranvagadh	T	283934	140397	143537
	R	283934	140397	143537
	U	—	—	—
Devbhog	T	76619	38065	38554
	R	76619	38065	38554
	U	—	—	—

The decennial growth rate of population of the district as a whole in relation to the State between the period 1991 and 2001 is presented below:

State/District	*Decennial growth rate of population (per cent) 1991–2001*		
	Total	*Rural*	*Urban*
Chhattisgarh	18.06	14.23	36.24
Raipur	18.97	9.14	49.77

LANGUAGES AND RELIGION

Main language spoken in the district are Hindi, Bengali, Gujarati, Marathi, Oriya, Punjabi, Sindhi and Urdu.

Main religion of the district are Hindus, Muslims, Christians, Sikhs, Buddhists and Jains.

GEOGRAPHY AND PHYSICAL FEATURES

The district is divided into two major physical divisions by the Mahanadi river which flows across the district from its south-western corner of the northern boundary. The country to the west of the river comprises north-eastern part of Dhamtari tehsil, the whole of Raipur tehsil and the western part of Baloda Bazar tehsil is part of the open Chhattisgarh plain, thickly populated and closely cultivated. The western boundary of the district runs along the Kharun river which flows to the north, and joins the Seonath about 8 kms south-west of Simga. The valley between the Mahanadi and the Kharun is marked by a long ridge of higher land extending from Kurud in the south to Lahud in the north-east direction. The top cover of the mounds have bhata land which is poor of laterite, red in colour and containing numerous little pebbles. It does not have much consistency and hardly retain moisture. The *Kanhar* is black soil which is very retentive of moisture. The *Matasi,* generally the yellow porous and sandy soil is not retentive of moisture, but gives good outturn of paddy with heavy rainfall.

The southern, south-eastern and eastern regions of the district contain good forests. The preponderant tree in the forest is Sal *(Shorea robusta).* Accompanying the Sal in the forests are the usual species. Suja *(terminalia tomentosa),* Kathua *(T. arjuna),* Bija *(Ptero Carpus Marsupium),* Dhwra *(Anogeissus Latifolia),* Bahera *(T. Belerica),* Harra *(T. Chebula),* Lendia *(Lagestroemia parviflora),* Salai

(*Baswellia*) serrata, Tinsa (*Ougeinia Delberg iodes*) Other Common varieties in the forest are Mahua (*Bassia Latifolia*), Tendu *(Diospyras melanoxylon)*, Chras *(Buchmania latifolia)*, Haldu *(Adina Cordifolia*) and Aonla *(Phyllan-thus emblica)*, Bamboo is found mostly in Bindranawagarh forest.

In the plain the common trees are *Babul (Acacia arabica) Palas (Butea frondosa) and Sirsa (Albizzia lebbek).*

RIVERS, CANALS AND WATERWAYS

Mahanadi is the principal river of the district. The general slope of the country is towards north. Consequently all important rivers and streams flow mainly in northern direction. Mahanadi rises in the Sihawa range. It flows north-east throughout its length in the district passing Dhamtari and Nawapara on its left bank and Rajim and Sirpur on its right bank until it reaches the northern boundary of Baloda Bazar tehsil. It then turns towards east and forms the district boundary with Janjgir Champa district. The important tributaries are the Pairi, the Seonath and the Jonk in Raipur district. The early course of the river is a hilly stream till it joins Pairi at Rajim. The river is dammed at Dudhawa and Hirakund. The Seonath touches the district 8 kms. above Simga where it is joined by the Kharun from the south. It forms the north-western and east-northern boundaries of the district separating it from Durg and Bilaspur respectively. River Kharun rises about 13 kms. to the west of Raipur town forming the boundary between the districts of Raipur and Durg. The river Pairi rises near Mainpur. After flowing for about 45 kms. it is joined by river Sondur on the left bank and itself joins Mahanadi at Rajim.

TOWNS, VILLAGES AND AMENITIES

The district at present comprises 13 tehsils and 14 towns.

The urban population of the district as percentage of total population in the census year 2001 is indicated below. It also shows the sex ratio (females per 1000 males) and density (population per sq. km.) in the urban population of the district in relation to the State:

State/District	*Urban Population as percentage of total population*	*Sex Ratio, 2001 (Females per 1000 males)*			*Density (Population per sq. km)*
	2001	*Total*	*Rural*	*Urban*	
Chhattisgarh	20.08	990	1005	932	154
Raipur	30.46	980	1004	926	230

COMMUNICATIONS

Raipur District is situated on the Howrah-Bombay main line of south-eastern Railway. National Highway No. 6 also passes through the district. Raipur is connected by air service with Bhopal, Delhi, Nagpur, Gwalior and Indore.

AGRICULTURE AND IRRIGATION

Percentage of total irrigated area to gross cropped area is 33.2 per cent. Canal is the main source of irrigation. Paddy is the main crop of the district. Wheat and gram are other important crops.

ANIMAL HUSBANDRY

Cows and buffaloes are common livestock found in the district.

INDUSTRIES

A large number of industries are established in and around Raipur. These include cement factories also.

Important Industries , 2000

Advani-Oerlikon Ltd. Raipur.

Manufacturer: Marketing of welding consumables and equipments, industrial electronic products, power and process control equipments. The company has foreign collaboration with M/s. Oerlikon Welding Ltd. Zurich, Switzerland. M/s. Ador Cooperheat Ltd., M/s. Ador Samia Ltd., M/s Semi Conductors Ltd and M/s. Advanced Welding Alloys Ltd. are the Subsidary Companies.

Allied Steels Ltd. P.O. Tatibandh, Raipur.

Manufacturer: Mild steel, carbon steel and spring steel billets and alloy steel.

Raipur Alloys and Steel Ltd. Plot No. 49, Opp. Urkura Rly. Station, Industrial Area, Raipur–492001.

Manufacturer: Mild carbon and alloys steel and also trading in rolled products.

MUSEUM

Mahant Ghasidas Memorial Museum, Raipur.

HANDICRAFT

Textiles (woven) works at Raipur.

TRADE, COMMERCE AND EXPORT

The following table provides information on important

commodities manufactured in, exported from and imported in the town of this district.

Name of town	*Most important commodities*		
	Imported	*Exported*	*Manufactured*
Bhatapara	Paddy	Rice	Cement
Bhatgaon	Wheat	Rice	Kosa cloth
Baloda Bazar	Paddy	Rice	Rice
Simga	Foodgrains	Paddy	Bricks
Tilda Nevra	Paddy	Rice	Cement
Raipur	Edible oil	Paddy husk	Rice
Arang	Paddy	Rice	Rice
Gobra Navapara	Paddy	Rice	Bidi

TOURISM

Rajiv Lochan temple located at Rajim is one of the very important place of tourist interest in the district.

Sitanadi: This district is famous for its Wild Life Sanctuary, it occupy an area of 553.36 sq. km. The tiger panther, different varieties of deer, blue bul, bear, and various other fauna is common in this sanctuary.

Udanti: Among the Wild Life lovers, this Wild Life Sanctuary is very famous tiger, panther, deers, bear are common fauna of it. During winter season migratory birds in big numbers use to land here.

HOTEL

Hotel Mayura (Government Approved) 3 star.

Access: 15 kms. from Airport, 2 kms. from Railway station, 1 km. from Bus stand.

Rooms: 52

FAIRS AND FESTIVALS

Important fairs and festivals organised in different parts of the district are mentioned below:

Chaitra Poornima, Bhatgaon Fair, Sarsiwa Fair, Dasahra, Magha Poornima, Shivratri, Kartika Poornima, Angar Mati Devi Fair, Rudreshwar Mahadev Fair, Deopur Fair, Rajim Fair, Mandai, Chitrakot Mela.

EDUCATION

According to 2001 census, total literates (excluding the population in the age group of 0-6 years) is 3009042 persons. Of these, 1520024 are male and 1489018 are females. In the rural areas of the district 2092567 persons (1044238 males and 1048329 females) are literate, and in urban areas 916475 persons (475786 males and 440689 females). The rate of literacy of this population to the total population, excluding 0-6 years age group according to 2001 census is shown below:

	Persons	*Males*	*Females*
Total	68.98	82.41	55.3
Rural	63.82	79.36	48.42
Urban	80.35	88.8	71.08

COLLEGES 2000

Arts and Commerce Girls Colleges, Devendra Nagar, Raipur (Established 1982) Enrolment 455, Teachers 34 (Affiliated College)

Adarsh Arts Commerce College, Nai Ganj Mandi, (Established 1995). Enrolment 143. (Affiliated College)

DES's Vivekanand College, Raipur (Established 1993), Enrolment 236. Teachers 9. (Affiliated College)

Government Arts and Commerce College, Khoka, (Established 1984), Enrolment 421, Teachers 10. (Affiliated College)

Government Badri Prasad Arts and Commerce College, Arang (1965), Enrolment 524, Teachers 12. (Affiliated College)

Government Chhattisgarh College, Raipur (Established 1938), Enrolment 2606, Teachers 76. (Affiliated College)

Government College of Engineering and Technology, Raipur (Established 1956). (Affiliated College)

Government College of Education, Raipur (Established 1956), Enrolment 201, Teachers 15. (Affiliated College)

Government College Gariaband (Established 1984), Enrolment 233, Teachers 7. (Affiliated College)

Government College, Shankar Nagar, (Established 1989), Enrolment 235. (Affiliated College)

Government College, Abhanpur (Established 1989), Enrolment 234, Teachers 7. (Affiliated College)

Government College, Simga (Established 1989), Enrolment 152, Teachers 6. (Affiliated College)

Government College, Bhatgaon (Established 1989), Enrolment 103 Teachers 12. (Affiliated College)

Government DSV Sanskrit College, Raipur, (Established 1955), Enrolment 103, Teachers 12. (Affiliated College)

Government DB Girls PG College, Raipur (Established 1958), Enrolment 2730, Teachers 71. (Affiliated College)

Government DK Arts and Commerce College, Balodabazar (Established 1963), Enrolment 991, Teachers 27. (Affiliated College)

Government GNA Degree College, Batapara (Established 1964), Enrolment 816, Teachers 24. (Affiliated College)

Government Girls College, Balodabazar (Established 1989), Enrolment 196, Teachers 7. (Affiliated College)

Government Model College of Science, Raipur (Autonomous) (Established 1948).

Government NPA Ayurvedic College, Raipur (Established 1955), Enrolment 19.

Government Naveen Girls College, Purani Basti, Raipur, (Established 1986), Enrolment 225, Teachers 11. (Affiliated College)

Government Pt. JNM Medical College, Raipur (Established 1963), Enrolment 14. (Affiliated College)

Pt. Harishankar Shukla Memorial College, Shankar Nagar, Raipur, Enrolment 14. (Affiliated College)

Raipur Institute of Technology, Near Nalghar, Raipur, (Established 1995), Enrolment 136, Teachers 5. (Affiliated College)

Sau KTD Law College, Raipur (Established 1951), Enrolment 1388.

Smt P.G. Daga Girls College, Raipur (1987), Enrolment 595, Teachers 27.

St. Vinsent Palloti College, Byron Bazar, (Established 1995), Enrolment 64, Teachers 21. (Affiliated College)

Chanakya College of Commerce and Business Administration,

Pandavi Gana Sewa Samiti, Raipur (Established 1994), Enrolment 86, Teachers 8. (Affiliated College)

(Above named colleges belong to Pt. Ravi Shankar Shukla University, Established 1964. Raipur.)

MEDICAL

376 inhabited villages (9.37 per cent) have one or more medical facilities.

MEDIA

AIR Station. All India Radio, Raipur.

Newspapers

Dainik Agradoot, Hindi daily, published from Raipur, circulation 92287.

Nav Bharat, Hindi daily, published from Raipur, circulation 87690.

Aaj Ki Jandhara, Hindi daily, published from Raipur, circulation 61881.

Amrit Sandesh, Hindi daily, published from Raipur, circulation 51813.

Deshbandhu, Hindi daily, published from Raipur, circulation 54322.

Highway channel, Hindi daily, published from Raipur, circulation 25300.

Parakhar Samachar, Hindi daily, published from Raipur, circulation 33458.

Swadesh, Hindi daily, published from Raipur, circulation 28941.

Tarun Chhattisgarh, Hindi daily, published from Raipur, circulation 32436.

Samata Abhiyan, Hindi weekly, published from Raipur.

ADMINISTRATION

Administrative Division: Raipur

Tehsils: Simga; Bhatapara, Blodabazar; Plari; Kasdol; Bhilaigadh; Arang; Abhanpur; Raipur; Rajim; Tilda; Bindranwagadh; Devbhog.

Towns and Urban Agglomerations with their Population, Sex Ratio, Decadal Growth and Literacy Rate (2001)

Town	*Population*	*Percentage decadal growth 1991–2001*	*Sex Ratio*	*Literacy*
Bhatapara (M)	50080	10.14	962	75.80
Bhatgaon (TP)	8221	- 4.84	997	69.73
Baloda Bazar (TP)	22853	31.54	947	80.56
Simga (TP)	13137	- 3.06	987	71.26
Tilda Nevra (UA)	26911	30.78	974	74.93
Tilda Nevra (M)	26637	29.44	975	74.76
Uria (CT)	9359	—	820	70.14
Birgaon (CT)	23352	—	845	75.84
Gogaon (CT)	10453	—	893	70.22
Raipur (UA)	699264	51.13	921	81.66
(i) Raipur (MCI)	605131	37.96	925	82.42
(ii) Bhanpuri (CT)	16357	265.27	890	78.68
(iii) Moeva (CT)	13697	131.56	891	78.79
Arang (TP)	16593	16.38	976	75.77
Banarsi	10648		929	83.26
Gobar Navapara (MCI)	25604	21.91	986	77.40

(i) Parliamentary Constituencies along assembly segments (2001):

Number and Name of Parliamentary Constituencies:
16. SARANGARH 17. RAIPUR, 18. MAHASAMUND.

16. SARANGARH

Number and Name of Assembly segments of Sarangadh Parliamentary constituency which lies within the jurisdiction of Raipur District.

134. Pallari (SC)--Pallari and Lawan RICs in Baloda Bazar and the forest villages in the area.

135. Kasdol—Kasdol and Bilaigarh RICs in Baloda Bazar tehsil and the forest villages in the area.

136. Bhatgaon (SC)—Bhatgaon RIC in Baloda Bazar tehsil

and the forest villages in the area; and Bhanwarpur RIC in Mahasamund tehsil.

Number and Name of Assembly Segments of Raipur Parliamentary Constituency which lies within the jurisdiction of Raipur district

17-RAIPUR

126. Raipur Town (Gen.)—Raipur town (excluding wards 20 to 24, 29, 0, 34 and 35 and non-ward municipal area).

127. Raipur Rural (Gen.)—Wards 20 to 24, 29, 30, 34, and 35 in Raipur town including non-ward municipal area; Raipur-II RIC and Raipur-I RIC (excluding P.Cs. 111, 112 and 115) in Raipur tehsil.

128. Abhanpur (Gen.)—Abhanpur and Nawapara RICs in Raipur tehsil.

129. Mandhirhasod (Gen.)—Mandirhasod RIC and P.Cs, 111, 112 and 115 in Raipur-I RIC in Raipur tehsil.

130. Arang (SC) (Gen.)—Arang and Kharora RICs in Raipur tehsil.

131. Dharsiwa (Gen.)—Dharsiwa-I, Dharsiwa-II and Tilda RICs in Raipur tehsil.

132. Bhatapara (Gen.)—Simga RIC and Bhatapara RIC (excluding P.C.s 34 to 38) in Baloda Bazar tehsil.

133. Baloda Bazar (Gen.)—P.Cs. 34 to 38 in Bhatapara RIC and Baloda Bazar and Jarod RICs in Baloda Bazar tehsil.

The community wise break up [OBE] in Raipur is Muslims [2%], Scheduled Castes []16%], Telis [18%] and Ahirs [15%]. Kewats, Kurmis and Malis are around 5% each. Brahmins are also present in numbers. Satnamis/Chamars [11%] and Gandas [3%] are dominant among the Scheduled Castes.

Number and Name of Parliamentary Constituency which lies within the jurisdiction of Raipur district.

18-MAHASAMUND

141. Rajim (Gen.)—Rajim RIC, Chhura RIC (excluding P.Cs. 31 to 35) and P.Cs. 36 to 39, 41 and 42 in Gariaband RIC in Bindranawagarh tehsil.

142. Bindranawagarh (ST)—Deobhog RIC, Gariaband RIC

(excluding P.Cs. 36 to 39, 41 and 42) and P.Cs. 31 to 35 in Chhura RIC in Bindranawagarh tehsil and the forest villages in the area.

Mahasamund was in Baloda Lok Sabha seat in 1957. The community wise break up [OBE] in Mahasamund is Scheduled Castes [13%], Scheduled Tribes [29%] and Telis [10%]. Others in sizable numbers are Ahirs, Malis, Kewats, and Kurmis. Satnamis/Chamars [9%] and Gandaș [2%] among the Scheduled Castes and Gonds [19%] and Kawars [4 %] among the Scheduled Tribes are dominant.

OBSERVATIONAL ORGANISATION

Surface Observatories

Raipur district lies within the meteorological sub-division, Madhya Pradesh, East. This facility is available at Raipur and Mana. The instrument lies in

Raipur

Latitude	:	21.23° North
Longitude	:	81.65° East
Altitude	:	298 m
Date of starting	:	1-1-1870

Mana

Latitude	:	21.23° North
Longitude	:	81.65° East
Altitude	:	318 m
Date of starting	:	26-3-1979

Agricultural Meteorological Stations

This station provide on a routine basis meteorological information. The meteorological elements observed at these stations include rainfall, air temperature, humidity, soil temperature, soil moisture, wind speed and direction, evaporation, sunshine hours, the occurrence of weather phenomenon like thunderstorms, hailstorms, frost, high wind and micro-climatic observations. This faccility is available at Labhandi and the instrument lies in,

Latitude	:	21.26° North
Longitude	:	86.6° East
Altitude	:	289 m
Date of starting	:	23-2-1946

Hydrometeorological Stations for Climatological Purposes

This facility is available at Manipur. The instrument lies in,

Latitude	:	22.28° North
Longitude	:	82.23° East
Altitude	:	472 m
Date of starting	:	3-2-1948

Upper Air Observatories

This facility is available at Raipur. The instrument starting functioning from 15–7–1944.

Aeronautical Meteorological Observatories

This instrument facility is available at Raipur.

MINERALS AND ORES OCCURRENCES

Building Materials

Chandrapur sandstones of lower Vindhyan age occurs in the district at various places.

Limestone

Purple limestone in association with dark occurs near the tank east of Bhatapara Railway station (21.74, 81.95) and also to the south of milepost 1 on the Bhatapara Balodabazar road.

Squalls

5–6 May 1981, two chldren and one woman died in house collapse, trees and electric poles uprooted, more than 200 huts collapsed, standing crop destroyed.

DISASTROUS WEATHER EVENTS

Drought

September 1981, 3rd and 4th week, Kharif crop badly affected, aridity was less than 25 per cent.

Thunderstorm

11 May 1981, one child died due to electrocution, several villages affected, electric supply disrupted.

Floods

August 1982, 4th week, there was flood in the Mahanadi river, people reported died, thousands of villages affected.

Heavy Rains

On 16 August 1984, 4 persons died and 12 injured in house collapse

On 22 August 1984, persons reported died due to house collapse.

13 September 1985, several hundred people rendered homeless, hundreds of huts washed away, Indian Airlines flights suspended.

Drought

February to May 1992, acute shortage of drinking water, crops badly affected.

Thunderstorm

31 March 1992, continuous thunder and lightning, heavy rains, wind speed was more than 120 km per hour, 2 persons died, hundreds of houses, trees, electric poles damaged.

DISTRIBUTION OF *SCHEDULED CASTE* POPULATION BY SEX DISTRICTWISE (1991)

	POPULATION Total	Males	Females
RAIPUR	5,63,577	2,81,872	2,81,705
Audhelia	135	73	62
Bagri, Bagdi	151	74	77
Bahna, Bahana	20	8	12
Balahi, Balai	2,056	1,109	947
Banchada	29	18	11
Barahar, Basod	975	486	489
Bargunda	46	27	19
Basor, Burud, Bansor, Bansodi, Bansphor, Basar	895	445	450
Bedia	15	6	9
Beldar, Sunkar	1,365	660	705
Bhangi, Mehtar, Balmik, Lalbegi, Dharkar	3,262	1,612	1,650
Bhanumati	153	78	75
Chadar	59	30	29
*Chamar, Chamari, Bairwa, Bhambi, Jatav, Mochi, Regar, ...	3,97,947	1,98,886	1,99,061
Chidar	1,190	593	597
Chikwa, Chikvi	303	154	149
Chitar	216	125	91
Dahait, Dahayat, Dahat	45	22	23
Dewar	2,488	1,257	1,231
Dhanuk	275	157	118
Dhed, Dher	19	9	10
Dohor	69	42	27
Dom, Dumar, Dome, Domar, Doris	1,488	745	743
Ganda, Gandi	92,292	46,039	46,253
Ghasi, Ghasia	14,233	6,957	7,276
Holiya	8	3	5
Kanjar	360	183	177
Katia, Patharia	827	418	409
Khatik	133	62	71
Koli, Kori	237	134	103
Khangar, Kanera, Mirdha	592	288	304
Kuchbandhia	90	45	45
Mahar, Mehra, Mehar	33,503	17,010	16,493
*Mang, Mang Garodi, Mang Garudi, Dankhni Mang, ...	278	149	129
Meghwal	170	93	77
Moghia	120	59	61
Muskhan	18	11	7
Nat, Kalbelia, Sapera, Navdigar, Kubutar	632	313	319
Pasi	75	42	33
Rujjhar	348	164	184
Sansi, Sansia	135	61	74
Silawat	26	15	11
Zamral	13	7	6
Unclassified	6,286	3,203	3,083

(Contd.)

DISTRIBUTION OF *SCHEDULED TRIBE* POPULATION BY SEX DISTRICTWISE (1991)

	POPULATION Total	Males	Females
RAIPUR	7,14,087	3,52,561	3,61,466
Agaria	241	121	120
Andh	75	38	37
Baiga	41	23	18
Bhaina	388	200	188
*Bharia Bhumia, Bhuinhar Bhumia, Bhumiya, Bharia, ...	314	148	166
Bhattra	76	35	41
Bhil, Bhilala, Barela, Patelia	5,657	2,690	2,967
Bhil Mina	122	87	35
Bhunjia	7,350	3,602	3,748
Biar, Biyar	241	133	108
Binjhwar	48,406	23,218	25,188
Birhul, Birhor	116	54	62
Damor, Damaria	83	39	44
Dhanwar	2,435	1,143	1,292
Gadaba, Gadba	282	157	125
Gond; Arakh, Arrakh, Agaria, Asur, ...	4,79,822	2,37,668	2,42,154
Halba, Halbi	16,106	8,303	7,803
Kamar	16,473	8,081	8,392
Karku	339	179	160
Kawar, Kanwar, Kaur, Cherwa, Rathia, Tanwar, Chattri	65,793	32,481	33,312
Khairwar, Kondar	2,972	1,376	1,596
Kharia	4,161	2,011	2,150
Kondh, Khond, Kandh	4,974	2,310	2,664
Kol	598	283	315
Kolam	389	227	162
Korku, Bopchi, Mouasi, Nihal, Nahul, Bondhi, Bondeya	1,651	917	734
Korwa, Kodaku	802	387	415
Majhi	2,595	1,305	1,290
Majhwar	79	42	37
Mawasi	13	9	4
Munda	1,049	530	519
Nagesia, Nagasia	62	36	26
Oraon, Dhanka, Dhangad	1,785	962	823
Pao	71	36	35
Pardhan, Pathari Saroti	419	214	205
*Pardhi; Bahelia, Bahellia, Chita Pardhi, ...	978	472	506
Parja	40	23	17
Sahariya, Saharia, Seharia, Sehria, Sosia, Sor	219	90	129
Saonta, Saunta	202	95	107
Saur	6,591	3,214	3,377
Sawar, Sawara	31,189	15,182	16,007
Sonr	8,312	4,174	4,138
Unclassified	516	266	250

(Contd.)

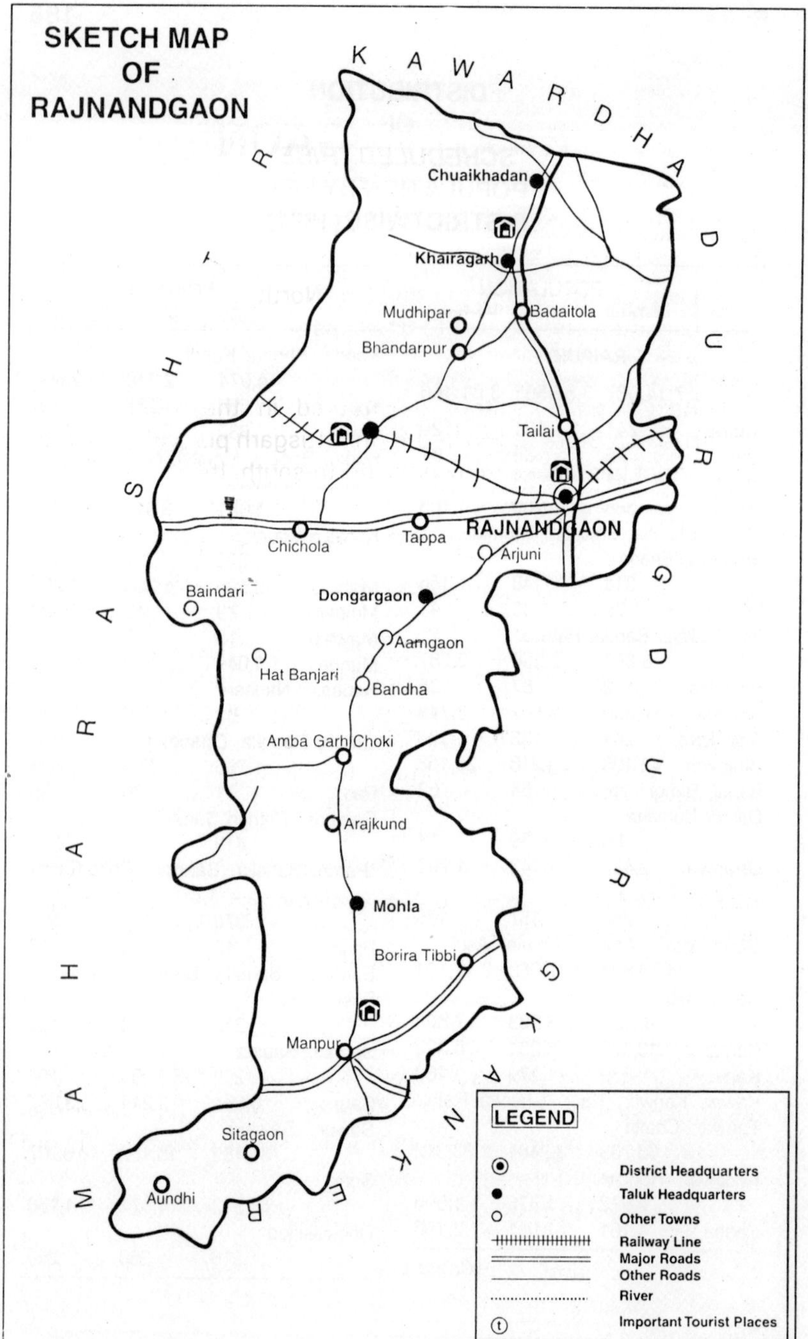
SKETCH MAP OF RAJNANDGAON
KAWARDHA
DURG
KANKER
MAHARASHTRA
Chuaikhadan
Khairagarh
Mudhipar
Badaitola
Bhandarpur
Tailai
RAJNANDGAON
Chichola
Tappa
Arjuni
Baindari
Dongargaon
Aamgaon
Hat Banjari
Bandha
Amba Garh Choki
Arajkund
Mohla
Borira Tibbi
Manpur
Sitagaon
Aundhi
LEGEND
District Headquarters
Taluk Headquarters
Other Towns
Railway Line
Major Roads
Other Roads
River
Important Tourist Places

RAJNANDGAON

LOCATION AND AREA

Latitude : 20.05° North to 21.5° North
Longitude: 80.5° East to 81.2 East
Altitude: 330 m

Rajnandgaon District is situated in the west part of Chhattisgarh State. It lies in the Chhattisgarh plain of the State. The district has large extent in the north-south. Its greatest length in the north-south is about 185 kms, while its width in the east-west extends about 80 kms, The total area of the district is 8355 sq kms.

The district of Rajnandgaon came into existence on 26th January, 1973. It was carved out of the then Durg district. The three tehsils which now constitute the Rajnandgaon district were constituent units of the then Durg district. Durg district of 1971 was bifurcated into Durg and Rajnandgaon districts. The present district constitutes Rajnandgaon tehsil, and Khairgarh tehsil. Besides this 497 villages of Chowki, Mohala and Manpur Revenue Inspectors Circles of Sanjari Balod tehsil were transferred to Rajnandgaon tehsil. The district is bounded in the east by Durg district and in south-east the kanker district, makes its boundary. Maharashtra State form the western boundary of the district. The district headquarters is located at Rajnandgaon.

HISTORY

The area of Rajnandgaon was ruled by Vaishya kings. The name Nandgaon is said to have originated from 'Nand', i.e., father of Lord Krishna and 'gaon' meaning village. The name was probably given by the Bairagi family who were devotees of Lord Krishna and ruled the State. Another interpretation is that Nand means ant-hill in the local dialect and Nandgaon means "The villages of ant Hills". The history of the establishment of the State is interesting. A shawl merchant from Punjab, Prahlad Das Bairagi by name came to Ratanpur in Bilaspur district towards the end of 18th century. He became a wealthy man and on his death his property devolved on his disciple Hari Das who in addition on being the spiritual guide of seven Ranis of Maratha Chief Bimbaji started money lending and in this business he secured the *Zamindari* of Pandadah. After Hari Das's death, his disciple Ram Das continued the money-lending business and he secured Nandgaon *Zamindari* in satisfaction of a loan advanced to a Mohamadan *Zamindar* thereof. Mohgaon was conferred on the fifth mahant the Bhonsalas and whose estate was divided between the chiefs of Nandgaon and Khairagarh as a reward for their help in putting down the revolt. These various acquirements, i.e., Pandadah, Nandgaon, Mohgaon and Dongar-gaon formed the feudatory State of Nandgaon in 1865. Ghasi Das, the seventh Mahant was married and the government decided that his son could succeed him to the feudatory State's throne. His son was Raja Balram Das who contributed to the construction of Raipur and Rajnandgaon water works.

POPULATION

Total population of the district according to 2001 census is 1281811 persons, comprising 633292 males and 648519 females. Rural population of the district is 1050150 persons (516030 males and 534120 females) and urban population is 231661 persons (117262 males and 114399 females).

The Tehsil-wise population break-up, i.e., rural-urban and male-female population distribution is represented according to 2001 census in the following table.

Tehsil	*Total/ Rural/ Urban*	*Total Population*		
		Persons	*Males*	*Females*
Chuikhadhan	T	139447	68944	70503
	R	121167	59871	61296
	U	18280	9073	9207
Khairagarh	T	156283	77207	79076
	R	141134	69523	71611
	U	15149	7684	7465
Dongargarh	T	174262	86057	88205
	R	139822	68601	71221
	U	34440	17456	16984
Ranjandgaon	T	453591	225361	228280
	R	309864	152397	157467
	U	143727	72964	70763

Dongargaon	T	110730	54482	56248
	R	99159	48568	50591
	U	11571	59114	5657
Mohla	T	75968	37174	38794
	R	75968	37174	38794
	U	—	—	—
Manpur	T	77165	38460	38705
	R	77165	38460	38705
	U	—	—	—
Ambagarh	T	94364	45607	48758
	R	85871	41436	44435
	U	8494	4171	4323

The decennial growth rate of population of the district as a whole in relation to the state between the period 1991 and 2001 is presented below:

State/ District	*Decennial growth rate of population (per cent) 1981–91*		
	Total	*Rural*	*Urban*
Chhattisgarh	18.06	14.23	36.24
Rajnandgaon	17.70	18.50	14.20

LANGUAGES AND RELIGION

Hindi is the main language spoken in the district and the main religion of the district are Hindus, Muslims, Christians, Sikhs, Buddhists, Jains.

GEOGRAPHY AND PHYSICAL FEATURES

Physiographically the district can be divided into three distinct parts: (i) Hilly part of the west, (ii) Southern plateau, and (iii) Plain region of eastern part. The ranges of Maikal and Mangata are spread in western part of the district.

The ranges in the west of Chhuikhadan are the highest in the region. The Maikal ranges in the district are known by different names *viz.,* in Khairagarh tehsil Singbora, Zilmili, Malharghat, Banjari, Lachhana and in Rajnandgaon tehsil-Chhuria, and Kasam. The area is thickly covered with forests. Southern part of the district is a plateau. This part is undulating and higher than the Chhattisgarh plain in altitude. The area is woody and thinly cultivated. In the south-eastern part is Rajhara hills which extends in Durg district.

Sal, Teak, Saja, Dhawda, Harra, Tendu and Mahua are the species commonly met within the forests of the district. Among the wild animals Tiger, Tendua, Bear and Sambhar are common species.

RIVERS, CANALS AND WATERWAYS

The general slope of the district is towards east. All the rivers of the district flow in eastern direction. Sheonath is the most important river, the important tritbutaries of the river are Amner, Jonk, Ghumriya, Pairi Zura and Hanf.

TOWNS, VILLAGES AND AMENITIES

The district at present comprises 8 tehsils and 7 towns. The urban population of the district as percentage of total population in the census years 2001 is indicated below. It also shows the sex ratio (females per 1000 males) and density (population per sq km) in the urban population in the district in relation to the state:

State/ District	*Urban population as percentage of total population*	*Sex ratio 2001 (Females per 1000 males)*			*Density (Population per sq km)*
	2001	*Total*	*Rural*	*Urban*	
Chhattisgarh State	20.08	990	1005	932	154
Rajnandgaon	18.07	1024	1035	976	159

Amenities

Number of villages having one or more amenities in the district, these are Education, Medical, Drinking water, Post and Telegraph, Market and Hat, Communications, Approach by Pucca Road, and Power Supply.

COMMUNICATIONS

Rajnandgaon is the nodal point in the district and many arteries of communication pass through Rajnandgaon town. Rajnandgaon is situated on the Howrah-Bombay main line of South Eastern Railway. National Highway No. 6 also passes through the district and Baghnadi, Bhanpuri, Tumdibod, Somni and Anjora are some of the important villages situated on this road. Some of the important road links are as below.

Rajnandgaon-Pandariya Road—This road originates from Rajnandgaon and leads towards north connecting Khairagarh,

Chhuikhadan, Gandai, Sahaspur-Lohara and Kawardha.

Rajnandgaon-Manpur Road—It leads in the south from Rajnandgaon town connecting important places like Dongargaon, Chowki, Mohla and Manpur.

Rajnandgaon to Chandpur—This road originates from Rajnandgaon and passing through Chowki, Mohla and Manpur leads to Chandrapur in Maharashtra State.

Rajnandgaon-Bhanupratappur Road
Rajnandgaon-Mandla Road
Rajnandgaon-Balaghat Road.
Rajnandgaon-Baihar.
Rajnandgaon-Nagpur.

AGRICULTURE AND IRRIGATION

Percentage of total irrigated area to gross cropped area is 12.1 per cent. Canal is the main source of irrigation. Main crop grown in the district is paddy. Wheat, gram are also grown in the district in good quantity.

ANIMAL HUSBANDRY

Cows and buffaloes are common livestock found in the district.

INDUSTRIES

Textile mill and oil mills are important industries in the district.

TRADE, COMMERCE AND EXPORT

The following Table provides information on important commodities manufactured in, exported from and imported in the towns of the district.

Name of town	*Most Important Commodities*		
	Imported	*Exported*	*Manufactured*
Gandai	Cloth	Handloom cloth	Handloom cloth
Chuikhadan	Oil	Handloom cloth	Handloom cloth
Khairagarh	Medicine	Vegetables	Handloom cloth
Dongergarh	Tobacco	Bidi	Bidi
Rajnandgaon	Paddy	Rice	Cloth
Dongargaon	Tobacco	Bidi	Bidi
Ambagarh Chowki	Rice	—	Earthen pots

TOURISM

Khairagarh. The ruling family of this ex-feudatory State claimed descent from the Nagvanshi Rajput king of Chhota Nagpur and the first in line, Laxminidhi came here and established himself at Kholewa. Shiaghan was the *Zamindar* of Kholwa in 1740. Other terrories were acquired in 1740. Other territories were acquired as follows: Khamaria on the north-east was seized from the Kawardha chief at the end of the 18th cenury in lieu of a small loan. Khairagarh tract was received at an early date from the Mandla Rajas. Dongargarh was received from the Bhonsalas because the chief helped the Marathas in suppressing the revolt by the *Zamindar*.

Chhuikhadan. The name of this ex-feudatory State means 'quary of white clay'. The nucleus of this ex-feudatory state was formerly the Khondka tract which was acquired from the *Zamindar* of Parpodi in satisfaction of loan by Mahant Rupdas, a *baniya,* who was founder of this State about the middle of the 18th century. The states of the feudatory chief was conferred on the chief in 1865. It is said that Rupdas was a near relation of the Maharaja of Udaipur who, owing to some ill feelings arising in the family, turned a *bairagi* and settled at Panipat where he attracted a following. He came to Bhonslas at Nagpur as a trader in horses and was made a cavalry chief in which capacity he suppressed the revolt by the *Zamindar* of Khondka.

FAIRS AND FESTIVAL

Kunwar Achhariya Mela, Magha Poornima, Bhoram Deva Ka Mela, Shivaratri, Pritampur Mela, Navratri, Dasahra, Berla Mela, Worship of Shiva, Kali Mai Urs Sayad Baba Atalshah, Urs Hajrat Baba Abdul Rehman Shah Kabali.

EDUCATION

According to 2001 census, total literates (excluding the population in the age group of 0–6 years) are 829463 persons. Of these, 460853 are males and 368610 are females. In the rural areas of the district 662220 persons (367691 males and 294529 females) are literates and in urban areas 167243 persons (93162 males and 74081 females) are literates. The rate of literacy of this population to the total population, excluding 0–6 years age group according to 2001 census is shown below:

	Persons	Males	Females
Total	77.58	87.54	67.92
Rural	76.35	86.64	66.05
Urban	82.85	91.29	74.23

COLLEGES

Government Digvijay College, Rajnandgaon (Established 1957). Enrolment 2484, Teachers 52. (Affiliated College)

Government Degree College, Dongargaon (Established 1984). Enrolment 349, Teachers 6. (Affiliated College)

Government Degree College, Khairagarh (Established 1983). Enrolment 388, Teachers 15. (Affiliated College)

Government Degree College, Chuikhdan (Established 1989). Enrolment 134, Teachers 6.

Government Degree College, Manpur (Established 1989). Enrolment 138, Teachers 3. (Affiliated College)

Government Degree College, Gandai (Established 1989). Enrolment 124, Teachers 5. (Affiliated College)

Government KD Girls College, Rajnandgaon, (Established 1963). Enrolment 567. Teachers 18. (Affiliated College)

Government KL Law College, Rajnandgaon (Established 1968). Enrolment 433, Teachers 7. (Affiliated College)

Government Nehru Degree College, Dongargarh (Established 1964). Enrolment 737, Teachers 16. (Affiliated College)

(Above named colleges belong to Pt. Ravishankar Shukla University, Established 1964).

MEDICAL

A ratio of 1.59 beds per 1000 of population of urban areas of the district is observed. Higher ratio of 4.89 beds per 1000 population is observed in Khairagarh town while lowest ratio of 1.16 is found in Dongargarh town.

ADMINISTRATION

(i) Administrative Division: Raipur

Tehsils : Chhuikhadan, Khairagarh, Dongargarh, Rajnandgaon, Dongargaon, Mohala, Ambagarh, Manpur.

Towns and Urban Agglomerations with their Population, Sex Ratio, Decadal Growth, and Literacy Rate (2001)

Town	*Population*	*Percentage decadal growth 1991–2001*	*Sex Ratio*	*Literacy Rate*
Gandai (TP)	11862	15.46	1017	69.44
Chuikhadhan (TP)	6418	3.70	1011	81.08
Khairagarh (TP)	15149	11.64	971	83.10
Dongargarh (M)	34440	9.48	973	83.78
Rajnandgaon (MC)	143727	14.64	970	83.28
Dongargaon (TP)	11571	24.19	957	83.45
Ambagarh Chowki (TP)	8494	27.31	1036	89.76

(ii) Parliamentary Constituencies along assembly segments (2001):

No. & Name of Parliamentary Constituency:

22-RAJNANDGAON.

No. & Name of Assembly Segments of Rajnandgaon Parliamentary Constituency, which lies within the Jurisdiction of Rajnandgaon district

169. Chowki (ST)—Manpur and Mohala RICs and Chowki RIC (excluding P.Cs. 99 to 105) in Rajnandgaon tehsil.

170. Khujji (Gen.)—Chhuria and Khujji RICs and P.Cs. 99 to 105 in Chowki RIC in Rajnandgaon tehsil and the forest villages in the area.

171. Dongargaon (Gen.)—Dongargaon RIC in Rajnandgaon tehsil; and Lal Bahadur Nagar RIC (excluding P.C. 88) in Khairagarh tehsil and the forest villages in the area.

172. Rajnandgaon (Gen.)—Rajnandgaon RIC in Rajnandgaon tehsil.

173. Dongargarh (SC)—Ghumka RIC in Rajnandgaon tehsil; P.C. 88 in Lal Bahadur Nagar RIC and Dongargarh RIC and P.Cs. 52 and 55 to 61 in Pandadah RIC in Khairagarh tehsil.

174. Khairagarh (Gen.)—Khairagarh and Chhuikhadan RICs, Pandadah RIC (excluding P.Cs. 52 and 55 to 61 and Gandai RIC (excluding P.Cs. 6 and 8 to 14) in Khairagarh tehsil and the forest villages in the area.

Rajnandgaon was in Raipur Lok Sabha seat in 1957. The communitywise breakup (OBE) in Rajnandgaon is Scheduled Castes (10 per cent), Scheduled Tribes (11 per cent), Telis (18 per cent) and Ahirs and Lodhs around 10 each. Of the Schduled Castes, Satnamis/Chamars (8 per cent) and of the Scheduled Tribes, Gonds (8 per cent) are dominant.

OBSERVATIONAL ORGANISATION

Surface Observatories

The district Rajnandgaon lies under meterological sub-division, Madhya Pradesh, East. This instrument facility is available at Rajnandgaon. The apparatus located in

Latitude	:	21.1° North
Longitude	:	81.03° East
Altitude	:	330 m
Date of starting	:	30-11-1980

Hydrometerological Stations for Climatological Purposes

This facility is available at Khairagarh. Khairagarh lies in

Latitude	:	21.41° North
Longitude	:	80.98° East
Altitude	:	
Date of starting	:	15-4-1971

MINERALS AND ORES OCCURRENCES

Arsenic

Lenticular deposits rich in arseno pyrite in felsite near its junction with the granite batholith, south of Handitola (20.81, 80.65).

Bauxite

Bauxite occurring in bands and irregular segregations in the laterite covering an area of about 2 kms., on a hill, one mile east of Bhave (21.51, 80.75).

Building Materials

Occurrence of flaggy calcareous shale are reported from Anjur (21.1, 80.9) Sonesarar (21.5, 80.96), Sukhri (21.1, 80.96),

Ghorda (21.1, 80.95) and Rampur (21.05, 80.96) for use as building stones.

Clay

Occurrence of a band of white clay has been reported from half a mile N.E. of Musalijob (21.05, 80.81). The clay is more than 15 ft. in thickness. White clay is also reported along a *nala* on the eastern side of the path leading from Charbhata (21.1, 80.56) to Mohanpur (21.11, 80.56). The clay is sofft and gritty and has low plasticity.

Another small occurrence of greenish clay is recorded in a *nalla* bed at Karelagarh (21.45, 80.87). Occurrences of considerable quantities of whie clay in the Cudappah shales at Harakota white clay (20.9, 80.7) occurs on the ridge near Kariagondi (20.75, 81.00). Buff or yellow clay has been recorded at (20.81, 81.45) and Kosagondi (20.83, 81.00). Buff or yellow clay has been recorded at Pankibhat (20.81, 81.45) and Kosagondi (20.83, 81.45) near the Dhamtari Railway station. The clay lies below 15 ft. of laterite capping and the reserves are estimated about 300,000 tons of non-refractory clay which find use as filler in paper, paint, etc.

Copper

Small quantities of green carbonate of copper were noted by Blanford in quartz vein containing galena, exposted about 5 kms. to the west of Chicholi (21.05, 80.66). Similar traces were found by Ball in a quartz vein at Wararband (21.05, 80.83).

Lead and Silver

Some quartz veins with galena have been noticed in the laminated shales at Karamtara (20.7, 80.8) close to the junction of shales with granite and porphyry.

Ochre

The ferroginous shales S.E. of Kankapur (20.7, 80.9) are rich in Ochreous material.

Stetite

Potstone is reported to occur in abundance west of Kilekera (20.7, 81.01) and is worked locally for making utensils. The material is found in pockets is from 3 to 8 ft. thick. It is dark grey and pink in colour and is very impure.

DISASTROUS WEATHER EVENTS

Floods

On 13th August 1989, there was severe flood in Karra river, 8 persons including 3 women drowned.

Heavy rains

21–23 August 1990, Number of hoses damaged in Rajnandgaon, vehicular traffic completely disrupted, at some places telephone lines damaged, people reported died due to house collapse.

12–13 July 1994, people reported died due to house collapse, standing crops damaged, electric poles, telephone lines and trees uprooted, cows and oxen perished.

DISTRIBUTION OF *SCHEDULED CASTE* POPULATION BY SEX DISTRICTWISE (1991)

	POPULATION Total	Males	Females
RAJNANDGAON	1,48,018	73,446	74,572
Audhelia	2	2	0
Bagri, Bagdi	59	36	23
Bahna, Bahana	14	4	10
Balahi, Balai	130	71	59
Banchada	6	4	2
Barahar, Basod	446	231	215
Bargunda	2	2	0
Basor, Burud, Bansor, Bansodi, Bansphor, Basar	790	388	402
Bedia	3	2	1
Beldar, Sunkar	137	78	59
Bhangi, Mehtar, Balmik, Lalbegi, Dharkar	1,471	725	746
Bhanumati	67	37	30
Chadar	13	6	7
*Chamar, Chamari, Bairwa, Bhambi, Jatav, Mochi, Regar, ...	89,667	44,523	45,144
Chidar	187	87	100
Chikwa, Chikvi	62	35	27
Chitar	81	49	32
Dahait, Dahayat, Dahat	6	3	3
Dewar	1,063	505	558
Dhanuk	33	16	17
Dhed, Dher	6	5	1

	POPULATION Total	Males	Females
Dohor	10	4	6
Dom, Dumar, Dome, Domar, Doris	146	80	66
Ganda, Gandi	5,414	2,610	2,804
Ghasi, Ghasia	1,010	532	478
Holiya	1	1	0
Kanjar	13	5	8
Katia, Patharia	434	226	208
Khatik	207	111	96
Koli, Kori	144	79	65
Khangar, Kanera, Mirdha	21	16	5
Kuchbandhia	41	23	18
Mahar, Mehra, Mehar	44,007	21,783	22,224
*Mang, Mang Garodi, Mang Garudi, Dankhni Mang, ...	104	55	49
Meghwal	70	34	36
Moghia	138	58	80
Muskhan	5	4	1
Nat, Kalbelia, Sapera, Navdigar, Kubutar	340	170	170
Pasi	35	21	14
Rujjhar	100	35	65
Sansi, Sansia	23	14	9
Silawat	6	4	2
Zamral	5	2	3
Unclassified	1,499	770	729

(Contd.)

DISTRIBUTION
OF
SCHEDULED TRIBE
POPULATION BY SEX
DISTRICTWISE (1991)

	POPULATION Total	Males	Females
RAJNANDGAON			
	3,62,355	1,77,703	1,84,652
Agariya	608	296	312
Andh	54	23	31
Baiga	16,788	8,301	8,487
Bhaina	8	5	3
*Bharia Bhumia, Bhuinhar Bhumia, Bhumiya, Bharia, ...	22	15	7
Bhattra	55	22	33
Bhil, Bhilala, Barela, Patelia	1,814	959	855
Bhil Mina	6	3	3
Bhunjia	4	2	2
Biar, Biyar	26	9	17
Binjhwar	113	57	56
Birhul, Birhor	90	53	37
Damor, Damaria	645	337	308
Dhanwar	190	91	99
Gadaba, Gadba	75	31	44
*Gond; Arakh, Arrakh, Agaria, Asur, ...	2,42,759	1,19,099	1,23,660
Halba, Halbi	45,806	22,385	23,421
Kamar	5	0	5
Karku	64	28	36
Kawar, Kanwar, Kaur, Cherwa, Rathia, Tanwar, Chattri	48,057	23,384	24,673
Khairwar, Kondar	46	19	27
Kharia	4	3	1
Kondh, Khond, Kandh	5	3	2
Kol	40	19	21
Kolam	303	158	145
Korku, Bopchi, Mouasi, Nihal, Nahul, Bondhi, Bondeya	176	108	68
Korwa, Kodaku	3	3	0
Majhi	84	50	34
Majhwar	3	0	3
Mawasi	1	1	0
Munda	14	9	5
Nagesia, Nagasia	5	2	3
Oraon, Dhanka, Dhangad	1,109	581	528
Pao	5	2	3
Pardhan, Pathari Saroti	853	406	447
*Pardhi; Bahelia, Bahellia, Chita Pardhi, ...	571	269	302
Parja	9	3	6
Sahariya, Saharia, Seharia, Sehria, Sosia, Sor	9	3	6
Saonta, Saunta	9	4	5
Saur	62	30	32
Sawar, Sawara	87	45	42
Sonr	279	153	126
Unclassified	1,489	732	757

(Contd.)

SKETCH MAP
OF
SURGUJA DISTRICT
UTTAR PRADESH
JHARKHAND
KORIYA
BILASPUR
KORBA
RAIGARH
JASHPUR
Sanaval
Dumarpan
Pal
Charaikund
Khobir
Vadrafnagar
Khond
Krishnanagar
Ramanujganj
TamorPingla
Moran
Manpur
Tatapani
Juva
Tamki
Barti
Kaura
Ramkola
Ghuai
Samarsoth
Karcha
Mahan
Khormul
Pratappur
Chanderpur
Jriyo
Sarhari
Kandri
Mahan
Palmau
Samri
Patna
Umko
Sirsi
Raipur
Kuiluja
Karanji
Depadih
Kusmi
Sidhma
Manpur
Tulsi
Rehra
Surajpur
Dhorpur
Jainagar
Rapuri
Lundra
Pilkha
Ambikapur
Barbaspur
Bargidih
Lahaptara
Darima
Sirmina
Bakali
Lachmanpur
Khukhri
Ramgarh
Chotadamali
Parsa
Karabel
Barima
Soor
Mainpat
Kadnai
Sitapur
LEGEND
District Headquarters
Taluk Headquarters
Other Towns
Railway Line
Major Roads
Other Roads
River
Important Tourist Places
Wild Life Sanctuary

SURGUJA

LOCATION AND AREA

Latitude: 22.5° North to 24.01° North
Longitude: 82.5° East to 84.05° East
Altitude: 611 m

District Surguja is situated in the extreme north corner of Chhattisgarh State. The district is surrounded by Uttar Pradesh and Jharkhand in the north, Palamau district of Jharkhand in the east, Raigarh and Korba districts in the south and Koriya district on its west.

Total area of the district is 18017 sq. kms. The district headquarters is located at Ambikapur.

HISTORY

The constitution of present Surguja district is older than the territorial constitution of the Madhya Pradesh, Surguja district was constituted in 1951 by merging the three feudatory States, namely Chang Bhakhar, Koria and Surguja. Since the erstwhile feudatory State Surguja was biggest amongst the three feudatory States, the newly constituted district was named as Surguja. There is no town or village of this name. The etymology of the term "Surguja", according to some local people is that it might have come from two words 'Sur' and 'Guja' meaning the land where the Gods revelled.

The early history of the district is obscure. Because of its hills and forests and lying away from routes of invading armies, the area now constituting the district escaped the usual turmoil. This tract appears to have been unknown to the Moghal Government from the remains of extensive rock excavations supposed to be temple and monasteries discovered in village Harohouka in Bharatpur tehsil in 1870-71, it appears probable that in early times, i.e., before the Gonds and Kols took over that part of the district ws occupied by a civilized race. Who these people were and what the period of their stay was remains unknown. It is likely that the district was divided up into many petty principalities each under its own chief, who were constantly at war with one another. In his "A Statistical Account of Bengal" (Vol. XV. 1877) Hunter describes the history of erstwhile Surguja State as follows. For many generations, however, the Kol and the Gond territories of eastern and western Surguja have been united under the present reigning family, who call themselves Raksel Rajputs. According to local traditions in Palamau, the Raksel Rajputs governed that part of the country up to 1613 A.D. when they were ousted by the Cheros in a strange fashion. In 1612, Bhagwant Rai, the head of the Chero tribe, then a fugitive from Chainpur took service with a large body of Chero retainers under Mansingh, the Raksel Raja of Palamau, intending, on first opportunity, to seize the supreme power.

In the following years Mansingh went to Surguja to celebrate the marriage of his son with the daughter of the Surguja chief. Taking advantage of the absence of Mansingh Bhagwant Rai rose with all his followers, murdered Mansingh's family and made himself the first Chero Raja of Palamau. Mansingh made no attempt to regain his kingdom, but in his turn murdered the Surguja chief and took the possession of the Raj. This was the origin of present Raksel dynasty. As against this the CHHATISGARH. FEUDATORY States GAZETTEER (1909) states : "These petty chiefs carried on internecine was one with another and finally some 1700 years ago were attacked by a Raksel Rajput from Kundri in Palamau district who invaded their territories and reduced them to subjection." If the latter source is to be taken as correct the Raksel dynasty started in Surguja about 200 A.D. which appears to be very unlikely. The account given in the Feudatory States Gazetteer may be based on traditions kept by the Raksel dynasty who extended their hold to the south as far as banks of the Mahanadi, be that as it may, it may be likely that in early times the chief of Surguja exercised a feudal authority reaching beyond the limit of erstwhile Surguja State. At one time the Surguja chief was the overlord of other neighbouring States Jashpur, Udaipur, Korea and Chang Bhakhar.

The authentic history of the district commences about the year of 1758, when a Maratha army in progress of the Ganges overran half of the district (that is Surguja State) and compelled the chief to acknowledge himself a tributary of the Barar

Government. But beyond this and imposing a heavy fine they did not do anything else.

In 1872, the attention of British Government was directed towards Surguja because of the Surguja chief's annexation of a *pargana* of Chhota Nagpur and subsequently aiding a rebellion in Palamau against the British. This led to an expedition into Surguja by one Colonel Jones. A Treaty was, however, effected later between the British and the Barar Government, i.e., there was some disorder Marathas. But, after the British withdrew which again prompted the British to interfere. Things, however, did not improve much and lawless state prevailed until 1818. In this year the three erstwhile feudatory States (Korea, Chang-Bhakhar and Surguja) which constitute the district, were ceded to the British Government under the provisional agreement with Appa Sahib Bhonsla. The British force under Captain Sinnock restored order and Amar Singh was declared Raja of Surguja.

Between this period and 1951 when the three feudatory States merged with Madhya Pradesh there was nothing of any historical importance to be mentioned here.

POPULATION (GENERAL SC/ST)

Total population of the district according to 2001 census is 1970661 persons, comprising of 999196 males and 971465 females. Rural population of the district is 1833442 persons (927160 males and 906282 females) and urban population is 137219 persons (72036 males and 65183 females).

The tehsil-wise population break-up, i.e., rural-urban and male-female population distribution is represented according to 2001 census in the following table.

Tehsil	*Total Rural Urban*	*Persons*	*Total population Males*	*Females*
Pal	T	224357	113971	110386
	R	214503	108832	105671
	U	9854	5139	4715
Wadrafnagar	T	130480	66535	63945
	R	130480	66535	63945
	U	—	—	—

Pratappur	T	122560	62160	60400
	R	122560	62160	60400
	U	–	–	–
Samri	T	154870	78282	76588
	R	154870	78282	76588
	U	–	–	–
Surajpur	T	537408	272295	265113
	R	501062	252964	248098
	U	36346	19331	17015
Ambikapur	T	400881	204338	196543
	R	309862	156772	153090
	U	91019	47566	43453
Rajpur	T	88706	44908	43798
	R	88706	44908	43798
	U	–	–	–
Lundra	T	101305	51264	50041
	R	101305	51264	50041
	U	–	–	–
Sitapur	T	210094	105443	104651
	R	210094	105443	104651
	U	–	–	–

The decennial growth rate of population of the district as a whole in relation to the State between the period 1991 and 2001 is presented below:

State/ District	*Decennial growth rate of population (per cent) 1991–2001*		
	Total	*Rural*	*Urban*
Chhattisgarh State	18.06	14.23	36.24
Surguja	24.58	22.52	60.65

LANGUAGES AND RELIGION

Main languages spoken in the district are Hindi, Bengali and Urdu and main religions of the district are Hindus, Muslims, Christians, Sikh, Buddhists and Jains.

GEOGRAPHY AND PHYSICAL FEATURES

Surguja district is a great tableland of numerous hills and plateau. The two prominent physiographic features of Surguja district are the Mainpat (Plateau) and the Jamirpat. Pat is the local word which is used for the tableland, isolated hill ranges and peculiar physiographic formation. The Mainpat is a magnificent tableland 28.8 kms long and 9.6 to 12.8 kms broad, and rising to the height of 1152.45 metres. This Mainpat forms the southern boundary with Raigarh district. The Jamirpat is about 3 km (2 miles) wide, long winding range plateau. It forms the eastern boundary of Surguja with Jharkhand State. The elevation of isolated hill range and high plateaus which has risen from Jamirpat is 1066.8—1219.2 metres.

The district is in the belt of Sal forest and the Sal trees are the predominant species. Sal (*Shorea robusta*) is also known locally as *Sakhun.* Some other species in the forest of district are Saja of asan *Khawara, Tendu, Amla, Bahera, Harra, Char, Khair, Kauha* and *Palas,* etc.

Collections of *tendu* leaves the major economic activity of the district, other forest products of the district are namely, *Amla, Harra, Bahera, Tendu, fruit, Charo, Kauha, Khair, Sal Seeds, Resin, etc.*

Timber—Sal, Saja, Bhawara, Kauha, Bija, Amla, Kusam, Palas.

Tendu, Khair, Saguan, Teak, Bamboo and *Sisham* are the species supplying timber to the district.

Bamboos and Eucalyptus are used for paper pulp which are mainly found in the district. Due to land diversion plan percentage of area under forest are rapidly decreasing and area under cultivation are increasing.

RIVERS, CANALS AND WATERWAYS

The principal rivers of the district are the Kanhar, the Rihand (REND), the Morna, the Mahan, the Geur, the Gager, the Neur, and the Gej. There are two distinct drainage systems in the district. The one is northernly and the other is southernly.

Northward flowing rivers from the drainage system of Son. The Kanhar rises in Jashpur tehsil of Raigarh district, flowing northward forms the eastern boundary of the district. The Rihand also referred to as the REND rises from the region of Mainpat plateau and flows toward north, through the central part of the district.

TOWNS, VILLAGES AND AMENITIES

The district at present comprises of 9 tehsils and 7 towns.

The urban population of the district as percentage of total population in the census years 2001 is indicated below. It also shows the sex ratio (females per 1000 males) and density (population per sq km) in the urban population of the district in relation to the State:

State/ District	*Urban population as percentage of total population*	*Sex ratio 2001 (Females per 1000 males)*			*Density (Population per sq km)*
	2001	*Total*	*Rural*	*Urban*	
Chhattisgarh state	20.08	990	1005	932	154
Surguja	6.96	972	977	905	125

Amenities

Number of villages having one or more amenities in the district as per 2001 census are Education, Medical, Drinking Water, Post and Telegraph Market and Hat, Communications, Approach by Pucca road, and power supply.

COMMUNICATIONS

Since the railways run for a short length in the district, the economy of the district is more or less dependent on road transport. At present Ambikapur is the artery, where buses from 18 important routes coveraging Raigarh, Ambikapur, Katghora, Ambikapur *via* Udaipur, Lakhanpur, Manendragarh, Baikunthpur, Surajpur, Ambikapur, Chhirmiri Collery to Ambikapur, Rewa to Ambikapur Janakpur to Ambikapur *via* Manendragarh, Kalhari, Varanasi to Ambikapur *via* Batappur Wadrafnagar.

AGRICULTURE AND IRRIGATION

There are some local variations in the soil of the district. The terms prevalent in the eastern half part of the district are the same as those in Raigarh district and other area of the Chhatisgarh; such as *Matasi* (a yellowish soil) *Kanhar* (black soil), *Dorsa* (mixture of *Kanhar* and *Matasi*) *Palkachhar* (an alluvial soil), *Patparakachhar* (a sandy alluvium) and *Bhata* (poor laterite detritus). *Matasi* is the most common type soil in the eastern half, which is adopted for growing paddy.

The *bahara* land, also known as *kanhar* or *dhondhi* is considered to be the best land for paddy, *chaura* and *sitai* are the

second-class paddy land. *Tanr* and *tikra* are not considered suitable for paddy. *Dand, Darha, Dandi* or *gora* is the third class paddy land, Nar is the term for small *baharas* and *gabhar* is the term for flat land. *Bahara* is considered to be the best position land.

ANIMAL HUSBANDRY

It is seen that though, the number of buffaloes in Surguja district is more than that in Raigarh district, the number of males over 3 years used for work is less in Surguja district than Raigarh district whereas the number of the buffaloes in Surguja district is much greater than Raigarh. This indicates that male buffaloes are not as popular here as in other district for ploughing but Surguja district produces larger quantity of milk and milk products. It also appears that she-buffaloes are retained and he-buffaloes are exported outside the district. Though the sheeps are very few in number in the district but number of goats is highest in Bilaspur division. The horses and ponies seems to have decreased in comparison to 1961, camels and mules population was nil. The poultry population is just doubled.

INDUSTRIES

There is no major industry in the district.

TRADE, COMMERCE AND EXPORT

The most important commodities manufactured in the towns of the district are *kattha, bidi,* poles, paper, edible oil and rice. The most important commodities imported in the towns of district are sugar for Ambikapur and Surajpur towns, and *Kirana* for Ramanujganj town.

The following table provides information on important commodities manufactured in, exploited from and imported in the towns of this districts.

Name of Town	*Most important Commodities*		
	Imported	*Exported*	*Manufactured*
Ramanujang	Cement	Plastic shoes, chappals	Edible oil
Surajpur	Iron sheets	Bucket	Bucket
Vishrampur	Petrol, diesel	Coal	Steel furniture
Ambikapur	Cloth	Alluminium Utensils	Aluminium Utensils

TOURISM

Ramgarh. The most important archaeological sites are the temples of Ramgarh hill. This hill is about 13 km to the west of village Lakhanpur and about 62 km from Ambikapur district headquarters. It is rectangular mass of a sandstone rising abruptly from the plains. There is a natural tunnel here known as Sita Bengera Jogi Madha.

Shrigarh. There is an old fort situated in Ambikapur.

Dipadih. This is in the way of Kusmi (Samri) to Shankargarh. There are ruins of broken images.

Tatapani. It is in the Ramanujganj (Pal) tehsil of the district where there is a hot water stream which flows continuously throughout the year. It is believed that its water contains sulphur, therefore, people take bath for the relief of skin diseases.

Tomar Pingla: It is a famous Wild Life Sanctuary, located in the part of the district and spread over an area of 608.52 sq. km. Tiger, Panther, Sambhar, Chital, Blue bull and Wild Hogs are the famous faunas of this sanctuary.

Samarsot: The Samarsot wild life sanctuary is located in the North eastern portions of the district. It occupies an area of 340.35 sq. km, Tiger, Panther and varieties of Antelope are the faunas available in this sanctuary.

FAIRS AND FESTIVALS

Important fairs and festivals organised in different parts of the district are mentioned below:

Ganga Dasahra, Ramnavmi, Dasahra, Shivratri, Kartik Poornima, Urs, Gahar Guru, Jatna Fair.

EDUCATION

According to 2001 census, total literates (excluding the population in the age group of 0-6 years) is 886255 persons. Of these, 553595 are males and 332660 are females. In the rural areas of the district 785595 persons (496443 males and 289152 females) are literates and in urban areas 100660 persons (57152 males and 43508 females) are literates. The rate of literacy of this population to the total population, excluding 0-6 years age group according to 2001 census is shown below:

	Persons	Males	Females
Total	55.37	68.19	42.17
Rural	53.01	66.23	39.47
Urban	84.86	91.81	77.18

COLLEGES 2000

Government College, Ramanujganj, Enrolment 102 (Affiliated College)

Government College, Wadrafanagar, Enrolment 74 (Affiliated College)

Government College, Pratappur (Established 1989), Enrolment 137, Teachers 7 (Affiliated College)

Government Girls College, Ambikapur, Enrolment, 198, Teachers 6, (Affiliated College)

Government Postgraduate College, Ambikapur, (Established 1971), Enrolment 3169, affiliated college, teachers 75.

(Above named colleges belong to Guru Ghasidas University, Established 1983)

MEDIA

Air Station. All India Radio, Ambikapur

ADMINISTRATION

(i) Administrative Division: Bilaspur

Tehsils: Pal, Wadrafnagar, Pratappur, Samri, Surajpur, Ambikapur, Lundra, Sitapur, Rajpur.

Towns and Urban Agglomerations with their Population, Sex Ratio, Decadal Growth and Literacy Rate (2001).

Town	Population	Percentage decadal growth 1991–2001	Sex Ratio	Literacy
Ramanujganj (TP)	9854	25.79	917	78.45
Telgaon (CT)	7145	—	877	77.41
Surajpur (TP)	16835	29.01	886	77.80

Vishrampur (CT)	12366	9.31	874	87.75
Ambikapur (UA)	91019	71.00	914	86.96
(i) Ambikapur M.Cor	65999	24.00	901	87.05
(ii) Phundardihauri (CT)	16106	445.97	952	87.61
(iii) Namnaklan (CT)	8914	—	940	85.04

(ii) Parliamentary Constituencies and assembly segments 2001:

No. & Name of Parliamentary Constituency :

12-SURGUJA (ST).

No. & Name of Assembly Segments of Surguja Parliamentary Constituency which lies within the jurisdiction of Surguja district.

89. Premnagar (ST)—Premnagar RIC and Ramanujnagar RIC (excluding P.Cs. 73 to 80) in Surajpur tehsil; and Udaipur RIC and P.Cs. 55, 57, 58 and 65 in Lakhanpur RIC in Ambikapur tehsil and the forest villages in the area.

90. Surajpur (ST)—Surajpur and Bhaivathan RICs and P.Cs. 73 to 80 in Ramanujnagar RIC and Chandramedha RIC (excluding P.Cs. 17 to 26) in Surajpur tehsil.

91. Pal (ST)—Basantpur, Ramchandrapur and Chalgali RICs and Ramanujganj Town and P.Cs. 32 to 34A and 34B in Balrampur RIC in Pal tehsil.

92. Samri (ST)—Samri tehsil and the forest villages in the area; and Balrampur RIC (excluding Ramanujganj Town and P.Cs. 32 to 34A and 34B) in Pal tehsil.

93. Lundra (ST)—Lundra and Rajpur RICs in Ambikapur tehsil and the forest villages in the area; and P.Cs. 39 to 42 in Pratappur RIC in Surajpur tehsil.

94. Pilkha (ST)—Pilkha RIC, Pratappur RIC (excluding P.Cs 39 to 42), and P.Cs. 17 to 26 in Chandramedha RIC in Surajpur tehsil and the forest villages in the area.

95. Ambikapur (ST)—Ambikapur-I and Ambikapur-II RICs and Lakhanpur RIC (excluding P.Cs. 55, 57, 58 and 65) in Ambikapur tehsil and the forest villages in the area.

96. Sitapur (ST)—Sitapur and Batauli RICs in Ambikapur tehsil.

The communitywise breakup (OBE) in Surguja is Muslims (3 per cent), Christians (3 per cent), Scheduled Castes (5 per cent],

Scheduled Tribes (62 per cent) and Ahirs (5 per cent). Gonds (25 per cent), Oraons (11 per cent), Kawars (10 per cent), and Nagasias (5 per cent) are dominant among the Scheduled Tribes.

OBSERVATIONAL ORGANISATION

Surface Observatories

The district Surguja lies under meterological sub-division, Madhya Pradesh, East. This facility is available at Ambikapur. The instrument lies in

Latitude	:	23.16° North
Longitude	:	83.25° East
Altitude	:	611 m
Date of starting	:	14-12-1950

MINERALS AND ORES OCCURRENCES

Bauxite

Bauxite is exposed to the south of Chutai (23.36°, 83.86°). Another deposit was found a furlong S.W. of the Chutai deposit and north of Amarth (23.33°, 83.83°). The bed is 6 to 8 ft. thick Bauxite also occurs to the S.E. of Titijharia (23.38, 83.88). The thickness of the bauxite varies and the reserves are estimated to be about 150,000 tons.

Good deposit of bauxite occurs north of Gopatu (23.38, 83.93) traceable for a distance of 500 ft. About a mile south of Bagbota (23.36, 84.03), bauxite occurs for a distance of half a mile in the hill slope. The thickness varies from 2 to 6 ft.

In the northern portion of the Jamirapat plateu, near Nawadih (23.53, 83.8), a bed of bauxite with an average thickness of 3 ft. is seen for a distance of about 300 ft. West of Nawadih, near the head of a stream, there is another patch of bauxite. Good bauxite occurs S.E. of Asanpani (23.21, 84.05) with an average thickness of 3 ft.

Bauxite is often found associated with laterite on the main *Pat* in the catchment areas of the Rehar in IB Rivers. Several long band of bauxite are found near Sapnadand (22.86, 83.35) and Parpatia (22.85, 83.23) also near Kudaridih (22.76, 83.33), Barma (22.76, 83.33) and Dankishora (23.8, 83.13) in the eastern part near Samri (23.4, 83.93), Seraipat (23.46, 83.96) and at Joka (23.55, 83.66). On the Surguja Tashpur Border and cut Kunakel

923.01, 83.5) and Jarangpat (23.2, 83.53). The results of chemical analyses show that this material is suitable for the extraction of aluminium, even though the Hitania content ranges from 9 to 12 per cent.

On the main *Pat* south of Ambikapur (23.11, 83.18) and at heights of 3,500 ft, or higher also to the east. Bauxite deposits have also been recorded from Satpathrikhar Pahar (22.66, 83.01) Perta Pahar (22.68, 82.96), Sarjom (23.38, 83.95), Dumarkholi (23.45, 83.96) and Barpat (23.36, 84.05).

Lead and Silver

At Bhelaunda (23.86, 83.33). The discovery of a vein of galena in a hill named Pattia near the village of Pelawa or Bhelaunda.

Mica

Deposits of mica have been worked sporadically at Paharkarwan (23.6, 83.21). Haldibaria (23.9, 82.83). Kantra (23.55, 82.75), Pendari (23.83, 82.76). The mica-bearing pegmatites vary in thickness from 5 to 35 ft. Generally the mica is of the ruby variety and at places greenish mica are also obtained. The mica books range in size up to 2 ft. across, but a fair portion of them are badly stained. Large quantity of mica are reported to have been produced from some of the mines.

Several thin pegmatite veins are recorded near Kajia (23.3, 83.9), Nawadih (23.53, 83.88) and Gadion (23.31, 83.91). Books of mica about 8 inches across are found, but they are badly cracked.

Mineral Waters

At Tatapani (23.68, 83.71). Not less than a score of springs occur on or near a ridge of psedomorphic quartz and breccia marking a line of fracture. Temperature of water varies from 54°C to 88°C and discharge of water is copious. Water deposits silicious sinler and emits a strong odour of H_2S.

An occurrence of a spring is reported from near Lanjit (23.51, 82.95) where the spring has a steady flow. However, the water is luke warm and has no smell in sulphur.

Ochre

A deposit of red ochre occurs on the laterite capped hills near Laba (22.78, 83.21). The material is slightly giretty and belongs to the standard second grade.

Pyrites

Occurrences of pyrites have been reported from near Churka (23.81, 83.13) and Lanjit (23.51, 82.95). At Churka pyrites crystals are found disseminated in Barakar sandstones. Pyrites occurs as lenses and pockets in sandstones near Lanjit.

Heavy Rains

6 July 1986, Machinery worth Rs 10 crore damaged at Bishrampur mines of South Eastern Coalfields Ltd.

DISTRIBUTION OF *SCHEDULED CASTE* POPULATION BY SEX DISTRICTWISE (1991)

	POPULATION Total	Males	Females
SURGUJA	1,14,832	58,673	56,159
Audhelia	50	29	21
Bagri, Bagdi	38	20	18
Bahna, Bahana	4	4	0
Balahi, Balai	76	42	34
Banchada	90	47	43
Barahar, Basod	1,771	888	883
Bargunda	7	5	2
Basor, Burud, Bansor, Bansodi, Bansphor, Basar	5,884	2,955	2,929
Bedia	10	8	2
Beldar, Sunkar	194	125	69
Bhangi, Mehtar, Balmik, Lalbegi, Dharkar	930	480	450
Bhanumati	348	194	154
Chadar	54	26	28
*Chamar, Chamari, Bairwa, Bhambi, Jatav, Mochi, Regar, ...	60,777	31,073	29,704
Chidar	305	164	141
Chikwa, Chikvi	6,249	3,144	3,105
Chitar	70	34	36
Dahait, Dahayat, Dahat	41	20	21
Dewar	53	24	29
Dhanuk	193	108	85
Dhed, Dher	16	9	7
Dohor	28	16	12
Dom, Dumar, Dome, Domar, Doris	2,683	1,343	1,340
Ganda, Gandi	1,556	840	716
Ghasi, Ghasia	26,260	13,227	13,033
Holiya	61	31	30
Kanjar	38	18	20
Katia, Patharia	95	57	38
Khatik	453	303	150
Koli, Kori	761	398	363
Khangar, Kanera, Mirdha	18	16	2
Kuchbandhia	16	11	5
Mahar, Mehra, Mehar	736	407	329
*Mang, Mang Garodi, Mang Garudi, Dankhni Mang, ...	34	16	18
Meghwal	27	16	11
Muskhan	15	8	7
Nat, Kalbelia, Sapera, Navdigar, Kubutar	27	19	8
Pasi	522	281	241
Rujjhar	39	15	24
Sansi, Sansia	16	12	4
Silawat	5	2	3
Zamral	4	1	3
Unclassified	4,278	2,237	2,041

(Contd.)

DISTRIBUTION OF *SCHEDULED TRIBE* POPULATION BY SEX DISTRICTWISE (1991)

	POPULATION Total	Males	Females
SURGUJA	11,17,577	5,65,719	5,51,858
Agariya	28,806	14,513	14,293
Andh	172	75	97
Baiga	14,168	7,115	7,053
Bhaina	281	155	126
*Bharia Bhumia, Bhuinhar Bhumia, Bhumiya, Bharia, ...	50,290	25,276	25,014
Bhattra	54	30	24
Bhil, Bhilala, Barela, Patelia	75	46	29
Bhil Mina	92	60	32
Bhunjia	76	47	29
Biar, Biyar	2,439	1,235	1,204
Binjhwar	1,745	877	868
Birhul, Birhor	130	63	67
Damor, Damaria	94	53	41
Dhanwar	2,243	1,170	1,073
Gadaba, Gadba	121	67	54
*Gond; Arakh, Arrakh, Agaria, Asur, ...	4,40,425	2,23,227	2,17,198
Halba, Halbi	71	31	40
Kamar	43	26	17
Karku	103	61	42
Kawar, Kanwar, Kaur, Cherwa, Rathia, Tanwar, Chattri	1,67,773	85,255	82,518
Khairwar, Kondar	38,725	19,590	19,135
Kharia	555	276	279
Kondh, Khond, Kandh	81	40	41
Kol	5,916	3,009	2,907
Kolam	588	295	293
Korku, Bopchi, Mouasi, Nihal, Nahul, Bondhi, Bondeya	575	304	271
Korwa, Kodaku	53,120	26,845	26,275
Majhi	15,059	7,739	7,320
Majhwar	17,344	8,717	8,627
Mawasi	126	74	52
Munda	1,340	689	651
Nagesia, Nagasia	51,377	25,947	25,430
Oraon, Dhanka, Dhangad	2,08,340	1,05,124	1,03,216
Pao	2,672	1,343	1,329
Pardhan, Pathari Saroti	1,456	724	732
*Pardhi; Bahelia, Bahellia, Chita Pardhi, ...	468	232	236
Parja	30	21	9
Sahariya, Saharia, Seharia, Sehria, Sosia, Sor	2	1	1
Saonta, Saunta	760	388	372
Saur	2	0	2
Sawar, Sawara	201	100	101
Sonr	970	455	515
Unclassified	8,669	4,424	4,245

(Contd.)